D0500297

Toward An Efficient Energy Future

Volume Three in the
INTERNATIONAL ENERGY SYMPOSIA SERIES
A 1982 WORLD'S FAIR EVENT

Toward An

Efficient Energy Future

Proceedings of the
International Energy Symposium III
May 24-27, 1982

Edited by

MARY R. ENGLISH • ROBERT A. BOHM • LILLIAN A. CLINARD

Energy, Environment, and Resources Center
The University of Tennessee

Ballinger Publishing Company • *Cambridge, Massachusetts*
A SUBSIDIARY OF HARPER & ROW, PUBLISHERS, INC.

International Standard Book Number: 0-88410-878-3

Library of Congress Catalog Card Number: 82-24280

Printed in the United States of America

Library of Congress Cataloging in Publication Data

International Energy Symposium (3rd : 1982 : Knoxville, Tenn.)
  Toward an efficient energy future.

  (International energy symposia series ; v. 3)
  1. Energy policy—Congresses. I. English, Mary R.
II. Bohm, Robert A. III. Clinard, Lillian A. IV. Title.
V. Series.
HD9502.A2I5785 1982   339.79   82-24280
  ISBN 0-88410-878-3

As the final communiqué of this Series notes, participants from many nations, with an extraordinary diversity of economic status, resource availability, technological sophistication, and political background, have contributed to these Symposia. The commonality of views on energy issues has been remarkable. Although national problems differ, the fundamental challenge is so deeply shared that continued international cooperation and interaction are imperative if the world's nations are to achieve the goal of a just and sustainable energy future.

S. H. Roberts, Jr.
President
The 1982 World's Fair

Editors' Preface

This volume contains the *Proceedings* of the last in the three-part International Energy Symposia Series sponsored by The 1982 World's Fair. The first two Symposia's *Proceedings* were released in October, 1981, and May, 1982, respectively, appearing under the titles *World Energy Production and Productivity* and *Improving World Energy Production and Productivity.* They are available from the Series' publisher, Ballinger Company of Cambridge, Massachusetts.

As in the prefaces to the prior *Proceedings*, this preface attempts to summarize the rationale and framework of both the Symposium at hand and the Series as a whole. In doing so, some of the prior prefaces' contents are given here in abbreviated form, together with new material on Symposium III's organization and the Series' culminating message. However, it should be noted that this can only convey a general sense of the Series; for a full understanding of the range of views and expertise represented, the *Proceedings* themselves should be consulted.

Purpose and Structure of the International Energy Symposia Series

The intent of the International Energy Symposia Series (IESS) was to provide a broad-based forum for addressing basic concerns about mankind's need for energy. Carried out under the auspices of an international energy exposition entitled The 1982 World's Fair, the IESS began with Symposium I held October 14–17, 1980. Symposium I was followed by Symposium II held November 3–6, 1981, and the Series concluded with Symposium III held May 24–27, 1982, shortly after the Fair officially opened.

The IESS was designed to enable consideration of alternative energy policies. Its broad theme, "Increasing World Energy Production and Productivity," was global in scope and provided room for analysis of both energy supply and energy demand. Set within the context of the World's Fair, a symbol of worldwide cooperation and sharing of knowledge, the IESS sought to help rectify world energy problems by bringing many different viewpoints together in order to assess areas of conflict and reach areas of agreement. The IESS thus undertook an evaluation of energy issues that included but went beyond solely technical considerations, addressing energy issues in light of the human condition as a whole. Its impact was intended to be three-pronged, affecting the work of scientific and technical personnel on energy issues, the public's understanding of the international energy situation, and policymakers' decisions on both a national and a global basis.

As structured by the Program Committee, the Organizing Committee, and the Symposia staff (see Appendix III), each Symposium in the Series was to complement the others. The first Symposium focused on defining the nature of the global energy problem. Building on the results of Symposium I, Symposium II served as the Series' analytical component from which considerations and recommendations were carried forward to Symposium III. Deliberations at Symposium III were directed toward specifying ways to help manage the world's energy problem and resulted in a final communiqué of the Series.

Organization of the Symposia

Symposium I. To fulfill its task of issue identification, Symposium I was organized into a sequence of four plenary sessions, each with a predetermined topic about world energy production and productivity: the nature of the problem; the role of technology; critical paths, conflicts, and constraints; and alternative policies. At each half-day session, two papers were presented, followed by discussion among the participants and a summary by a designated integrator.

Symposium II. The focus of Symposium II was a series of seven concurrent two-day work sessions, each with a comprehensive position paper and a separately authored case study or special paper. Four of the sessions were organized around world divisions according to national perspective: industrialized nations with market economies, industrialized nations with nonmarket economies, energy-surplus industrializing nations, and energy-deficit industrializing nations. The remaining three sessions centered on issues of global importance: the role of nuclear power, biomass and its energy/nonenergy conflict, and energy for rural development. Participants—some new, some of whom had attended Symposium I—were assigned to work sessions based upon their areas of expertise and interest but were free to shift among sessions, and throughout, extensive debate was encouraged. The sense of each work session was summarized by its chairmen/integrator at the Symposium's closing plenary session.

In addition, Symposium II included three plenary session papers on broad-ranging topics: alternative energy futures, including the case for electricity and appropriate energy strategies for industrializing countries; and the development of international institutional arrangements for increased energy production and productivity.

Symposium III. This Symposium was designed to conclude the Series' work by moving from technical, economic, social, and environmental considerations to government policy issues. Although a number of participants from the prior Symposia were present, the emphasis here was on ministerial/cabinet-level participants who could represent their nations' energy strategies.

The first day of Symposium III was directed toward providing continuity: a comprehensive technical paper highlighting salient issues was presented, followed by statements from Symposium II's seven chairmen/integrators and general discussion among the Symposium III participants. The next day was devoted, first, to presentations of national energy policies, and then, to discussion and refinement of the communiqué to be delivered at the Symposium's closing session. To add to the breadth of the conference, two special papers were also given: a case study of Italy's public/private cooperation in energy technology transfer and a discussion of international energy cooperation from a European Community perspective.

More detail about Symposium III's program and participants is contained in Appendices I and II. Additionally, in this *Proceedings*, special organizational and editorial considerations are noted at the beginning of each of the book's six sections.

The Symposia Series' Message

Because of the diversity inherent in the Series, it is impossible to reduce what occurred to a brief statement. Instead, the reader is referred to the summaries of past Symposia integrators, to the synopses in the past prefaces, and, most particularly, to the *Proceedings* papers and discussions.

And just as the Series' process cannot readily be summed up, so too is its value complex and multifaceted, resisting distillation to a single message. Failing that possibility, it nevertheless is appropriate to address one central outcome: the final communiqué presented at the closing session on May 27, 1982. Although the Symposia had a number of results—many intangible but important, especially insofar as a new spirit of understanding was attained—the communiqué merits special attention as a cooperative attempt to reconcile differences and synthesize a sense of the Series. Its text appears in full in Chapter Nineteen; an abstract of it is given below.

> The communiqué states that the essential world energy problem is to manage wisely the existing conventional resources while, through continued attention, accomplishing the decades-long transition to sustainable, affordable energy sources and highly productive energy uses. It categorizes the options available to industrialized and less industrialized countries over the next twenty to thirty years and beyond to make this transition, and it notes that strong government leadership coupled with private sector choices are necessary, as are trade and cooperation among nations. It further notes that although some progress has been made, the record is mixed and the future rate of progress will determine the future energy problem's scope.
>
> The communiqué recommends (a) that each nation recurringly assess, first, its options to achieve its own best mix of energy supplies and uses—a process that can be helped by international cooperation and assistance—and second, its impact on the world energy picture; (b) that the least fortunate countries be given technical, financial, or material assistance with their energy problems by those well endowed with technology or other resources; and (c) that existing international organizations as well as bilateral and multilateral arrangements be used to facilitate the transition to sustainable energy sources and efficient end uses. Finally, it recommends that the IESS be continued through biennial meetings, the first of which should address the topic "Managing the Energy Transition."

General Editorial Considerations

Although editorial changes have been held to a minimum in the *Proceedings*, some alterations have been necessary to ensure consistency among the papers and the prepared or spontaneous remarks. Throughout, however, the overridding aim has been to retain the original tone and intended meaning. Insofar as this has been achieved, the editors extend thanks to the authors and other participants for their cooperation. Insofar as this aim has not been fully met, the editors request the understanding of those involved, who undoubtedly realize the complexity of the task and the rapidity with which it had to be executed.

Acknowledgments

Our sponsoring organization, The 1982 World's Fair, is to be commended for assuming the demanding task of hosting the International Energy Symposia Series. Through the Fair's unfailing support, this Series has been able to make a much more substantial contribution to the body of knowledge about energy policy and prospects than would otherwise have been possible. In addition, the editors would like to acknowledge the important support of the Symposium's cosponsors: the International Energy Agency and its parent organization, the Organisation for Economic Co-operation and Development; the United States Department of Energy; the Tennessee Valley Authority; and The University of Tennessee. The International Energy Symposia Series has been facilitated by a grant from the United States Department of Energy and by the support of its offices and officials. The International Energy Symposia Series is also cosponsored by a diverse group of foundations, organizations, and corporations concerned with the global energy problems that are associated with high levels of demand coupled with uncertain future supplies.

The *Proceedings* could not have been completed without the enthusiastic and professional efforts of the staffs of The 1982 World's Fair and The University of Tennessee's Energy, Environment, and Resources Center. Our editoral team included Jim Billingsley, who developed the book and cover design and layout specifications; Joyce Rupp Troxler, who prepared graphics; Carolyn Srite, who provided editorial assistance; Dan Hoglund and Sylvia Hoglund, who proofed several drafts of this volume; and Rica Swisher, Peggy Taylor, and Nancy Gibson, who prepared manuscripts.

A special thanks is offered to Earl Williams and to Tana Lawson and the rest of the Williams Company staff, who patiently worked with us to typeset and compose this volume on a very tight schedule. Finally, to those at the Ballinger Company with whom we worked—Carol Franco, Editor; Gerry Galvin, Production Manager; Robert Entwisle, Marketing Director; and Leslie Zheutlin, Marketing—we would like to express our appreciation for their professional support.

MRE, RAB, and LAC
Knoxville, TN
November 1, 1982

Contents

Figures

Tables

Abbreviations

ASEAN	Association of South East Asian Nations
bbl	barrel
bpd	barrel per day
Btu	British thermal unit
BWR	boiling water reactor
CANDU	Canadian deuterium-uranium reactor
cm	centimeter
CPE	centrally planned economy
ECM	European Common Market
EEC	European Economic Community
ESCAP	Economic and Social Commission for Asia and the Pacific
FAO	UN Food and Agricultural Organization
FRG	Federal Republic of Germany
FY	fiscal year
GDP	Gross Domestic Product
GJ	gigajoule
GNP	Gross National Product

GW	gigawatt
ha	hectare
IAEA	International Atomic Energy Agency
IEA	International Energy Agency [an agency of the Organisation for Economic Co-operation and Development]
IIASA	International Institute for Applied Systems Analysis
IMF	International Monetary Fund
INFCE	International Nuclear Fuel Cycle Evaluation
ISFM	International Spent Fuel Management
kcal	kilocalorie
kg	kilogram
km	kilometer
kw	kilowatt
kwh	kilowatt-hour
LDC	less developed country
LNG	liquefied natural gas
LPG	liquefied petroleum gas
LWR	light-water reactor
m^3	cubic meter
Mbd	million barrels per day
Mbdoe	million barrels per day of oil equivalent
Mtce	million tons of coal equivalent
Mtoe	million tons of oil equivalent
MW	megawatt
MWe	megawatt-electric
NPT	nuclear nonproliferation treaty
OECD	Organisation for Economic Co-operation and Development

OLADE	Organisaçion Latinoamericana de Energia [the Latin America energy organization]
OPEC	Organization of Petroleum Exporting Countries
PWR	pressurized water reactor
quad	quadrillion (10^{15}) British thermal units
R&D	research and development
RD&D	research, development, and demonstration
SNG	substitute natural gas
t	metric ton [1000 kilograms, or 2,205 pounds avoirdupois]
tce	ton of coal equivalent
therm	100,000 British thermal units
toe	ton of oil equivalent
TPE	total primary energy
TW	terawatt
UNCTAD	United Nations Conference on Trade and Development
UNEP	United Nations Environment Programme
UK	United Kingdom
US	United States
USSR	Union of Soviet Socialist Republics
W	watt
WAES	Workshop on Alternative Energy Strategies
WCC	World Council of Churches
WOCOL	World Coal Study

The following terms and prefixes have been used to express quantities given in powers of ten:

Quantity	Term	Prefix
10^{15}	one quadrillion	peta
10^{12}	one trillion	tera
10^{9}	one billion	giga
10^{6}	one million	mega
10^{3}	one thousand	kilo

Unless otherwise specified, all tons refer to metric tons and all dollars [\$] refer to US dollars.

SECTION I

Opening Session

Editors' Note

Symposium III's opening session, held the evening of May 24, 1982, included the keynote address by Imelda Romualdez Marcos and a number of brief salutations by officials associated with the Fair or the Symposium. The latter have been excluded from the *Proceedings* because of space limitations. The address of Symposium III's chairman, Armand Hammer, was planned for the opening session but was delivered the following morning due to scheduling conflicts. However, it has been included here because it is most appropriate to this section of the *Proceedings*. Appreciation is extended for the significant contributions that both the keynote address and the chairman's address have made to the Symposium.

CHAPTER ONE

Keynote Address:
The Summons
to Energize the
Global Political Will

Imelda Romualdez Marcos
Minister of Human Settlements
Republic of the Philippines

In Nairobi, I had the privilege to share a vision—a vision of the new human order, a vision which suggests that solutions to the current predicament of mankind cannot be found fragmented in economic or technological solutions as many of us have been wont to believe.

Humanity must advance to a new and unprecedented order of totality, to the disciplined consciousness of authentic destiny. A long-term perspective must begin to exert stronger counterbalancing forces to short-term conflict.

For it is only when people are total and whole, reconciled with the universe within them—their inner being—that the awesome powers of their creativity can liberate them from the shackles of nature and from fellow humans.

Today, I am honored to speak on the so-called energy crisis, not as a situation that could paralyze the collective will of mankind but rather as one of those rare opportunities that occurs from time to time to call forth human genius.

A TRANSITION IN CONSCIOUSNESS

The so-called energy crisis is not only a crisis about energy but also a crisis of consciousness about energy and material needs, a crisis of deep-seated assumptions about the way to satisfy those needs.

The temptation is great for the economic or technological mind to regard the energy crisis solely as a problem, or even worse, to perceive it simply as an economic or political problem imposed

5

on us by somebody else, whether they be the oil producers or oil companies or lawmakers or the rich or some whimsical force beyond our control.

Often the energy crisis is diagnosed as a problem of supply availability, security, and cost. Such thinking is not only a perceptual dead end; it also follows a destructive and possibly tragic course because it leads to solutions that do not go beyond, for example, more oil exploration, more efficient cars, more energy taxes, more oil stockpiles, more energy R&D, and so forth.

For in truth, as it is said, nature has enough for mankind's NEEDS—but not for greed.

The energy crisis, like a providential hand, has presented mankind with a challenge, not a problem; with a lesson, not a scourge. The call, the challenge, the opportunity before humanity is not simply to solve the energy problem, not simply for the global economy to undergo an energy transition—it is also for mankind as a whole to undergo a transition in consciousness.

What do we mean?

First, we see a subtle but distinct and inevitable change in our management orientations and in our attitudes toward nature, both personal and cultural. As the world economy steadily shifts from primary reliance on nonrenewable fossil fuels to renewable forms like solar and biomass energy well into the twenty-first century, a profound transformation in attitudes and orientations will also take place. Extracting from nature is vastly different from nurturing her.

The psychological and cultural frameworks engendered by capture production systems like mining, hunting, catching, and logging are vastly different from the psychological and cultural frameworks engendered by culture production systems like agriculture, aquaculture, and silviculture or dendrothermal plantations. A chasm separates the attitudes and habits of those taking a nonrenewable resource from those caring for or cultivating a renewable resource.

We can see an analogy in human development, from a child with its grasping and taking instincts to a mature adult trained to take on responsibilities for husbanding, cultivating, and sustaining anything from a plant, a livelihood system, an ecosystem to social institutions.

We believe that in the next century the change which began thousands of years ago when primitive humans gave up hunting and gathering and started cultivating crops, domesticating animals, and husbanding livestock will essentially be completed. We can, at our present stage, only speculate on the more profound changes that will possibly take place in world cultures and in the human psyche as this final weaning away from the primitive hunter is accomplished.

Second, the energy crisis is not only introducing structural changes in economic systems; it is also having the very important effect of contributing to a quantum reorientation in developmental values, toward the establishment of a balanced ecoculture.

The industrial model of development which was pioneered in England slightly over two hundred years ago has begun to lose its widespread persuasiveness and appeal. Serious doubts are expressed on the feasibility of fully and successfully replicating the model elsewhere. Historians in the distant future may regard the industrial phase of human civilization as experienced between approximately 1760 and 2000 as a fortunate aberration—arising as it did from the favorable conditions of cheap energy, access to colonial markets, and a head start in technological development—conditions which can no longer be repeated.

The model of the modern industrial society is increasingly under scrutiny and question. To mention some of its weaknesses:

- *It results in vulnerability arising from excessive energy intensiveness and materials intensiveness.*
- *Its conventions for determining the allocation of factors and the distribution of revenues worsen income distribution and tend to emphasize material output or efficiency criteria over human welfare or human resource development criteria.*
- *Its structural defects in the definition and delineation of accounting units result in externalities which, for example, allow rather than control environmental damage.*
- *It produces disjunction between workplace and family, or between factory and community, which results in an erosion of community values on the one hand and a growth of alienation in factory environments on the other.*
- *It separates the flow of materials from natural ecosystem biomaterial flows, modifying or disrupting the latter or introducing alien or deleterious materials into them.*

In focusing the modern mind on fundamental questions and in pressing governments and business firms to entertain the hypothesis that manmade structures, institutions, or conventions may have gone dangerously astray, the energy crisis is thus greatly contributing to a worldwide ferment. It is a creative ferment that is mysteriously and wonderfully transforming human values and consciousness in the macrocosm outside.

AFTER A DECADE OF THE ENERGY CRISIS

During the past decade, the energy issue has been the dominant focus in every major decision—more than any other issue in recent memory. Its importance is such that regional and possibly even global stability will be threatened unless problems concerning it are resolved. The lifestyle of the industrial societies faces severe modification, while the continually worsening situation of the oil-importing developing countries has serious implications for survival.

The industrial countries have a stake in assisting the developing countries to develop new energy systems, for in doing so the former will help to stabilize their own economic systems. The oil-importing developing countries cannot separate the energy question from the overall issues of terms of trade, debt, and technology transfer. There is also little recognition of how closely the energy prospects of the industrial and oil-importing developing countries are tied together. Therefore, the most immediate concern for the industrial countries must be the overall impact of the developing countries' inability to pay their growing debts and the implication this has for the international financial system and the world economy in general. Some 30 to 40 percent of these debts are derived from loans for oil purchases—loans that the commercial banking community is now nervous about. The interdependence between the developed and developing countries makes the latter's oil indebtedness all the more critical.

A compelling motive for assisting developing countries in their energy problems also arises out of the convergence of environmental problems associated with the development process. Intractable food problems also threaten the stability on which so much of the industrial world's investments rely. It is important that the citizenry and leadership of the industrial countries understand the vital connection between these problems and the impact of scarce energy resources on the global environment.

The international financial position of oil-importing developing countries is a precarious one. An increasing share of their national wealth is devoted to paying oil bills, and as a consequence growth has slowed dramatically in a number of these countries. At the same time, the credit of some of these developing countries has been stretched far beyond the limits of their realistic capacity to pay. *They now find it difficult to obtain international credit on top of their existing debts. An indication of this financial burden imposed by these oil imports becomes evident when the cost of energy imports is measured against merchandise export earnings.*

Of course, the impact of these rising fuel oil bills has also been greater in developing countries than in the industrial countries, because the former's development process is firmly locked on a path that increases or decreases with oil consumption.

The increasing scarcity of fuelwood directly threatens both the quality of life and life itself in the less developed countries' rural areas. A massive increase in permanent damage to renewable resources can also arise from this fuelwood crisis. *All of these conditions are due to the fact that developing countries, as a whole, are even more dependent on oil than the industrial countries.*

For the industrial countries, the commitment of the entire community to a high-consumption lifestyle dramatically narrows the choices of political leaders. But for developing country leaders, the problem is not so much with the people's lifestyles or habits as it is with fulfilling their aspirations. How their hopes for a better life are to be met may be less important than the belief that these hopes will be fulfilled. However, very little has yet been done to establish and clarify choices for developing countries among alternative energy resources and technologies. *These countries face a dilemma of whether to adapt to the new energy realities by formulating national energy plans in accordance with imperfect alternative energy potentials or to wait until the price of oil forces decisions upon them.*

CREATIVE APPLICATION OF A NEW POLITICAL WILL

Obviously, tremendous political will—national as well as international—has been generated by the energy crisis. The force and magnitude of this political will appear to rival those typically generated only by war or the clear threat of war. Rarely does such an international opportunity occur during a time of peace.

This political will is a rare opportunity and a valuable resource—national and international. Exploit it fully we all must, and equally important, we must channel its expression along mutually desirable lines, taking care that this political will is not expressed in conflict or war—a potential danger in some oil-producing areas and in oil-bearing disputed areas.

With the pain and the anguish mankind has collectively

experienced over the past decade, the time has now come to creatively apply this political will deriving from the consciousness generated by the energy crisis not merely to seeking the development of energy alternatives. We are also summoned to apply this political will to the shaping of new communities, of a new social order.

From our part of the world, especially the Asian region where two thirds of the world's population live, the tropical forest is being renewed and maintained. In the Philippines, massive reforestation efforts have been linked to scientifically cultivated energy plantations. The development of biomass energy not only alleviates the country's oil bill; it also helps to sustain the planet's life-support system.

The Philippines' Ministry of Human Settlements has launched a people-oriented movement for development. It has focused on the human being as the center and the goal of development. Programs have been geared toward the fulfillment of man's basic needs, such as water, power, food, clothing, shelter, livelihood, medical services, sports and recreation, culture and technology, ecological balance, and mobility—the last meaning roads, bridges, posts, and communication.

In the Philippines, these programs have become a movement—a humanistic movement for self-reliance. We have sought to involve our people in every barangay—our smallest political unit—to participate in various development projects.

We have also established an innovative university called the University of Life whose task is to establish learning and educational networks that allow individuals to study and work not only in the classrooms but also in different towns and communities throughout the Philippines. This university does not simply seek to impart skills; it also seeks to foster commitment. In the University of Life, the world is the classroom; man and community, the course; and life's experience, the teacher. For it is not enough to have civilization; we need to humanize civilization.

In a profound sense, mankind must transcend this world to save it. The moral order manifests a total vision of life in this world. This vision is as vital and as life-giving as the sun. Without this real although intangible "sun," all life shall end.

The inner being of mankind is real and vital in a most urgent sense. The laws governing the personal relationships among people are essential to the maintenance of an elemental social order—an order which is as vital to this earth as is the magnificent order maintained by its physical laws.

We must make people whole. Address our programs and affections to their whole bodies, minds, and feelings. Commit our attention not to a fragment but to the whole.

In a sense, therefore, the response to the energy crisis is "creative human energy." By creative human energy, we do not, of course, mean that strength of people's brawn and muscle. It is puny compared to the power of the machines they have invented. By human energy, we mean the invisible but evident source of mankind's power, the fountainhead of its achievement: the human will. Our commitment should be not just to survive, but to prevail!

RECOMMENDATIONS FOR A PLAN OF ACTION

For this Symposium, the third in the International Energy Symposia Series, concrete recommendations and suggested methods of implementation are scheduled for discussion. We now take the liberty to make a few suggestions.

Balancing the Oil Trade with Water

Any measure that would correct the imbalance in the world oil trade should be an immediate objective in resolving the oil crisis. The present asymmetry in oil trade between the gulf states and East Asia, for example, presents the opportunity for such a solution while taking into account the legitimate aspirations of those developing oil-producing countries to prepare for the time when their oil resources decline.

The proposal calls for making use of the ninety to one hundred very large crude carriers (vLCCs) that ply the Middle East-Japan route every month, carrying crude oil on the eastbound trip and traveling under ballast on the return westbound trip, to carry fresh water as ballast on their back haul. *These vessels pass along either the western or the eastern coast of the Philippines, where there are abundant supplies of fresh water. The only additional cost of freight for the carriage of this water would be the minimal deviation and loading time required to take on water. Water thus carried could be treated according to the intended use at the point of discharge.*

This scheme would be of interest to countries in the Middle East because it could commit a dependable, reliable, long-term supply of significant quantities of fresh water for agricultural and industrial use at a price considerably lower than the current and projected cost of desalinated water. At the same time, it could build on a continuing trade relationship in which both sides would have a stake in something that neither side would wish to disrupt.

PL 480-Type Coal Program

World reserves of coal far exceed those of petroleum. It is estimated that some 2 trillion tons of proven reserves are recoverable and that the industrial countries account for some 90 percent of its production and use.

Coal production is expected to grow more rapidly than oil during the 1980s.

Replacing oil with coal is a more immediate option for the industrial countries than it is for the developing countries. Many of the industrial countries' manufacturing processes were originally based on coal, and less conversion adjustment would be required to shift back to coal or to activate old coal mines that could again be competitive with oil, with oil priced at $34 per barrel.

For the next decade, all nations will be locked into oil as their primary source of energy, and this is particularly true for the developing countries of the Asia-Pacific region. *For this region's nations, with the exception of Indonesia and Malaysia in the region, this has created very serious balance of payments problems in that to meet their increasing crude oil import bills these countries are simultaneously experiencing a decline in their export receipts and an increased need to borrow externally. Consequently, they must divert more resources from needed development investments in order to pay for their necessary crude oil imports.*

All the alternative energy sources to oil have some drawback. For example, natural gas is usually found where one finds oil, and the long lead time required to develop hydroelectric power greatly limits it as a viable alternative.

To alleviate this dual problem—in other words, the energy problem as well as the funds constraint problem—I would encourage the United States, with its more than 250-year supply of coal, to consider formulating a coal export program similar to its PL 480 grain-exporting program wherein buyers of American coal could use the proceeds from the subsequent sale of coal to fund development projects and pay for the coal over stipulated periods of time. Multilateral development banks could administer such a program as a complement to resources that would be specific to the Asia-

Pacific region. *The coal-based PL 480-type program should be extended on a similar basis to other regions of the world if such was deemed financially feasible; otherwise, assistance in developing other energy sources that might be more appropriate should be considered.* Involving any of the multilateral development banks would encourage Australia, Canada, China, and other countries with surplus coal to participate in a development trust fund that would be used to internalize the transport cost of the coal. *A two-tier price in its acquisition cost and such additional investment as might be required for its use should have a predetermined life of, say, ten years, after which it should be phased out.*

Surplus coal could be used both as capital and as a means of generating capital for economic development in the region. The selective thrust of this special program would be to help the less industrialized countries to develop their exports in order to buy machinery and equipment from the United States and other countries exporting coal under a PL 480-type program. A continuous regenerating cycle of trade and economic development would restore a balanced supply of energy in the region that would benefit all and result in worldwide noninflationary economic development.

Coal would be a dominant export for the United States in the next decade—the speed with which this export would materialize would depend on how fast the developing countries could make the large capital investments in infrastructure and conversion costs. Multilateral development banks could fund the capital costs, with the United States initially financing the coal. In the long run, these developing countries would be able to finance the coal from their own resources, once they were somewhat free from the oil burden and their balance of payments had reached equilibrium. Hence, for the United States the program can be considered as a long-term market strategy in the nation's own economic interest.

Notably, it should be pointed out that cofiring coal with wood eliminates the problems associated with sulfur pollution. It so happens that most developing countries are situated favorably with regard to growing tree plantations. The geography of sunshine correlates well with the geography of hunger. The solar energy ratio is between 2:1 and 3:1 in favor of the tropics.

The foregoing proposal therefore not only offers the opportunity for developing countries to enhance and strengthen their programs of renewable energy development but also offers a market for high-sulfur coal with the capability of controlling its pollution side effects. It is therefore an effective bridge to a viable energy future.

Export Options for the US Nuclear Power Industry

The emotion that has surrounded nuclear energy has clouded the fact that it is an established energy source and that commercial nuclear power has been with us for a quarter of a century.

The first commercial-scale nuclear power plant went into operation in 1956. Around the world, there are currently more than 250 commercial nuclear power reactors in operation with an aggregate power capacity of 135 thousand MW producing 8 percent of the world's electricity. *With the nuclear plants currently under construction or in the planning stage, it is expected that nuclear power will provide 11 percent of the world's power by 1985 and 13 percent by 1990, and that the total installed nuclear capacity will reach nearly 450 thousand MW in 1995.*

Although the United States today leads the world with 72 nuclear plants installed and operating, other countries depend on nuclear energy for a larger share of their electric power. *Against the United States' 12 percent, Belgium depends on nuclear plants for 22 percent of its power; Sweden, 23 percent; Switzerland, 25 percent; France, 7 percent; and Japan, 13 percent. France is currently embarked on a very aggressive program to quadruple its nuclear power generating capacity.*

In the Asia-Pacific region, Japan is quietly but similarly embarked on an aggressive program to increase its nuclear generating capacity to 78 thousand MW to provide 28 percent of its electricity by 2000. South Korea and Taiwan have similar aggressive programs. *Korea's first nuclear power plant, which is of the same design as the Philippines' own nuclear power plant under construction in Bataan, went into operation in 1978 and has already generated over 10 billion kwh. The cost differential between power generated by this plant and the higher cost of oil-based electricity is so great that this first Korean nuclear power plant has paid back in only thirty months the foreign exchange required to build it. A second nuclear power plant is scheduled to go into operation next year, and seven more are in various stages of construction.*

Despite the safety questions raised by the Three Mile Island incident and the regulatory and political problems in some countries, nuclear power is playing an increasingly important role as an energy source around the world. *By the end of 1980, 235 pressurized water reactors, 116 boiling water reactors, and 38 heavy water reactors had been ordered by noncommunist countries.*

Solving the problem of the ultimate disposal of nuclear waste would probably do much to further increase the reliance on nuclear energy as a power source. The technology to safely handle, process, and dispose of nuclear waste is already available; is being refined in a number of countries; and will eventually provide permanent solutions to the disposal problem.

Actually, the volumes of high-level radioactive wastes from nuclear power plants are small and manageable. The nuclear fuel cycle is well developed. Uranium is readily available in the world market at prices considerably below what they were five years ago. Nuclear power is not dependent on a single supplier or any one country. Enrichment, fuel fabrication, and reprocessing exist and are available in many countries of the world.

There are many countries with nuclear plants that have not solved the problem of the ultimate disposal of their spent fuel or that have not been able to operate them because of a conditional need to first solve this disposal problem. The establishment of a regional nuclear fuel enrichment plant combined with a disposal facility that would provide an assured alternative source of nuclear fuel as well as a spent-fuel disposal site would greatly facilitate the development of nuclear energy as a power source in that region. One of the developing countries in such a region could put up the site for the enrichment plant as its equity contribution. *The Japanese, with some thirty-six nuclear power plants expected to be in operation by the end of the 1980s, could be interested in taking the lead in both the construction and the financing of a combined regional nuclear enrichment/disposal facility. South Korea, with nine nuclear power plants to be in operation by 2000, could be an alternative to Japan.* This will help create a positive climate for the revival of the US nuclear power industry, at least until such time as the domestic problems that have held back the growth of nuclear power in the United States can be sorted out. Technology and engineering can provide for the safe disposal of spent fuel; however, should this matter be politically untenable, an alternative disposal site could be worked out in any island in the Asia-Pacific acceptable to the proximate countries.

Joint Energy-Food Production by a Rural Community Corporation

Food and energy are critically interlinked issues that have to be considered and addressed together.

On the one hand, acceleration of food production to keep abreast of population growth cannot continue indefinitely to rely on the expansion of cultivated land. Competing land uses, the increasing marginal costs of developing new agricultural lands, and eventual physical limits will not allow indefinite expansion of agricultural land areas. Intensification of agricultural production, on the other hand, requires inputs such as mechanization, irrigation, and nutrient supplements or fertilizers which themselves require energy.

Biomass is both the traditional and the future key energy resource for many rural locales in oil-importing Third World countries. However, biomass energy sources tend to compete with food as well as cash crops for available land. As energy costs and urban energy demands continue to escalate, there is a real danger that some food and cash crops may be priced out of the reach of rural households.

We in the Philippines are implementing an innovative social energy/food farming system in an attempt to avoid the energy versus food dilemma and in a bold experiment to radically correct some flaws of the western industrial system. *We propose to establish an agroindustrial community corporation in a rural setting in Central Luzon, based on the joint production of food and biomass energy.* Culturally valid lifestyles and work ethics as well as commitment to the national community would be developed by creating corporate conditions wherein as farm workers or employees, local residents could acquire an integral stake in the national social and economic system.

The creative conditions designed to actualize this process are as follows:

- *After a reasonable period of productive operation (e.g., ten to fifteen years), by which time investors shall have paid their loans and obligations and realized reasonable returns on their investments, the entire agroindustrial complex would be sold at book value to its deserving farm workers and factory employees, with repayments to come from the continuing proceeds of the corporation.*
- *During the interim period, deserving employees or their children would be trained in technical, managerial, and entrepreneurial skills preparatory to the eventual takeover by the*

community of the enterprise's ownership and management. Through the medium of productivity circles, workers and employees would gradually develop an integral stake in the enterprise through participation in its management and improvement.

• *Transfer of ownership would be equitably determined from the accumulated earned credits of workers/employees computed by individual performance, productivity, length of service, innovativeness, and participation in community development. Earned credits would replace shares of stock as claims to, or a modified form of ownership of, the corporation's assets.*

This project is part of a national movement launched last year by President Marcos: The Movement for Livelihood and Progress (Kilusang Kabuhayan at Kaunlaran). The strategy behind this movement involves the transformation of rural communities into productive systems where the farmers and workers eventually become responsible owners and effective managers of productive forces of society.

These suggested modes of action do not exhaust the possibilities, but they may serve to galvanize a global political will that would energize a new humanity—a new human order.

CONCLUSION

In conclusion, we must apply ourselves to designing and creating the components of a world society with new institutions, conventions, and procedures that will respond to the problems now facing human societies.

Technological changes and new institutional devices are needed. Less manifest but more important are internal changes— revisions in our outlooks and perceptions, attitudes and habits; radical transformations in our consciousness. The global plan of action must be permeated with a new spirit; it must include concrete personal transformations in all of us.

It is fitting to call attention to this spirit—this vital force, this creative energy—here in Knoxville, Tennessee, for the origins of America were decidedly of this spirit. The new world of America meant a new way of looking at mankind. Beyond America's material prosperity, it has principally been its spirit which has made it an inspiration for all peoples of the world. It is a spirit with which we can all identify.

Today, all the world's peoples—from Europe, Asia, and Africa—are represented here in America. And as President Marcos said in Cancún, America may not be able to solve the problems of the world, but the world's problems cannot be solved without America.

The summons to America is to lead in inspiring humanity to achieve peace tempered with justice, to build a new human order that fulfills man, to use the nation's great political strength and will to energize humanity.

And on this new spirit of humankind, the Eagle shall fly with wings of hope — as high as love can soar, as far as dreams can see, and as we, your friends, continue to pray that God bless America. For in so doing, He also blesses the world.

CHAPTER TWO

Chairman's Address

Armand Hammer
Chairman of the Board and
Chief Executive Officer
Occidental Petroleum Corporation

It gives me great pleasure to serve as the chairman of Symposium III, the important concluding session of the International Energy Symposia Series, one of the highlights of this exciting World's Fair. I salute Jake Butcher, Bo Roberts, Walter Lambert, and all their hard-working colleagues, as well as the city of Knoville, for outstanding efforts in making this fair such a resounding success. As Symposium III's chairman, I also want to express my appreciation on behalf of all of us to Mrs. Marcos for her thought-provoking keynote address which officially opened the conference last evening.

This third gathering in the Energy Symposia Series truly has an international flavor, and this is as it should be, because the nature of energy problems is certainly global. World energy supplies, now and in the future, and their equitable distribution at free-market competitive prices among all the peoples of the world, is one of the greatest challenges we have. It will continue to haunt us—during the remainder of this century, at least—and we must seek solutions to this problem.

Speaking of looking for answers, I am reminded of the story of a man who went up for his first parachute jump. He jumped from the plane at 20,000 feet, and as per instructions, he grabbed the main ripcord, counted to ten, pulled the cord—and nothing happened. Following emergency instructions, he grabbed the emergency cord, continued to count to ten, pulled the cord—and again nothing happened. Now, he was plunging from a height of 20,000 feet toward the earth. And as he was falling, he noticed, about a hundred feet away, a man with his hands at his side, head flung back, shooting straight up in the air. He called out to the man, saying, "Hey, do you know anything about parachutes?" The man called back, "No, but do you know anything about butane gas stoves?"

Obviously, appearances can be deceiving, and I believe that this is especially true about the world energy situation as we look at it today. For the past year there has been a so-called glut on the international oil market, and oil prices have fallen somewhat. Complacency has set in, and many people have been led to the mistaken conclusion that the energy crisis is over. Nothing could be further from the truth.

Let's not be lulled by false appearances. The OPEC nations are taking measures to cut back on production, and we must remember that history has a habit of repeating itself. Although Americans have made important strides in energy conservation, in part because of the recession economy, we still paid close to 80 billion dollars for imported oil in 1981, resulting in a trade deficit of 27½ billion dollars. The energy crisis that has plagued us for the past decade has not gone away; it is just catching a second wind. As long as we in this country rely on imported oil as our basic energy resource, we will continue to find ourselves dependent to varying degrees on a small group of countries—some of which are unfriendly—for a commodity we cannot do without, and this will remain true until our nation adopts realistic measures to meet this challenge. Now, conservation is fine, and we are all for it. But let's not delude ourselves: the more we conserve, the less OPEC will produce, thereby once again keeping us in short supply and continually raising prices.

And if this affects *us*, the United States, imagine how it affects other nations of the world, many of whom have economies much more fragile than our own. I have theorized in the past that the price of a barrel of oil could reach a hundred dollars during this decade, and despite the temporary glut which we have just experienced, I am not ready to back away from that grim forecast, unless we and the other nations develop alternate sources. Technically and tragically, many Third World countries find themselves in desperate straits. They continue to pay such exorbitant prices for oil that there is not enough money left in their national treasuries to buy even such things as fertilizers, farm equipment, and grain from time to time when it is needed to feed their populations. They continue to borrow money; their foreign debts soar and become a matter of diminishing returns.

Now, I saw mass starvation during my early days in Russia,

when I was a young physician and had my own hospital there during the famine. The memory of this has lived with me all these years, and it is something I hope never to see again. To many people in the Third World, famine is already a reality. They cry out to us, and we must respond if we are going to have international peace. Food, in my opinion, will be our crisis in the 1990s.

Years ago, the shah of Iran said that oil was too valuable to burn, and he was right. If you ask the average American family what the energy crisis means to them, they will probably tell you that their greatest concerns are gasoline for their car and oil for heating and cooling their home. Even in the halls of Congress, it is the direct consumption of energy that gets most of the attention. I am reminded of the little boy who ran to his father and excitedly said, "Dad, you ought to see the great lawnmower our neighbors have! It doesn't need gasoline or anything—all you have to do is push it!"

Understanding is so important. There is the story of the company president who called in one of those overly aggressive efficiency experts to straighten out some of his firm's problems. The efficiency expert called together all the division heads, and he said to them, "Now, gentlemen, as the first order of business, I want on my desk the names and positions of all your personnel broken down by sex." One of the responses he received a few days later read, "We found two with suspected drinking problems, but none broken down by sex."

What should we do about our energy problem? Winston Churchill once said, "Things don't get better by being left alone. Unless they are adjusted, they explode, with shattering detonation." During the past few years I have suggested four points which could help the United States both to become energy independent and to help the rest of the world, and I believe these points are still valid.

First, we should look to our neighbors to the south. We must continue to improve our relations with Mexico. Mexico has one of the largest oil deposits in the world, second only to Saudi Arabia. Mexico probably has proven reserves of approximately 150 billion barrels of oil, indicating that it could produce and export increasing amounts during this century. Mexico's domestic problems, however, have now become critical. Inflation has reached an annual rate of 60 percent. Half the working population is unemployed. The peso has recently been devalued drastically, and the Mexican foreign debt has soared. The time for us to work with Mexico is propitious—certainly, not to take advantage of its serious economic situation, but to help it. And it can in turn help us—the United States and the rest of the world. Businessmen should reassess their attitudes toward Mexico. The Mexicans are a proud people, and they are not going to be converted by their big neighbor to the north as they were earlier in the century. I propose that businessmen all over the world, and especially those of my own country, should follow the lead of our Mexicana Hooker Company, which we fully Mexicanized by selling 51 percent to the Mexican public. We are now making more money with 49 percent than we were previously with 100 percent. Although my proposal is not a quid pro quo for Mexican oil, I believe that in return for helping the Mexicans build their industrial base and improving the lot of their people, they would produce more oil and help to supply the needs of consuming countries. The Mexicans are now producing 2½ million barrels of oil per day, but I believe this production could be doubled or even tripled in a few years if we entered into a program of working closely with Mexico to help it with its economic problems.

I would like to turn now to coal. Besides oil, I believe that coal is the world's most important remaining source of energy which can be developed to meet what I foresee is a crisis ahead. We have shown that we can burn coal and still meet the most stringent environmental standards. We can put scrubbers on our stacks, and we can get rid of the sulfur emissions. We can learn from Japan. In a few years, not a single boiler in Japan will burn anything but coal. Now, Japan has very little natural energy resources of its own, and it must import all its oil and coal. In the United States, for example, we have enough coal to last more than a hundred years. We should continue to export our coal to countries that need coal, and we should see that coal replaces oil wherever possible. If Japan can do it, why can't we and other countries do the same?

Third, we must go ahead on coal liquefaction. In South Africa, they have proven that coal liquefaction is feasible. We had a delegation in South Africa recently, and they told me that you can drive up to a gas station, and there is a pump that says "Sasol," which is the gasoline produced from coal, right next to a Shell pump—and both fuels sell at approximately the same price.

My fourth proposal for a promising source of liquid fuel is shale oil. In this country alone, there is the equivalent of 1.8 trillion barrels of oil locked up in the Rocky Mountains in three states: Colorado, Utah, and Wyoming. Our company has been a pioneer in the development of shale oil. But I am sorry to say that this development by ourselves, Exxon, and others has been set back because of high costs and temporarily depressed oil prices. I believe that the US government should step in and lend support on a temporary basis in order to help build a synthetic fuels industry for shale oil. If we do that, the United States could become the supplier of shale oil to the whole world.

It is very interesting that Sheik Yamani said, "If the West invests heavily in finding alternate sources of energy, it won't be long before their dependence on our oil—that is, OPEC oil—as a source of energy will jeopardize our position." About ten years ago, when we were predicting that we could produce shale oil for as little as $3 per barrel, Yamani said that when oil prices went to $5 or $6 per barrel (this was when oil was selling at $2 and $3 per barrel), OPEC would be losing its market to synthetic oil. Now, since then oil has at one time reached $40 per barrel; it has gone from $27.50 to almost $34 per barrel in a matter of weeks—and we have done very little about developing this tremendous source of synthetic oil which we have in the United States.

I know I have been a voice in the wilderness, crying out for many years for the development of shale oil, and our company is one of the leaders in developing an in situ process whereby we develop shale oil underground. We have invested over $200 million in this venture and are partners with Tennaco. Recently, however, we had to cease production because of escalating costs, inflation, and the recent drop in the price of oil—but I consider this cessation only temporary. Exxon has had to do likewise. When I am told that shale oil development cannot be done so fast and that there are risks, I remind the speakers of what Franklin Roosevelt did to rally the American people during World War II, when the Nazis were sinking US ships that were bringing in natural rubber. I was then in the alcohol business, and I recall how we converted our plants almost overnight to develop the synthetic rubber industry that was so vital to the war effort. Who could have believed that we could do that in such a short time, or, for that matter, that the Manhattan project could be done in such a short time? When President Roosevelt was warned by timid members of Congress that he was going too fast with a crash program and that there might be costly mistakes, he replied, "If we don't act now, we won't have time to make mistakes."

As one world, we must begin to develop a sensible, pragmatic approach to dealing with the energy crisis on an international scale—and by that, I mean international cooperation to a far greater extent than it has occurred up to now. We must begin to recognize that the energy problem and crisis is a world problem rather than a collection of unrelated regional concerns.

Let me cite one example of promising international cooperation with which I have had some personal experience. Just a month ago, I returned from a one-week business trip to Peking—my third trip to the People's Republic of China in three years. I can report to you that I remain very optimistic about prospects for mutual cooperation with the Chinese. I had an opportunity to meet Chairman Deng Xiaoping for the third time, and I believe that he is steering China on a course of cooperation with the West and that he is inviting foreign nations to participate in building up China's economic situation and industries—and particularly to participate in developing China's coal and oil reserves. Our own company has signed a contract with the Chinese to build, under a joint venture, the largest coal mine in the world. This coal mine contains about 1½ billion tons of low-sulfur coal, is conveniently located to a seaport on a fairly good railroad system, and is all open-pit mining. The coal will be exported principally to the Pacific rim countries.

We also have another international energy venture—this one with Italy. As you know, Italy has no oil or coal. So we formed a company called Enoxy, which is a joint venture between a capitalist company, Occidental, and a government agency, ENI—Italy's energy agency. We sold them a half interest in four of our coal mines, and, with a capitalization of over a billion dollars, the business started on the first of January of this year and is doing very well.

There has been a lot of talk about cooperation with the Soviet Union in solving energy problems. I believe that the cause of peace will be served best if President Reagan and President Brezhnev meet at the Summit in October as has been proposed. I am honored to have a friendship with both of these world leaders, and I believe that if they meet and get to know each other, they will develop a better understanding and we will avoid the possibility of an armed conflict that could lead to a nuclear war and the destruction of both peoples. What difference does it make if we can destroy them ten times over and they can only destroy us five times over? I believe that each side has enough nuclear capability to destroy each other, and who wants to be destroyed even once?

For the next three days, you will be talking about international cooperation that will, we hope, help us to find some solutions to our energy problems. But our cooperative efforts should not end this Thursday when the Symposia Series' communiqué is released. Such cooperation must continue on a day-to-day basis and must grow if we expect to achieve results. No one said it would be easy; there are still many obstacles in our path. But I believe that the opportunities are within our grasp, and by all of us working together, we can help make the Knoxville World's Fair be a milestone event—and we can help the world's quest for energy independence, peace, and well-being for all its people.

Technical Paper
and Related Comments

Editors' Note

Those organizing Symposium III were faced with a particular problem—how to provide a bridge from the prior Symposia to this one. Important in any event, this bridge was especially crucial since, given the shift in emphasis from analysis to policy, many of the third Symposium's participants were new to the Series. A dual solution was identified: first, a comprehensive background, or technical, paper to highlight salient issues evolving from the prior Symposia; and second, statements by Symposium II's chairmen/ integrators reacting to that paper. To complete the bridge, opportunity was allowed for a broad-ranging discussion by Symposium III's participants of the paper, the subsequent statements, and related issues.

David J. Rose, John H. Gibbons, and Hans H. Landsberg were asked to coauthor the technical paper, since all three had been closely tied with the Series from its inception as both members of the IESS Program Committee and participants in the prior Symposia. Despite a shortage of time and the pressures of other commitments, they accepted and fulfilled their difficult task admirably, an effort which merits deep appreciation.

The Symposium II chairmen/integrators also deserve special recognition for their continued efforts at Symposium III. All but two were able to attend; those who could not authorized members of their Symposium II work sessions to speak in their stead. The following is a list of the Symposium II work session topics and the chairmen/integrators or their substitutes:

The Role of Nuclear Power	Marcelo Alonso for Harvey Brooks
The Biomass Energy/ Nonenergy Conflict	Philip H. Abelson
Energy for Rural Development	Ishrat H. Usmani
Industrialized Market-Economy Nations	Keichi Oshima
Industrialized Nonmarket-Economy Nations	Ioan Ursu
Energy-Surplus Industrializing Nations	James E. Akins for Mohammad Sadli
Energy-Deficit Industrializing Nations	Guy J. Pauker

As can be seen in Chapter Four, which contains the chairmen/integrators' statements, not all elected to speak on all parts of the paper. Several had prepared statements of considerable length for the morning session, after Parts A and B of the paper were presented; there was thus a sense of urgency at the afternoon session to move quickly from the presentation of Part C to the open discussion.

David le B. Jones, the afternoon session's chairman, is to be commended for his skillful orchestration of that session, especially the two-hour discussion among the participants. Our thanks to him and to Yumi Akimoto, the morning session's moderator, for their valuable contributions to Symposium III.

CHAPTER THREE

Technical Paper: International Energy Issues and Perspectives

David J. Rose
Professor of Nuclear Engineering
Massachusetts Institute of Technology

John H. Gibbons
Director
Office of Technology Assessment
United States Congress

Hans H. Landsberg
Senior Fellow
Resources for the Future

INTRODUCTION

Symposium III's technical paper was prepared jointly by its three coauthors but with each author assuming primary responsibility for the part he presented at the Symposium. Parts A and B were presented by David J. Rose and John H. Gibbons, respectively, at the May 25 morning session; Part C was presented by Hans H. Landsberg at the May 25 afternoon session. Assistance in preparing the paper was provided by staff of the University of Tennessee's Energy, Environment, and Resources Center.

PART A: OVERVIEW

Lewis Carroll's Alice asked the Cheshire Cat, "Would you tell me, please, which way I ought to walk from here?" And he replied, "That depends a good deal on where you want to get to." Like the Cheshire Cat, this paper will not prescribe where we ought to go from here—that is the collective task of this Symposium, which must decide where we want to go, if indeed any single direction can be defined. Instead, we try to give a context for that collective decision by providing a kind of map: the ground the Series has covered thus far and where the paths might lead.

Much of this synthesis will be done in the paper's latter two parts, of which the first reviews Symposium II's findings and the commonalities among nations springing out of those findings; the second, the findings' other, darker side—their implicit areas of tension—and some possibilities for resolution. This introduction, continuing the map metaphor, is a mere sketch with some main features—where are relatively smooth places, or especially rocky ones, and even places unexplored. Here we seek an overall perspective. The approach used in this part is to review a few essential ways in which this situation will be different in the future—basic observations but worth saying because they *are* basic—and then to indicate how far Symposia I and II have gone in addressing the ramifications of these changes.

Seven Basic Observations About How Things Will Be Different

1. The decreasing negotiability of energy. In the simplest terms, energy used to mean mainly oil—black gold, useful and used in free international trade. It is convenient to transport and easy to exchange for a variety of goods and services. In the future, however, energy resources will be more expensive, more tied down to fixed installations, harder to transport, and more limited in their applications. Energy thus will become a decreasingly transferable commodity, to be replaced in part by technological structures and expertise, a fact which will affect international financial markets and relationships between nations.

2. The increasing turbulence of the oil market. Oil is still the swing fuel (i.e., the one that fills energy gaps left by shortfalls in other sources). But the amount of freely negotiable oil declines, for several reasons. Thus, the open oil market is now smaller, but it must still fill in all the unevenness of supply versus demand. A 1-

or 2-percent change in coal (or even in conservation) has a much bigger effect on the oil market than it did previously, making it more turbulent.

3. The increasing importance of rational and effective energy use. We are not running out of energy, but the traditional sources have become expensive and will remain so. New energy sources are also expensive. All bring problems as well as benefits. Thus it becomes necessary to be sure that energy sources are being used providently rather than profligately. When energy supplies were cheap and abundant, how they were used or not used didn't much matter, but now every benefit must be wrung from them, to stretch them as far as possible. Waste not, want not, as the saying goes.

4. The ripple effects of environmental problems. Until recently, most environmental problems either *were* purely local concerns or were *perceived* as such. Now, the consequences increase, or tend to, because we are using more energy and (often) are switching to energy forms more difficult to handle. We tend to solve nearby problems when they annoy us sufficiently, but put at risk people who are farther away in space and time.

5. The increasing need for technology transfer and for information and education. In the past, energy production (with some exceptions) entailed relatively low levels of technology; energy consumption was a simple matter of filling a tank or flicking a switch. More and more, however, effective energy production and use requires technological sophistication. The content of this technological knowledge varies according to the producer or user group, as does the method of transmittal: transferring high-level technology requires high-level diplomatic commitments and commitments to joint programs of education and training; transferring basic information to an uninformed populace requires basic commitments to humanity. These efforts must be sustained if they are to be successful—in most instances, they cannot be treated as one-time cure-alls.

6. The continuing pressures of population. More than 4.4 billion people now; the prospect of 8 billion people in 2030. Particularly when coupled with higher energy demands per capita in the less developed countries as they seek to raise their people above subsistence levels, the effect of these global population figures cannot be ignored. Is this population growth inevitable, or can it be checked? What effects will the lag times between changes in birth and death rates and changes in population size have? (For we know that, like a supertanker, population growth takes a long time even to slow down perceptibly when the population base is as large as it is now.) What new energy demand patterns can we expect in the future, and how will these demands be met? Such questions must be addressed head on; a supply-side view is not enough.

7. **The increasing instability of the global society.** As people become increasingly less willing to tolerate their lot of hunger and poverty and as energy resources become less readily accessible and in greater demand, international destabilizing forces will grow increasingly strong. With these destabilizing forces comes the increased likelihood of war—war which already has been seen in localized conflicts and which includes the possibility of a global holocaust. In a world where making weapons is so easy and so dangerous, we must strive to make a world where people don't feel that they have to build bombs, and are in fact more secure without them.

Where We Are Now

The above observations are not solely my own: their structure was borrowed in part from Professor Roger Revelle. Furthermore— and more importantly—they are a distillation of the sense of the past two Symposia. As will be shown in the latter two parts of this paper, those Symposia went far toward elucidating the global energy problem and how it might be addressed. In particular, the following topics were well recognized and discussed:

- The fact that energy is more than technology: that it has social, economic, and other dimensions also.
- Nuclear power, particularly its fuel cycle.
- The need to continue dialogues and achieve action on the North/South, rich/poor conflict and to move toward a more just and sustainable global society.
- The importance of time perspectives, and especially of recognizing the middle- or long-term consequences of short-term solutions. Too often we paint over rust. We live in the long term of our past neglect.
- The fuelwood crisis: a crisis which is an example of the above point but is worth setting off since it illustrates how, with half of the world's population relying out of necessity on wood and agricultural waste products, vast areas are becoming denuded and depleted of their soil and nutrients.

A number of other points were brought up at the past Symposia but bear further consideration. In particular, these stand out:

- The tragedy of the commons: the fact that some actions which are benign or even beneficial when regarded narrowly or unilaterally have multilateral, sometimes disastrous drawbacks when regarded more broadly over space and time. Carbon dioxide build-up a hemisphere away and years removed from its sources is one example of this, but the "commons" metaphor is not limited to environmental issues—it applies to economic and social ones as well.
- The larger problem of managing the world's affairs, of which energy is only a part: the Europeans call it *le problematique.* Can our inevitably interrelated energy/water/soil systems be sustained unless we alter our methods to accommodate the connections? A country's ability to manage its energy concerns can indicate its capacity to manage these larger concerns—the mishandling (or adept handling) in one sector may signal its level of success in many others.
- The need for international collaborative programs to address the above and other issues: programs which are founded not on single interests, as those in the past often have been, but on holistic approaches.

Finally, some points which received only passing mention during the past two Symposia and merit further attention. Here are three that come particularly to mind:

- The root sources of global energy demand. As mentioned above, an understanding of population's effect on the demand side of the global energy equation is crucial, but thus far the Symposia have largely concentrated on energy supply. This focus is understandable: the economy of supply is simpler than the complexities of demand, so an unbalance of attention tends naturally to build. Rational and effective energy use needs more attention, everywhere.
- Urban rural energy needs and conflicts, especially in less developed countries. In the industrialized countries a sophisticated and complex mix of energy sources prevails in *both* the rural and the urban sectors—their energy modes are not markedly dissimilar. But in the less industrialized countries, a different situation prevails: the urban sector frequently has an overlay of the same complex mix seen in the industrialized countries, but with kerosene as its underpinning; the rural sector frequently has just two things—biomass and kerosene. Kerosene is thus a highly political fuel in such countries.
- The effects of cities on energy patterns. A corresponding subject of inquiry—one appropriate to both industrialized and less

industrialized countries—is how cities are *built*. Set down in concrete, cities last a long time—are the new ones now under construction and the old ones now being refurbished with updated infrastructures as efficient and livable as they might be? Our concern for the environment must extend to the *built* environment which surrounds so many of us.

Conclusion

To conclude this section, here are three simple facts—again, obvious, but worth sharing because they are.

First, we are going to need a lot more energy globally in the decades ahead. The industrialized nations have begun to reduce their per capita energy demands and, if we are fortunate, will continue to do so, but it is likely that a *substantial* change in their demands—one which involves profound changes in living standards—will not readily occur. It is also likely that the less industrialized nations, seeking to raise *their* standards of living, will raise their per capita energy demands, and that the global number of "capitas" will increase inexorably. Although this trio of probabilities can be tempered, there's no way to completely get around them: the world is going to need more energy, not less, in the years ahead.

Second, the transition from the old modes of energy production to new and more sustainable modes is going to be much slower than most people think. Equipment and capital stock change slowly, and so do ingrained habits.

Finally, this energy problem, like so many others, is full of paradoxes. Energy is not a problem with solutions that come with single or simple fixes; we are flooded with oversimple suggestions, most of which, when taken together, are inconsistent. But many of them are parts of a larger whole, and the parts, while preserving their identity and value, must give something to the whole. This paradox of parts and wholes is as old as all of literature. On its recognition, hear the Apostle Saint Paul nineteen hundred years ago: ". . . the body is one, and has many parts; and all the parts are one body: . . . If the ear should say because I am not the eye, I am not of the body—is it therefore not of the body? If the whole body were an eye, where is the hearing? If the whole were hearing, where is the smelling? . . . And the eye cannot say to the hand, I have no need of you: nor again the head to the feet, I have no need of you." So it is with supply and demand, conservation and exploitation, costs and benefits, and many other things in mutual constructive tension.

This problem will not go away; despite temporary respites, it will reappear in new and more intractable forms if not managed wisely. We cannot handle it alone, by unilateral and politically narrow actions. This Symposia Series, which has been marked by a lack of political divisiveness, shows the progress that is possible when issues are considered apolitically, although the issues themselves are political in the highest sense of the word, as they concern the world's body politic.

PART B: FINDINGS AND COMMONALITIES

This part is divided into two sections. The first contains *synopses* of the separate findings of the seven work sessions which ran concurrently through Symposium II. Three of those work sessions focused on selected issues of global importance (the role of nuclear power, biomass and its energy/nonenergy conflict, and energy for rural development); the remaining four were organized around world groupings according to national perspective.

The synopses are taken verbatim from the Editors' Preface of Symposium II's *Proceedings* and are, according to the editors, simply brief reportage jobs with no attempt to delve into either the wealth of diverse opinion at those work sessions or the implicit interplay among the sessions. They are included here to help bring those not present at that Symposium up-to-date, and we extend thanks to the editors for their efforts.

The second section of this part attempts to cull from the many papers and discussions of the past Symposia a sense of the commonalities we might be arriving at.

SYNOPSES OF SYMPOSIUM II WORK SESSION FINDINGS

The Role of Nuclear Power

Globally, nuclear power is in economic and political trouble. Its survival will depend on several factors: on an increased demand for electricity (forecasted in the special plenary paper entitled "The Case for Electricity," but not without debate); on the maintenance of a nuclear safety record sufficiently impeccable to assure the public that the technologies involved—including those dealing with spent fuel reprocessing or storage—are adequate and well under control; and on choices to be made on a country-by-country basis about the economic and environmental appropriateness of nuclear power. With regard to the last factor, it was found that in the past nuclear power has not seemed appropriate for most less developed countries (LDCs), but, with the advent of the LDCs' search for energy self-sufficiency and of the possibility of smaller nuclear plants more in proportion with these countries' electricity grids, this situation may change. With that change, the pros and cons of technology transfer and nuclear nonproliferation become major issues.

The Biomass Energy/Nonenergy Conflict

This conflict is potentially a major one, involving not only the deflection of biomass from its needed use as food for a growing global population but also the environmental degradation—deforestation, desertification, and loss of soil nutrients—that can occur if biomass is improperly managed. On the other hand, for those countries with rich biomass resources (and especially for LDCs that are otherwise resource poor), biomass offers the possibility of profitably utilizing lands that are unsuitable or only marginally productive agriculturally and of attaining a measure of energy independence. To reap the full benefits of biomass for energy while minimizing its drawbacks, decisions about employing biomass for such purposes should be made on a country-by-country basis and should be carried out at a decentralized (i.e., regional or community) level, employing multipurpose systems that integrate such end uses as food, fuel, feed, and fertilizer. While such approaches could greatly defuse the potential conflict, the issue of global food needs versus national interests remains a haunting one.

Energy for Rural Development

The problem of rural development in Third World countries is multifaceted, entailing not only energy inputs but inputs from many other sources (human, animal, environmental, financial, etc.). And above all, it entails the need to remove barriers that hinder socioeconomic development—barriers involving inadequate education and capital, customs and institutional infrastructures that are inconducive or antagonistic to development, and the tendency on the part of governments to favor large, prestigious projects over smaller but potentially more productive ones. Furthermore, a critical problem for many Third World rural people—one specific to energy but permeating their lives—is that of a fuelwood shortage. Approximately one-half of the world's population depends on wood, dung, and vegetative waste for its heating and cooking needs; as this population grows, these resources become increasingly scarce, to the severe detriment of both the people and their environments. To ameliorate this situation and to increase energy's contribution to rural development, two main possibilities (not necessarily mutually exclusive) are forseen: (1) the utilization of alternative energy sources such as the sun, the wind, and biogas; and (2) the establishment of decentralized electricity systems based on either small-scale hydro power or mini diesel-fired generators. In establishing these, the barriers to change noted above must be taken into account: a proposed rural energy project must be appropriate to the recipient group and its locality, and that group must be not just recipients but participants in the project. However, with even the simplest technologies, a lack of capital may be a major obstacle, particularly if the intended beneficiaries cannot afford even minimal new household or agricultural equipment.

Industrialized Market-Economy Nations

The primary problem for this group of nations is the transition from cheap to expensive energy—a transition which began with the 1973–74 oil crisis and which is likely to continue inexorably, despite respites from temporary oil gluts due to market imbalances. Such market-induced imbalances can work both ways, at times provoking false panic, at other times a false sense of security, and either way, they point out two key concerns for market-economy nations: (1) how to temper the effects of energy supply and demand imbalances on related economic factors, and, as an important part of this, (2) how, despite temporary supply gluts, to promote continued energy efficiency, conservation, and conversion from scarce to less scarce fuels. In both of these concerns, government plays a central but delicate role, attempting to correct market imperfections without dictating resource allocations or prices. Another equally important but equally delicate role of government is that of arbitrating among social goals involving economic growth, employment, equitable income distribution, national security, and environmental quality—goals that are all affected by energy needs and resources and that may all come into conflict. Finally, and most elusive to deal with, are the international equity questions, particularly that of the appropriate allocation between the developed and the developing nations of the world's dwindling petroleum resources.

Industrialized Nonmarket-Economy Nations

This category may be a misnomer: its work session emphasized that the nations included here—primarily East European centrally planned economies—do not operate on a uniformly nonmarket basis, and they are in various stages of development rather than being fully industrialized. While this indicates their lack of homogeneity, the latter point, especially, reveals a shared characteristic of these nations: many started industrializing as recently as World War II, and with the 1973–74 oil crisis and its aftermath, many were caught in mid stride. Their common problem, then, is not one of making adjustments in order to maintain the economic status quo (as in the case with many of the nations in the industrial market-economy group), but one of pumping growth into their economic systems in order to bring their development processes to maturation and raise their standards of living. However, the root problem—expensive energy—is the same for this group, as are many of the related issues: a past overreliance on oil and, as a corollary, energy infrastructures that are sufficiently well established to be difficult to change; a need for a mixture of solutions to attain resilient energy systems; and a need for attention to environmental problems that, if ignored, bode ill for the future. The roles of government obviously differ between the two groups, but this could be an asset: it could offer enlightenment about alternative political/institutional possibilities and their ramifications.

Energy-Surplus Industrializing Nations

This is another broad category which includes diverse nations: those with high per capita incomes, those with low; those with vast oil reserves, those with scant. But the commonalities they share are (1) they currently are able to derive export income from their oil resources and (2) those resources are eventually depletable. To the extent that the oil-exporting nations are otherwise resource poor, they thus must translate their ephemeral oil riches into more lasting forms of investment or development if they are to attain secure economic bases. Their needs in doing so are to some extent shared by other developing nations—in addition to needing opportunities for foreign investments, they need technological assistance and foreign markets for their domestically produced goods. However, their international relationships are subject to particular pressures: in terms of energy, they are seemingly the haves, the rest of the world's nations the have nots. They thus have an especial need for cooperation with regional and international institutions, in order to help resolve oil supply/price issues and to obtain the support necessary to attain stable socioeconomic systems. A central contradiction remains, however: it is generally in the best economic interest of these nations to maximize their oil returns by getting the highest prices possible over the longest period possible, but for the other nations of the world—especially for the LDCs, who need large and cheap energy supplies to initiate their development processes—this interest is

in direct conflict. In particular, it may cause the latter's development to founder unless ways (such as investment of petrodollars in
those countries) can be found to relieve the problem.

Energy-Deficit Industrializing Countries

As suggested above, these nations are caught in a twofold
dilemma: as noted in Symposium II's special plenary session paper
entitled "Appropriate Energy Strategies for Industrializing Countries," the financial burden of increasingly expensive oil imports is
particularly great for the LDCs since it absorbs such a great proportion of their GNPs, but in order to increase their GNPs, they need
energy to fuel their nascent development. This category of nations
includes both middle- and low-income developing countries; thus
their remedies to this dilemma differ. Nevertheless, their prerequi-
sites are similar: the need to obtain technological assistance; the
need to have foreign markets for their goods; the need to attract
foreign investments; the need for energy planning that incorporates multiple approaches, both of energy supply modes and of
their centralized or decentralized application. In the poorest of
these countries, however, their problems' severity makes those
problems particularly difficult. For example, the fuelwood crisis is
especially urgent in many such countries but has no ready solution, and while other forms of energy—for example, electrification—are considered imperative to raise living standards above
subsistence levels, these energy systems are in many instances
very difficult to adopt because of their expense. For the extremely
poor nations, then, direct aid and the transfer of basic technology
will continue to be critical.

COMMONALITIES: WHERE WE FIND CONSENSUS

This Symposia Series has brought together perhaps the most diverse representation of the world's nations that has ever been
assembled to analyze and search for consensus on energy issues.
We have explored the frontiers of energy technology and examined
the different geographic, economic, and political situations in
which the problems are imbedded . . . and from which solutions
must be constructed.

To be sure, we have recognized a range of issues on which we
find not even modest agreement—even in the remarkably
nonpolitical environment that has happily pervaded these Symposia. On the other hand, we have found substantial common ground

on a number of important topics . . . a consensus that arises from analysis and acceptance of the *facts* of science and technology, the *reality* of economics, the *force and validity* of social values, the *experience* of the past decade, and the *concern* we all share for our planet and its peoples.

Five Existence Theorems

(1) The fact of transition. Appealing as the thought may be, there is no convincing evidence to suggest that traditional sources of energy will ever again be plentiful and inexpensive for more than brief interludes, as obtained for the years prior to 1972. All nations face the challenge of accommodating a transition from an era of low-cost oil and gas to a new era of increased diversity and cost of supply and dramatically more efficient energy use. The transition will cover considerable time, perhaps decades, and consume enormous amounts of capital. Furthermore, we cannot expect this transition to be uneventful. It has already been turbulent and will likely continue to be so.

(2) There are many supply options but none that are easy. The world is running out of inexpensive sources of oil and gas—not in a year or a decade, but certainly in a few decades. Additional supplies of these premium fuels will be ever more expensive and require increasingly sophisticated technology to recover.

The world is not running out of energy in general. However, none of the alternatives to oil and gas are without problems of their own. There are numerous less attractive fossil fuels to choose from, most obviously coal, but use of these resources entails many adverse impacts—social and economic as well as environmental. On the other hand, solar energy *is* present in enormous amounts. Its nonfossilized forms include direct, biomass, hydro, and wind. These forms, when combined with clever technology, give cause for much hope. But the real is less rosy than the ideal. For example, major use of biomass for energy can cut into the amount of food and fiber available to us.

Nuclear fission is a significant and rapidly growing new source of electricity, but it is also beset with diverse difficulties, ranging from technical and economic obstacles to resilient concerns about social acceptability.

(3) Energy productivity. Many people still only grudgingly admit that the opportunities to use energy more efficiently are great. How often do we still hear "... of course we must all conserve energy, *but* . . ."—as though there were something unpatriotic about devising ways to use energy more productively. A continuing problem is the lack of widely accepted words to describe consumption and demand-side activities. The word "conservation" has been particularly misused, however unintentionally, by people who should know better, including high government officials. Conservation, which means wise and thoughtful use, is used by many to signify curtailment (i.e., a heroic response to minimize damage) or preservation (i.e., no consumption). Thus, many now use "efficiency" or "productivity" when referring to energy conservation. The term "productivity," purposefully used in these Symposia in counterpoint to the word "production," stands for a measure of how much useful service is derived from a unit of energy.

Improving energy productivity makes sense for all nations and regions—developed and less developed countries. Evidence presented at these Symposia has amply demonstrated the fact that the long-run demand for energy can be very elastic—that, given time, other ingredients can be substituted for energy in providing amenities—ingredients such as materials, labor, capital, time, and technology.

In the second Symposium, we noted that the energy intensiveness (energy input per unit of output) of a country first increases with industrialization but later peaks and then falls as technological sophistication enables energy productivity to rise. One unique outcome of these Symposia is our recognition that it is possible for developing nations to "tunnel through" the peak of energy intensiveness in their development if provided requisite technological assistance.

(4) Regional differences. The Symposia have illuminated the fact that, while accommodation to the new realities of energy is a common necessity and encompasses common strategies such as technology, different countries will have to employ different tactics. Indeed, the differences *within* countries—especially urban versus rural areas—are often greater than differences *between* countries. India, Brazil, and the United States share very similar needs to develop large electric power plants to serve big cities. They also share interest in improving biomass utilization. This latter interest is much less similar than the former, because of the differences in land use in these countries. But the basic science and technology skills to be applied are sufficiently similar that close multilateral cooperation is fully justified out of mutual self-interest.

(5) Linkages—the energy conundrum. Our attention to energy issues may appear to some observers as unjustified in the face of today's supply situation and the unquestioned physical existence of diverse additional resources. We argue that such a view is not valid. The emergence and subsequent analysis of energy issues, especially over the past decade, reflects the troubling reality that energy is only one aspect of a growing and interconnected set of issues of meeting human needs and fulfilling human aspirations. Population growth exacerbates the problem, in part because more than 90 percent of this growth is occurring in developing nations. Energy availability affects food, environment, economic growth, and world peace in very sensitive ways. For example, more energy production is needed to bolster agriculture and treat wastes, but that energy production simultaneously competes with food production and produces its own wastes—which in turn could alter global climate or erode human health. Learning to deal effectively with energy could give humankind the most valuable lesson ever learned about how to care and provide for ourselves in a way that is indefinitely sustainable. On the other hand, if the lesson isn't learned, the energy problem could be the initiating event leading to the indefinite decline of civilization.

What Have We Found to Be Required to Implement a Sound Energy Policy?—Three Requirements

(1) Substantial efforts over a long period of time is the first requirement. A new energy supply typically requires several decades to make the transition from scientific demonstration to significant commercial availability. On the demand side, efficiency improvements in existing energy-consuming equipment can be made relatively quickly, but the major cost-effective opportunities take more time—again, often decades. Thus, to view a few years' lull in the pressure on existing energy supplies as a cause to relax or abandon R&D in the areas of new supplies and increased productivity is folly.

There is an unfortunate mismatch between lengthening time requirements dictated by technology and shrinking time horizons dictated by economic ills and social/political expectations. This is a reality, virtually independent of political ideology, that must be taken into greater account in developing and implementing every policy.

(2) A second requirement, equally applicable to both supply and consumption, is the application of human *ingenuity* through science and technology and through *innovation* in our social institutions and political structures. Technology has never moved more rapidly than today, and much of it—applied genetics, geophysics, microelectronics, materials technology, to name a few— is directly applicable to easing energy problems.

(3) A third requirement is *capital* investment. An enormous amount is needed. Competition exists between supply-side and demand-side (productivity) investments. It is important, if not imperative, to identify and follow *least cost* paths.

What Works?

The role of price. Since there is little argument about the *existence* of many options for energy supply and efficient use, the energy problem can be viewed as one of choosing from alternatives. This contains the issue of economic efficiency: that is, which technologies will be most cost effective in the long run, when total cost is taken into consideration?

What seems to be required is an energy *pricing* system (or a nonmarket surrogate) that adequately signals the full cost of energy to both producers and consumers. From the dawn of commerce more than ten thousand years ago to every current society, price has been one of the most sensitive factors in the decisions of both producers and consumers, regardless of the form of governance under which they live. On the demand side, price changes can lead to altered efficiency of use and altered patterns of use. On the supply side, the same price change may alter production schedules and investment strategies.

Unfortunately, energy prices often do not reflect full costs. The most obvious case of a breakdown is when prices are set without reference to the forces of demand and supply. Resource misallocation can easily result, irrespective of whether the economy is based on private market forces or is centrally planned.

Private cost versus full cost. Private cost refers to the value of the individually identifiable products of the economic system. Such *"divisible"* products—for instance, electricity, cement, and steel—often have *indivisible* side effects or spillovers—the so-called externalities of economic activity. If these are ignored in the energy sector (as they often are), then energy prices will not reflect full costs, and attempts to select cost-effective energy systems for the future will be based on incorrect (i.e., incomplete) information.

The most pervasive spillover issue in the case of energy is environmental damage. Because environmental costs are often incurred collectively and are broadly distributed over space and time, they tend to be ignored or considered separately in energy analyses. Thus, the carbon dioxide or acid rain problems do not normally appear in the familiar coal versus nuclear cost analyses for new baseload electrical capacity, nor, on the other hand, do we find complete representations of the costs of nuclear waste disposal and the risks of nuclear accidents and proliferation. Whatever the energy alternative, the question must be asked: What are its hidden collective costs? No nation, and certainly no world of nations, can any longer afford to employ a definition of cost that ignores these types of "extra" costs.

What Else Works?

Rational interdependence. There still is much talk of national energy independence. To be sure, all nations must seek some degree of self-reliance. But, since both natural and technological resources are unevenly distributed around the world, it is good that nations trade. Nature has provided humankind with virtually inescapable interdependence. But, if nations are to make the most of their particular resources, they must understand and be responsive to each other's needs. For example, energy-exporting, developing nations must have opportunities to reinvest the proceeds of their sales in ways that provide for successors to their present wealth in energy resources. That includes not only imports of goods but also opportunities for external investment, development of domestic technology and industrial production, and, ultimately, export markets for their industrial products. Western Europe sells equipment and lends money to the Soviets and in return gets natural gas. The Soviet Union uses the revenue from gas sales for its economic development, and for major grain purchases from the United States. The United States uses the proceeds of its grain sales, plus technology sales, to purchase oil from other exporters.

Thus, the economics of energy interdependence represent an opportunity for closer international integration. Still, it is necessary to recognize political and social realities which lie outside the purely economic sphere. Where, for instance, are the acceptable limits of political interdependence?

Energy and economic development. The most natural goal for all countries is economic development. It was popular a few years ago to characterize the basic dilemma of economic development with a familiar quote from Lewis Carroll's *Through the Looking Glass:*

> "A slow sort of a country!" said the queen. "Now, *here*, you see, it takes all the running *you* can do, to keep in the same place. If you want to get somewhere else, you must run at least twice as fast as that!"

In other words, can a country's economy generate a sufficiently rapid growth in income to outpace population growth and hence achieve an improved standard of living as roughly measured by per capita income?

In the not too distant past, energy was not recognized as an important constraint in the economic development equation, primarily because it was abundant, inexpensive, and getting cheaper. A correlation, or "coupling," has been recognized for a long time between higher energy consumption and economic development.

But what about a world of energy scarcity and rising prices? In the industrialized countries, "decoupling" appears to be a possibility, with level or falling per capita energy consumption but with economic growth continuing. This phenomenon has demonstrated the claim of analysts that given time to respond, energy is a largely replaceable commodity. Examinations of energy required per unit of goods and services produced shows that in the United States, for example, advancing technology has enabled massive economic growth over the past half century simultaneous with a steadily declining rate of energy per unit output.

In the less developed countries, however, there is concern that economic growth cannot be separated from increased per capita consumption of energy, especially at the stages of development when energy is directly substituting for human labor and is improving basic human needs such as habitat, mobility, food, and illumination. Thus, the potential for major "decoupling" of energy growth from economic progress in the industrial world is not seen as likely for developing nations. Consequently, the eroded, if not dashed, hopes of the world's poorest nations to make economic progress using an engine of cheap energy should be a matter of concern for all the world.

We are aware that an exclusive concern with the need to supply energy for development can have unfortunate consequences. The case of biomass is already familiar. Without careful consideration of the entire biomass system, conflicts with the production of food and other essentials quickly emerge, as well as concerns about deforestation. The case of rural electrification is similar. In less developed countries, large rural populations living at or below subsistence levels are common. Rural electrification is seen by many as a means both of raising productivity (and income) in rural areas and of reducing the population pressure on over-crowded cities. To be sure, electrification can help provide ameni-ties to rural areas and perhaps lessen the relative attractiveness of the cities. At the same time, energy—fueling mechanization—eliminates jobs in rural areas and creates jobs in cities. The point is simply that, to paraphrase Orwell, all methods of energy invest-ment are not equal; some are much better than others, especially when measured in terms of social utility!

Questions of Equity

What about those people who have little to offer at the trading table? The planet is bulging with situations of natural resource depletion, driven by population growth and exploitation. What responsibilities do the rest of us bear to assist those who seemingly have few assets? Throughout the first two Symposia there was an undercurrent of concern about the issue of equity. Included in this category are the people in underdeveloped, resource-poor coun-tries—both current and future generations—as well as future gen-erations in industrial nations. In the high-stakes energy game, these groups have few cards to play.

Our search for ways to manage the energy problem has led us to the point where we can no longer separate our scientific analysis of the problem from our values and beliefs. An obvious issue is the fate of the resource-poor Third World. Another is nuclear power; however, the situation also exists in the biomass debate and the energy demand/population growth dilemma. We must consider not only the technical possibilities but also the normative issues. As the German physicist, Max Born, once remarked,

> Intellect distinguishes between the possible and the impossible. Reason distinguishes between the sensible and the senseless. Even the possible can be senseless.

Is it sensible to opt for a world in which the disparity of resources between peoples grows indefinitely? Is it sensible to rush toward an exhaustion of inherited options such as oil and gas in satisfying present desires, seemingly without thought for future generations?

It seems sensible that the plight of resource-poor nations should be shared by the more fortunate nations. Those with great technological wealth can share technical assistance without significant loss. This is probably the most helpful form of development assistance since it can help trigger latent indigenous human ingenuity. Those with bountiful energy resources can likewise share some of their special wealth. But at some point there must be a quid pro quo among nations and peoples of the world. Each who seeks an import, whether it be materials, technology, or energy, should provide something in exchange if they hope to retain their independence. But most of all, while we are engaged in meeting our own difficulties, we must not become insensitive to the plights of others. George Bernard Shaw reminds us:

> The worst sin toward our fellow creatures is not to hate them but to be indifferent to them: that's the essence of inhumanity.

What Next?

Many nations have developed over recent years a vastly improved knowledge of their energy supply and consumption systems. Many are making substantial progress toward achieving higher productivity in the use of energy. But the burden of energy imports remains major for many, and nearly catastrophic for others. The links between energy, material resources, economics, environment, and population are tightening. One feeling that emerges from these Energy Symposia is that we must do some more dispassionate, careful thinking together about how to understand these interrelated issues. The expansion and integration of knowledge offers our best hope for improving the human condition. Even if we manage to gain a clearer technical understanding we will find it socially and politically difficult to take advantage of that understanding, but at least it would be a good place to start. The Anglo-Indian scholar, Henry Derozo, said:

> The greatest of all wisdom is humility, because it teaches us about our ignorance.

But we must not let our search for understanding be taken as a substitute for action. More than twenty-four hundred years ago, Sophocles remarked:

> One must learn by doing the thing, for though you think you know it, you have no certainty until you try.

At the last, then, our common view is that the energy world *is* very different—the past is not prologue. The transition to the energy future will require much time and sustained attention—the future will be born slowly. In the interregnum, a variety of morbid symptoms are bound to appear.

PART C: POINTS OF TENSION AND OF RECONCILIATION

THE SEARCH FOR CONVERGENCE

The search for convergence, or more modestly, for minimizing divergence, in matters of energy policy has been long and frustrating. To be sure, any situation that confronts sellers and buyers has inherent conflict: one seeks to sell at the highest price, the other to buy at the lowest. In the case of energy, there are several aggravating circumstances. First, the oil market has changed from one in which the prevailing mode is for private parties to transact business to one in which governments have come to play an increasing role. Second, political aspirations and motivations, not necessarily associated with energy in any technical sense, loom large. Third, nuclear energy activities and decisions are deeply affected by various aspects of the nuclear weapons problem. Fourth, energy production, transportation, and consumption inevitably cause environmental degradation and raise cost and tradeoff issues, some of which transcend national boundaries. And fifth, past attempts at international "cooperation" have foundered due to highly ambitious aims, such as that of trying to tie the energy problem to a great many others that beset the world—the fate of other depletable resources, investment needs, technology transfer, balance of payments problems, protectionism, and so forth.

These five circumstances are well known, and several of them have already been touched on in the first two parts of this paper. However, it seems appropriate to view them now in a different light—as points of tension in the world's energy problem, matters that must be acknowledged and reconciled if we want to move successfully toward easing that problem. It thus seems worthwhile to separately consider each of these points: its genesis, its effects, and issues that are related to it.

1. Government intervention in the oil market. Government intervention—open or hidden—in the energy market is not altogether new. Surely, oil and politics have been close companions ever since oil first became a marketable commodity. Moreover, in some countries energy has always been the domain of government. In others, intervention gathered steam following World War I, with the realization of the importance of energy supplies to national security. Government's role became more extensive and widespread during the ensuing years: concern for national security in the military sense was extended to economic security, and more nations—oil producers as well as consumers—adopted it as a rationale for their governments' intervention in previously market-determined outcomes regarding supplies and prices. While such action may provide greater stability by tempering swings in the market, it can also have the opposite effect: that is, it may aggravate the unpredictability inherent in market forces, as governments work to counterpurposes and as their actions are shaped by outside nonmarket-related events.

Obviously then, energy policy as a political tool is not a recent invention. But there is a new element, added during the past decade: the emergence of governments not just as intervenors or regulators, mostly on the domestic scene, but as buyers and sellers in world markets. Thus, *international* trade has largely become *intergovernmental* trade, and trade disputes have tended to become political disputes.

This complicates other, related world energy issues that are already sufficiently complicated. These issues—again, points which have already been mentioned but are worth reiterating here—include as a minimum the following:

- The legitimate desire of oil exporters to get the highest value possible out of their resources versus the need of oil importers, particularly the less developed countries, to obtain adequate and affordable fuel supplies during their transition to a more sustainable energy basis.
- A correlated issue: the distribution of the energy pie, especially the depleting fossil fuel resources. In particular, as prices increase, are there or should there be limits to the extent to which ability to pay for these resources sets the pattern of allocation? Are there ways of identifying and assuring minimum needs?
- The huge boost in oil prices since 1973, which has played havoc with trade and payment balances, has fed inflation, and has slowed down growth. Governments are forever tempted to correct these imbalances by unilateral policies, including protectionist measures, foreign exchange manipulations, and so forth. In this game retaliation is the rule, and in the long run there are few winners.
- The effect of government intervention in the conventional fuels market on the development and adoption of nonconventional renewable energy and conservation technologies. Is the marketplace, as modified by government interventions such as subsidies and price controls, working to *aid* or *discourage* the transition to a more sustainable energy basis?

These are all important issues—issues which should be taken into account when considering appropriate forms of government intervention in the energy marketplace, or governmental policy where markets do not exist to begin with.

2. The effects of politics on energy supplies. This is closely—perhaps inextricably—tied to the above point, but it needs separate consideration. Government intervention in the energy market preceded what we might call the "politicization" of energy; that is, the flowering of energy as a subject of broad public interest and debate. Energy has become a major political and highly divisive issue only during the last decade, when energy supplies became more expensive and scarce and when large numbers of interest groups developed and advocated ideas of the place of energy in their schemes of things. To be sure, increased public participation is a fine thing, but it does complicate the decision process when attitudes are rigid and minds are closed to the intake of new information—not an uncommon phenomenon.

While issue politics can serve a valuable function by drawing attention to a situation that might otherwise go ignored, they can also have less desirable side effects. In the instance of the politicization of energy, several such side effects are likely: first, to the extent that government intervention increases unpredictability of future markets, this unpredictability may be further heightened; second, regulatory unpredictability may be increased; and third, compromising and consensus-forming, a basic ingredient in public decisionmaking, tends to become more difficult as individuals and groups cluster around packages of beliefs, including those concerning energy, that they are unwilling to surrender or see violated. These tendencies hinder the development of energy resources by giving mixed and unreliable signals to suppliers and consumers alike and by greatly prolonging and exacerbating the decisionmaking process. Thus, while issue politics can serve as a useful catalyst in illuminating fully a problem such as energy supply, in most instances they will find their way into and make more complex the final compound making up that solution, frustrating those who look for neat, apolitical processes and outcomes.

3. Nuclear power and nuclear weapons. Broadly speaking, transnational concerns on this subject include (1) the possible misuse of nuclear technology in those countries that do not now have it, and (2) the theft—or more likely the diversion—of weapons-grade enriched uranium from power plants in countries that *do* have a nuclear capacity, with the object of fashioning nuclear devices for internal or external offensive designs. These concerns have led to widespread reservations about nuclear power—in particular, reservations about the wisdom of letting nuclear power technologies, including fuel enrichment, be introduced into the first group and nuclear power capacities expanded in the second. Subsets of concern involve the disposal of radioactive waste, transportation of fuel and waste, and recycling of spent fuel; all of them offer the opportunity for accidents as well as for diversion of radioactive material to illegitimate ends. Together with economic and environmental considerations, these concerns have impeded the growth of the nuclear power industry almost everywhere and thus place in jeopardy what is a source of practically nondepletable energy. Are such concerns well founded, or are they irrational impediments? These questions, together with issues of what kinds of nuclear power plants are appropriate in what places (issues that involve the magnitude of electricity demand, level of centralization, and desirable plant capacity in relation to total grid size) must be resolved if nations—and their energy suppliers—are to know the extent to which they can expect nuclear power to meet their future electricity demand.

The lead time of a nuclear power plant, from commitment through construction to initial operation, is long: ten years or more in some countries. This is due largely to the many precautions that need to be taken but results in multitudes of studies and permits, and not infrequently changes in design, while construction is under way. In that period many of the underlying assumptions that led to the decision can change; obviously, enormous waste of resources is inevitable if those building the plants cannot count on a reasonably secure basis on which to proceed. The need for sensible and consistent regulations concerning construction and management practices is beyond dispute, but so is the conflict that arises out of these two sets of interest: to build and supply, and to regulate. It extends all the way from the design of the reactor core to the storage and eventual fate of radioactive waste. And, as Sigvard Eklund noted in his Symposium II paper, "Let us recall that thermal reactor systems only represent a temporary contribution to the energy provisions of the world. A long-term contribution presumes the development of fast systems, breeders, whereby nuclear energy could make a long-lasting contribution . . ." Although whether breeders or some other technological option represents the best long-term strategy is still debatable, all these strategies require long-term planning.

The issues surrounding nuclear power are highly complex, both technologically and politically, particularly since the weapon connection puts mankind's future as well as present at risk. For that reason, they should be dealt with in an atmosphere that is as thoughtful and unbiased as possible. But, since we first encountered nuclear fission as "the bomb," it is probably impossible to strip the nuclear debate of its emotional and moral guise.

4. Environmental degradation and international costs and tradeoffs. As David Rose noted in his presentation, many environmental problems arising from energy production, transportation, and consumption used to be purely local concerns—either in fact or as perceived. Now, however, the larger scale of production and more complex nature of energy technologies have earlier and more far-reaching effects. As we improve our understanding of those effects across space and time, it has become apparent that these environmental issues can no longer be contained in a box labeled "Local." Instead, what we have, more often than not, is a set of problems that do not respect state or national boundaries but cross them willy-nilly with complete disregard for jurisdiction. What bedevils the issue, apart from ignorance, is that those who cause the problem are not generally those who suffer the consequences; no market forces exist to bring producers face to face with consumers of environmental insults.

There are numerous examples of this: water pollution in inland water bodies, water rights along shared rivers, acid rain far from its sources, the oceans used as dumping grounds for radioactive and other toxic wastes. Many situations, as these examples show, involve water, for water is a fluid medium and a traditional demarcator of boundaries. But the examples are not limited to water: air pollution; the possibility of carbon dioxide buildup from combustion of fossil fuels, especially coal; waste discharged into space—all these are international concerns as well.

So too, in the end, are questions about how each nation uses or misuses its resources, though here the complexity of judging the issue is enormous. Consider the question of whether some nations should use part of their agricultural lands—even marginally arable ones—for fuel production while other nations are starving. Who is to say? It is a moot point in two senses: there is no obvious resolution, and in any case, it is at present without a doubt not a subject for international decision. Nonetheless it is worth thinking about.

But many of these cross-national environmental issues are *not*

moot, and the number of acceptable choices is limited. Again—and
we are returning to a major theme—politics can help. How? By
spreading and at the same time solidifying an understanding of the
larger ramifications of environmental issues, and by developing
international fora to deal with them. At the same time, however,
politics should stop short of setting down specifics. As noted
above, regulations must be even-handed, consistent, and reasonably predictable if they are to provide a framework within which
suppliers can rationally operate, and if they are to function effectively *over time*, so that long-term negative effects can be foreseen
and ameliorated.

   5. **Targeted versus comprehensive approaches.** In recognizing
interrelationships, one must resist the temptation to be comprehensive, lest one overload the circuits. Over the last decade or so,
there has been an increasing awareness that energy is related to
everything else—to other resources, to world economics, to dis-
tributive justice, to ethics, to social structures, and so forth. In the
words of this fair's theme, "Energy Turns the World"—a good
thing to keep in mind, but a bad one to guide the decisionmaker in
his daily tasks.
   How tight are these relationships? Can they be broken into
manageable components, and can the components be matched to
people who can effectively handle them? It is, in Hamlet's words,
"a consummation devoutly to be wished," for over the last few
years, there has been a growing awareness that all these problems
cannot be resolved in one fell swoop, most certainly not at any one
conference, however long and well attended; yet some action must
be taken.
   The inertia principle: if we tackle (and inevitably get bogged
down in) the complexities of the *total* problem, there will be little
chance or even enthusiasm for partial solutions. And while we
must not lose sight of the former, we must urgently move on the
latter. As just mentioned, disaggregation of the problem into manageable components, with simultaneous and coordinated attacks
on a number of fronts, is one approach. Let me try to describe it.

THE ELUSIVE SOLUTION AND CROSS-NATIONAL
MANAGEMENT POLICIES

   As a backdrop to this approach I begin by suggesting that the
energy problem is not something that has a "solution" followed by

a return to "normality." Rather, the energy problem is a complex set of issues that need to be managed. They can be managed well, or they can be managed poorly. In the latter case, there will be recurrent crises, resorts to "quick fixes," and the like. Good management will consist of policies that meet the needs of the short run without creating difficulties and foreclosing options for the long run; that balance the needs for energy with the demands for environmental maintenance; that reconcile meeting domestic challenges with consideration of claims and needs beyond national borders; and that are—and this is a big order—*economically efficient, socially equitable, administratively feasible,* and *politically acceptable.*

How should these management policies be determined? Many, as they must, deal mainly with domestic issues; these are important but they are not the focus of this Symposia Series. But many others involve crossing national borders; these are the concern of this Series. The Symposia have gone a long way toward identifying issues that must be dealt with transnationally; the formulation of policies to address the issues is the next step. Returning to the point made above, this formulation will not be possible if it becomes swamped by contingent relationships; neither, however, can it arbitrarily ignore all ties.

To deal with these considerations, we would suggest that the transnational issues illuminated at these Symposia be grouped topically, thereby preserving key interrelationships while dividing the total energy problem into more manageable entities. One of many possible groupings is given below, without any attempt to more than sketch in the barest identification:

Market and Government Supply/Demand Issues

- Short-term price and supply stability; long-term price and supply predictability—How can these be achieved? At what cost to whom? Across different political and social systems?
- The relationship of conventional fuels to renewable or sustainable energy sources—Are public policies concerning the former helping the transition to the latter?

Needs of Less Developed Countries

- Technology transfer, affordable oil, foreign aid, open foreign markets, investment opportunities—To what extent are these needed but inadequately provided, and if so, why? How can we do better, both in quantity and—often neglected—in quality?

Are these matters of political will, appropriate institutions, or moral suasion?
- The fuelwood crisis—How can international efforts most effectively assist those experiencing this problem? What is the framework within which the task can best be tackled: energy, agriculture, both, or neither?

Environmental Issues

- Cross-boundary environmental effects—How serious are they? How can they be controlled? Who bears the cost, and do we need new institutions for resolving conflicts?
- Regulatory predictability in order to allow efficient, least cost resource development—Is this a reasonable objective? If so, can it be achieved? If not, what means can be evolved to live better with uncertainty?
- The interrelated problems of energy/soil/water systems—Can they be disentangled, defused, yet managed with the consistency that reciprocal relationships demand?

Nuclear Power and Nuclear Weapons

- International safeguards to ensure the nonmilitary use of facilities dedicated to nuclear power generation—Are we on the right track and are there unattended issues? Are there technical solutions, or do we need stronger institutions?
- International management, or at leat control, of waste disposal, transportation, and other critical phases of the fuel cycle—Are we ready to try? What are the best ways, and where do we begin?
- Regulatory predictability—Is this an illusory goal?

Technologies for Efficient Energy Use and for Sustainable Energy Systems

- Is efficient use a proper subject for international consideration? If so, what are the means and institutions for pursuing the objective? Beyond education, what incentives or pressures are at hand?
- The characteristics of a sustainable energy system—Do we know and can we define it? How do we get there? What are the time dimensions?
- Technology transfer—What do we have in mind when we use the term? Who are the actors and what should be asked of them? Is it a proper topic for international discourse and negotiation?

If some such grouping seems reasonable and useful, we might

then consider what type of institution, if any, would be most appropriate to take the next step—a step wherein the issues would be further reviewed and management policies to deal with them proposed. Such institutions might be ad hoc or permanent, regional or global, political or apolitical, depending on the issue group. They might be existing—the United Nations Environment Programme, the International Atomic Energy Agency, for example—or newly created, although the advantages of the former (they already exist; therefore, they will probably cost less and start sooner) should be borne in mind. In any event, I suspect most of us here today would be content to feel that we have only begun to talk to one another, and that somehow a sequel is in the offing.

In conclusion, and at the risk of seeming needlessly insistent, I would point once again to the importance of dealing with energy as a process, not a crisis. The roots of the problem go back to the fifties and sixties: the rapid worldwide growth in energy consumption and the sharp shift to oil which by the early seventies had drained away any excess production capacity. The actions of OPEC in late 1973 and early 1974 greatly accelerated propelling energy into the "problem" category, but it hardly created it. As we look around, our conventional energy sources—least so, natural gas—are flawed: coal with its severe environmental impact from mining to combustion, nuclear with its radiation and proliferation risks, oil with its potential for causing international conflict. Yet, the brave new world of harmless, riskless, environmentally benign, abundant, and affordable energy sources is still on a far horizon, kept there by technological problems, costs,—such as high capital requirements for active solar energy facilities—and individual as well as institutional inertia. Only the more efficient use of energy, if one may call it a "source" of energy, is basically benign.

Thus, we are caught in a difficult transition period. On the one hand, to invert an old saying about bottled liquids, our attitude toward conventional sources should be "use well before shaking." On the other hand, the problems afflicting the conventional sources suggest that we move forcefully toward a better mix. There are, of course, different views on what courses of action should be taken—for example, some prescribe a "hard path," others a "soft path." But these viewpoints go far beyond the energy problem and represent divergent views of human existence. Therefore, while it is important to keep such differences in mind, it is also important to recognize that they are not resolvable. In fact, they make the process even more difficult, and meanwhile we must attend to managing the problem at hand. For the dimensions of the energy problem must, above all, be seen not as a crisis with a solution but as a difficult though doable task of continuous wise management. I would urge you all to approach the discussion of the remaining hours in that spirit.

CHAPTER FOUR

Symposium II Chairmen/Integrators' Statements*

MARCELO ALONSO

Statement Following Presentation of Technical Paper Parts A and B

I am the understudy for Harvey Brooks, and that is not an easy task. It is very difficult to step into his shoes, so I apologize, both to him and to the members of our Symposium II work session on nuclear power, for any deficiencies in my statement.

If there is something on which it is difficult to reach consensus, it is nuclear power. It entails a tremendous diversity of opinion, basically, because its issues are much more complex than for any other energy source, and second, because positions on it normally are emotionally charged. Perhaps our energy problems would be a lot easier if we had never harnessed nuclear power. But we did, and therefore we must decide in an intelligent way what to do with it. In that sense, I would like to start by quoting the governor of Pennsylvania, Richard Thornburgh, who said in the governors' commissioned report about the Three Mile Island accident, "Nuclear opponents who would shut down every nuclear reactor in the country tonight simply are not in touch with our needs for tomorrow, but nuclear advocates who would pretend that nothing has been changed by the vigil at Three Mile Island simply are not in touch with reality." [*Report of the Governor's Commission on Three Mile Island*, Commonwealth of Pennsyl-

*For an explanation of the Symposium II chairmen/integrators' roles at Symposium III, see the introductory note to this section.

vania (Harrisburg: February 26, 1980) p. ii] I think that is a very good summary of the situation.

I would like now to examine the major points we discussed in our work session at Symposium II. Figure 4–1 refers to the issues presented in the excellent technical paper prepared on the basis of our work session's discussion, that I believe are of particular relevance to our analysis of nuclear power. I am not going to elaborate on each of them. I think that it is imperative to formulate a global energy strategy that has as one of its major objectives moving away from oil and using energy in a more judicious way, but it will be extremely difficult to reach such a global strategy—such a strategy is sensible, but I believe it is impossible, given the conditions in the world.

1. THE NEED TO FORMULATE A GLOBAL ENERGY STRATEGY

- Reduce dependence on oil
- Increase energy use efficiency
- Take into account different nations' situations

2. INTERNATIONAL COOPERATION ON ENERGY MATTERS

- Technology R&D; technology transfer; new and more efficient ways of producing, distributing, and using energy
- Assurance of supply
- Stable pricing mechanism

3. INCREASING ROLE OF GOVERNMENTS IN ENERGY MATTERS

- Planning, analysis, regulation, pricing

4. POPULATION INCREASE

- Approximately 2% annually worldwide; more than 3% annually in less developed countries
- 4 billion in 1980; 8 billion by 2030?

5. TREND TOWARD URBANIZATION

- Approximately 40% (1.6 billion) urban in 1980; 70% (5.6 billion) in 2030?
- 4–6 kW/cap in urban areas vs. 0.1 kW/cap in rural areas
- 10 W/m^2 in urban areas vs. 0.1 W/m^2 globally

6. INEQUALITIES IN ENERGY USE

- Industrialized countries' energy use per capita is approximately 30–40 times more than less developed countries'

Figure 4–1. **Aspects Emerging from the Technical Paper that Are of Special Relevance to Nuclear Power**

International cooperation on energy is essential for our survival. I think we should actively look for a new international energy order. I do not know if we can reach that goal, even if we keep talking about it all the time, but nuclear power really needs some international cooperation if it is to become an important alternative for the generation of electricity.

Governments are paying more and more attention to energy, and nuclear power is one aspect of energy that is basically in the hands of the government. So, if there is one type of energy in which government plays and must play a very important role, it is nuclear power.

But I think that there are three major world problems that may affect the extended use of nuclear power. One is the growing world population. Currently, the world population is a little over 4 billion, but is it going to increase to 8 billion in the next fifty years? Will it level off, or will it continue to grow? These are serious questions affecting the use of resources, energy in particular.

The second problem is the trend toward urbanization. Is this trend going to continue? At present, about 40 percent of the world's 4 billion people, or 1.6 billion, live in urban centers, but for the year 2030, urbanization is forecast at about 70 percent of 8 billion people, or 5.6 billion. So, we are confronted with a tremendous urban population explosion with an equally tremendous impact on energy use, in terms of both energy use per capita and energy use per unit of area, since urban centers are more energy intensive than rural areas.

I will give you one simple example. Mexico City today has about 15 to 17 million people—nobody really knows for sure how many Mexicans live there—but it is forecasted that by the year 2030 it will probably be the largest city in the world, with about 30 million people. One of the energy implications of that population explosion is water supply: Mexico City will need 120 cubic meters per second of water. Most of this water will have to be brought from 200 kilometers away, and will have to be raised 2,000 meters. Thus, if Mexico City's projected growth materializes, 3,000 mw of electric power will be required just to bring water to the city. Three nuclear power plants would be needed to provide that energy, because I do not believe that water can be obtained through rain or through the direct use of solar energy.

The third major problem is the one of inequalities in energy use. To understand this situation, we have to recognize that on the average, the less developed country uses thirty to forty times less energy than the industrialized country, and that Latin America uses about one-tenth the energy per capita of that used in North America. Energy use therefore must increase much more in the less developed countries than in the developed countries. That means that nuclear power might be an option for some less developed countries. I do not think I can give a prescription for that—I leave you all to think about it for yourselves—but I think it is important to keep that option in mind when planning for future energy supplies.

Next, let us examine what the general issues are that affect nuclear power and that need further clarification. These are listed in Figure 4–2. One issue is the trend toward an increase in total energy demand. Is the world's energy demand going to go from the 9 TW of today to 16 TW in 2030, as Professor Columbo mentioned in the second Symposium, or to 30 TW, as the study of the International Institute for Applied Systems Analysis (IIASA) has suggested? In the first case, we will have a steady society which will continue using energy at the current rate of 2 kw per capita and thus will maintain most of the current inequities unless the industrialized countries substantially cut their per capita consumption and give a chance to the less developed countries experiencing large population increases and thus needing more energy per capita, while in the second case the world will more than treble the present level of energy demand, with another set of consequences.

1. INCREASE IN TOTAL ENERGY DEMAND

- **Approximately 9 TW in 1980; 16–30 TW in 2030?**

2. STRUCTURE OF ENERGY DEMAND

- **Electricity's share in total energy demand:**
  industrialized countries—27% in 1980; 40–45% in 2000
  less developed countries—25% in 1980; 30–35% in 2000
- **Percentage of people without electricity:**
  industrialized countries—less than 10%
  less developed countires—approximately 60%
- **Centralized/decentralized mix of power generation**

3. ALTERNATIVES FOR GENERATING ELECTRICITY

- **Nuclear power compared with others**

Figure 4–2. **General Issues Affecting Nuclear Power that Need Further Clarification**

A second issue is what the structure of energy demand is going to be, especially the energy demand that can be met best by nuclear power. A related issue is what role electricity will play in this energy demand expansion. Electricity is perhaps the most refined and versatile form of energy, and in my opinion, electricity is essential to assure a certain quality of life. And nuclear power is particularly suited for generating electricity.

But an important point usually forgotten is that many people today do not have electricity, and they live mostly in the less developed countries—in Latin America alone, the rate is about 50 percent. For that reason, one of the major objectives in the less developed countries' energy plans is to provide electricity to as many people as possible. The question is *how*. For example, should electricity generation be centralized, decentralized, or some combination of the two? There is no general prescription for this, either. In some places it has to be centralized; in others, such as remote or sparsely populated areas, it may have to be decentralized. When it has to be centralized, what should the degree of centralization be? That is, how big can the grid be that will carry the energy? Only after considering such questions as these can you decide whether you need nuclear power or not, whether or not you should include it in your energy plans. For example, in Latin America only eight countries have electric systems larger than 1,000 MW—the rest of the countries currently cannot use nuclear power because their systems are too small. Of the eight countries, only three have systems larger than 10,000 MW, and only they can carry out comprehensive nuclear power programs; the remaining five countries probably can afford only one nuclear power plant each in the next twenty or thirty years.

Thus, if we agree that all countries need more electricity, what are the alternatives for generating electricity? Of course, nuclear power is one, but it must be compared economically and technically with the others. Which alternative should be chosen? First, countries must be prepared to *make* the choice. Unfortunately, not all countries yet have people and institutions prepared to make such a choice—a particularly serious problem for the less developed countries.

The most we can say is that in many places there exist conditions for an expanded use of nuclear power because of the foreseeable increase in electricity demand. I want to emphasize, however, that I am not saying that if those conditions exist, nuclear power *must* be used. All I am saying is that if those conditions exist, then nuclear power may be more relevant, more important, and therefore its use must be seriously regarded.

Let us now consider some conditions for expanded energy demand and thus pertinent to nuclear power (see Figure 4-3). A first condition is economic recovery and stability. Stability is very important, because expanding an energy supply takes a long time.

1. ECONOMIC RECOVERY & STABILITY

- 10-year lead time for planning and developing energy supply (low case)

2. INCREASED DEMAND FOR CENTRALLY PRODUCED ELECTRICITY

- Size of grids, resources

3. FAVORABLE COMPARATIVE ECONOMICS

- Structure of electricity generation costs
- Market vs. nonmarket criteria
- Capital

4. FAVORABLE COMPARATIVE RISKS

- Feasibility of assessing *total* risks associated with particular energy forms
- Environmental degradation associated with particular energy forms and processes (extraction, processing, transportation, use, disposal)

5. TECHNICAL FIX

- Siting and safety measures
- Back end of fuel cycle (temporary storage, reprocessing, permanent waste disposal)

6. DECOUPLING OF NUCLEAR POWER AND NUCLEAR WEAPONS

- Nonproliferation treaty (NPT): essential but not sufficient
- New fuel cycles (see International Nuclear Fuel Cycle Evaluation—INFCE)
- International facilities (industrialized countries vs. less developed countries)

7. PUBLIC ATTITUDES

- Information, media, roles of elected officials and technical bodies

8. REACTOR TECHNOLOGY

- Small reactors (less than 400 MW)
- Use of low-grade ores
- Converters, breeders, perhaps fusion

9. REGULATORY SYSTEMS

- National and international

10. QUALITY ASSURANCE AND MANAGEMENT OF NUCLEAR POWER SYSTEMS

Figure 4–3. **Conditions for Expanded Use of Nuclear Power**

As has been mentioned many times, building a nuclear power plant takes at least ten years, and building a big hydroelectric plant requires at least as many years. So you have to forecast what is going to happen to energy demand with a certain degree of certainty, in order to plan your energy system accordingly. For example, we know very well what has happened in the United States and in many places where a certain degree of economic uncertainty—an uncertainty that nobody could foresee or resolve quickly—has reduced the trends in energy demand somewhat.

The second condition for the use of nuclear power is an increasing demand for centrally produced electricity, as I have already mentioned.

A third point is that of comparative economics. The cost structures of electricity are, as you know, very different for a nuclear power unit, a hydroelectric unit, and a conventional thermal unit. In order to make a decision, one must compare these cost structures, which vary from place to place. Another important economic factor is that of market versus nonmarket criteria. In the nonmarket criteria, the social component (e.g., how to provide electricity, regardless of cost, to the people who need it most, or how to attain a safe degree of energy independence) carries more weight than in the market criteria. Finally capital, which is extremely difficult to find these days, except in one part of the world, is a key element in the economic considerations of energy supply.

A fourth aspect that affects the use of nuclear energy is comparative risk. One question that was discussed in depth at Symposium II is the extent to which it is possible to assess the total risk associated with a particular energy source. All kinds of risks must be compared, and that is very difficult; I do not think there is a general prescription for such comparison, and this is an area that needs further analysis. One important risk is environmental deterioration, because there is the danger of degrading the environment in an irreversible way. Every form of energy affects the environment, each one in a different way. How can we determine and assess the environmental impact of each form of energy in comparison with nuclear power?

The next point I wish to examine is the technological question. In my opinion, the crucial technological problem for nuclear power at this moment—one also recognized by our group in Symposium II—is the back end of the fuel cycle. Of the three major aspects of the nuclear fuel cycle's back end—temporary waste storage, fuel reprocessing, and permanent waste storage—temporary storage is technically the simplest, but in the United States, for example, because of delays in reprocessing, we may soon run out of temporary storage space. And reprocessing, while a fairly well-known technology, is a complex one: its safe execution and economical feasibility need further analysis. Next we have permanent waste disposal, which is probably the hottest issue and the one most difficult to resolve. Some see it as having been solved technically; others think that a satisfactory solution has not yet been found. So, these are technological issues that affect the future of nuclear power.

The sixth point concerning the use of nuclear power is the need to decouple nuclear power from nuclear weapons. On one side we have the nonproliferation treaty (NPT), which is recognized as essential, as a good tool, for preventing the spread of nuclear weapons capabilities, but is also seen as not sufficient. An aspect of the NPT that is crucial is that of safeguards: To what extent can they be enforced and improved and inspections made more effective? The role that the International Atomic Energy Agency has to play in preventing nuclear proliferation is an issue that still has to be decided by its member governments. How can one design new fuel cycles that are proliferation resistant? As you know, the International Nuclear Fuel Cycle Evaluation (INFCE) was an exercise carried out a few years ago in which many countries participated. An excellent report was produced, but perhaps has to be reexamined, and something has to be done about its implementation. In connection with nonproliferation, one interesting consideration might be the internationalization of nuclear facilities. Not every country that may want or need nuclear power is going to cover all aspects of the nuclear fuel cycle, for reasons of economics and size and for reasons of common sense. Thus, international fuel cycle facilities might be a very useful concept for such countries.

The next point to be considered is the problem of public attitudes toward and perceptions on nuclear power—a subject which has been discussed in many places. Is the public properly informed, and does it have the right perception about nuclear power? What are the most appropriate channels to provide the public with meaningful and objective information about all energy issues, and, in particular, nuclear power? In this regard I would like to quote three professors from the Department of Statistics of the Wharton School of Business. As you know, the US Court of Appeals in Washington, DC, recently ordered the Nuclear Regulatory Commission not to permit the Three Mile Island plant to be started up again until the psychological impact that such a start-up would have on nearby residents had been determined. In connection with this most unusual court decision, the aforementioned professors from the Wharton School of Business have stated that "it is important to examine the extent to which the psychological disturbance of residents in the vicinity of Three Mile Island has resulted from misunderstanding, misinformation, and 'antinuke' propaganda . . . We suggest that residents in the vicinity of Three Mile Island learn whether they have been misinformed regarding the alleged hazard of low-level radiation emission from the TMI facility, and whether they may have recourse for the psychological and other consequences of such information." [R. J. Hickey, E. J. Bowen, and I. E. Allen in *Nuclear News*, May 1982, p. 28] This clearly states the other side of the matter: the right to be objectively informed and the liability of those who misinform. It clearly is important to determine whether technical and governmental bodies can meaningfully interact with the public to provide proper information and guidance and in turn to receive input from the public. These are issues that were raised during our work session to which there are no simple solutions, either.

Another point that our work session examined is that of nuclear reactor technology. There are several reactors whose technology is well proved and whose performance is highly satisfactory, but for economic reasons their sizes are relatively large. Can we provide small reactors—say, of 400 MW or less—or reactors of adequate size, to countries that need nuclear power to produce electricity because of a lack of other energy resources but whose grids are too small to use 600-MW reactors? There currently are four or five designs in the market, but are they appropriate? Also, how can we optimize the use of the uranium resources? Should we use lower and lower grade ores, as may be required, particularly if breeder reactors are not adopted? This in turn presents another problem; more land would have to be used for mining, with its associated environmental impact. Thus should we design new types of reactors that use uranium more efficiently or breed new nuclear fuel?

Other points which our work session discussed but on which I will not elaborate included how to improve nuclear regulatory systems, at not only national levels but also an international level, and how to improve quality assurance and management of nuclear power systems. Although time does not allow me to elaborate on these matters, we are all aware of the problems that have arisen because of poor management and poor quality assurance while a nuclear project is being built.

This is my interpretation of what was discussed at Symposium II in relation to nuclear energy.

Statement Following Presentation of Technical Paper Part C

First, I would like to mention that energy cannot be isolated from all the other economic parameters. In particular, nuclear power cannot be seen in isolation from the rest of the energy resource issues, something which many people unfortunately tend to do. This is something I would like to emphasize. Second, since one of the tasks of this Symposium is to point out things that should be done in the future or lines along which concerted effort is required, and since nuclear power is the area on which I was asked to report at this Symposium, I would like to point out some ideas that the Symposium III participants might wish to consider as short-term actions and which could be used as part of the draft communiqué that will be submitted for discussion tomorrow (see Figure 4–4).

1. **Better understanding and assessment of trends in energy demand (particularly electricity)**

2. **Reorientation of energy demand and improvement of energy efficiency**

    $$I = E/G$$

    $$\propto = (\Delta E/E)\,(\Delta G/G)$$

    Where I = energy intensity,
    **   E = energy use,**
    **   G = GNP, and**
    ** $\propto$ = elasticity of change in E to change in G**

3. **Active exploration of all possible energy alternatives; increased R&D on nuclear technology (reactor design, performance, efficiency, reliability, safety, cost; nuclear fuel cycles)**

4. **Increased assistance and technology transfer to less developed countries for energy assessment, planning, new technologies, demonstration projects, nuclear parks, etc.**

5. **Decoupling of nuclear power and nuclear weapons; reinforcement of the NPT and IAEA**

6. **Improved public awareness of energy issues**

Figure 4–4. **Short-Term Actions**

Short of a global energy strategy which I mentioned this morning—and which I indicated is almost impossible to attain—I think international cooperation in energy is essential, and it is even more fundamental in the case of nuclear power. The fact that the world is divided into countries introduces a serious geopolitical element in relation to energy, because of the aspirations held by almost every country to be energy self-sufficient or energy independent, aspirations that are very difficult to fulfill, given the lack of correlation between the political structure of the world and the geographical distribution of energy resources. For example, I have figured out that if energy could flow without any restrictions in the western hemisphere—North and South America—we would have plenty of energy to take us until the end of the next century, and the energy problem of the western hemisphere would be completely different from what it actually is. We would not even be thinking of an energy crisis. If we imagine Latin America as a single political entity, the energy situation would be even better, and we would not have to differentiate among Latin American countries that have abundant and accessible energy resources and those that do not. So countries must realize the need for collaboration in all aspects related to energy. The concept of international cooperation is somewhat broader than energy interdependence, but it certainly includes it. However, many people do not like to think about energy interdependence, because they feel that then countries depend on the interdependence, and this brings a new kind of dependence. I think, nevertheless, that this is an issue that should be stressed by this Symposium.

Now, in relation to the nuclear power issues which I discussed this morning, I would like to emphasize four or five areas which I think are relevant for further analysis and short-term actions. The Symposium is not going to resolve all the issues related to nuclear power; that is impossible. But I think it can clarify some of them, and it can point out areas in which further analysis and further efforts within an international cooperation context are essential.

One is a better understanding and assessment of the trend in energy demand in general and of electricity in particular. We keep talking about energy supply. I think we tend to forget that the supply is intended to meet a demand. How can we understand that demand better, in particular, in regard to electricity?

Second, how can we *reorient* energy demand while improving energy efficiency? This is another area that is worth discussing. There are two classic indicators which relate energy to economic activity: energy intensity and energy elasticity. Although efforts are being made to reduce them, how to do so most effectively remains a big question, because their parameters are not well understood yet.

The third point is that we obviously have to explore all possible energy alternatives in planning energy supplies. Specifically, with regard to nuclear power, we have to increase R&D on nuclear technology (reactor design, performance, efficiency, reliability, safety, and cost; nuclear fuel cycles; etc.)

In terms of assistance and technology transfer to the less developed countries, I think it is especially important to help them in the following areas: making energy assessments, developing energy planning capabilities, incorporating new technologies, and executing demonstration projects as effectively as possible. In addition, in the case of nuclear energy, it is important to determine, as I said this morning, how we can internationalize different aspects of the nuclear fuel cycle, assuring a safe use of nuclear power.

Another point which has been emphasized several times in this Symposium and elsewhere is the need to decouple issues involving nuclear power from those involving nuclear weapons, reinforcing in whatever ways are appropriate the nonproliferation treaty and the IAEA and other institutions that could help in that effort. Thus, further analysis in this area is most desirable.

Finally, an area that deserves special attention is improved public awareness and knowledge of energy issues—not just on nuclear power but on all the energy issues.

These are some of the areas in which substantial effort is required if nuclear power is going to play an effective role in the future supply of electric energy, and, I repeat again, international cooperation is desirable in addressing these areas. There are several agencies—for example, the International Energy Agency within the Organisation for Economic Co-operation and Development, or the International Atomic Energy Agency—that play an important role in international cooperation on energy issues, but I feel that we still need stronger mechanisms for more or intensified international cooperation in order to look into those energy issues and many others.

PHILIP H. ABELSON

Statement Following Presentation of Technical Paper
Parts A and B

This statement will differ considerably from the comments which I made at the conclusion of Symposium II last November.

Since that time there have been new developments in bioenergy and I have become aware of substantial recent progress in agricultural research.

During the decade when oil was very cheap, its low price and availability served to surpress the development of alternative sources of energy and especially to discourage research on them. But the new price structure has created incentives for research and development on biomass. This is beginning to affect the international energy situation.

One of my tasks is to comment briefly on the competition between needs for food and needs for energy. The competition will be present, but my current viewpoint is that during the remainder of this century there will be no widespread shortage of food on this earth. There will be local problems due to weather and perhaps to the outbreak of some special pest, but prospects are substantial that there may even be a surplus of food, despite the increasing population. I say this because of information I gained during a visit to the International Center for Improvement of Maize and Wheat located in Mexico. I am also optimistic about the research productivity of the other major agricultural research centers.

The group in Mexico was one of the two that brought on the green revolution; the other was the International Rice Research Institute in the Philippines. The improvement in crops has not made a dramatic jump in the last few years, but improvement has been steady. Production of food worldwide has increased faster than the rate of population increase.

I visited wheat fields in Obregon in Sonora this March and saw thousands of plots that were devoted to breeding better wheat. The improvement in the amount of wheat produced per hectare goes on and on, and at the same time research to establish resistance to various diseases continues. I also saw the research on triticale, which is a manmade, genetically engineered cross of wheat and rye. This new variety is steadily being improved. It is pest resistant and capable of thriving in somewhat saline environments. It is also being grown in the Cerrado of Brazil—an area of some hundred million hectares where there is adequate rainfall and a soil that is tillable but acidic. Varieties are being improved to cope with the acid soil there. Other research efforts include crosses of wheat with wild grasses that are capable of living in marine environments. I am confident that with the experience which the people at the center in Mexico have had, they will achieve breakthroughs in the development of plants that can thrive in many of the large marginal environments around the world. Another development has been the improvement in the nutritious quality of maize. The protein in the new maize is excellent for human nutrition.

In summary, my observations and interviews in Mexico lead me to believe that the world food problem is not going to be a great one during the next twenty years. Of course, population cannot go on expanding exponentially indefinitely, but there is some breathing time for taking care of other problems, and there are signs that some nations such as China are slowing population growth.

During the past six months I also visited Brazil and saw what they are doing on their alcohol program. We did touch on that in our Symposium II panel discussion, but it was interesting to go there and get some feeling for it. In São Paulo all the automobiles have at least 20-percent alcohol in the fuel, and some several hundred thousand automobiles burn straight alcohol. A cruise down the highway in São Paulo is like participating in a very heavily drinking cocktail party. The fumes are reminiscent of that. The Brazilians will succeed because they both are determined and have the technical capability to do it. Furthermore, exploitation of their Cerrado will make a very great difference. Brazil is likely to become such a large producer of food that it will be able to use biomass for production of the many products that can be obtained by fermentation.

After Mrs. Marcos spoke last night, I read her book which was distributed. I recommend it. From it you will get a profound impression of things that are happening in the Philippines. The Philippines are well on the way to cutting their dependence on imported oil. They project that by 1989 their imports will be negligible. They are moving ahead in three major ways. One is to develop further their geothermal for electricity, and they project that they will be the world's leader in the use of geothermal before the decade is over. They are also moving ahead strongly in the cultivation of trees. There is a nitrogen-fixing tree suitable for the Philippines that matures in four years, grows to as much as 6 inches in diameter in that time, and is therefore a tremendous producer of biomass. They have two plans for it. One is simply to burn the wood in small decentralized plants, so that the problem of gathering fuel will be small. Many jobs will be created for the rural population. The second thrust using the wood is to convert it into various liquid fuels.

All of us are impressed by examples. When the developing countries see the examples of Brazil and the Philippines moving ahead, where the environments are quite different, they will be impressed. This is likely to lead to a great deal of interchange and imitation in the rest of the world. Various countries will be on notice that biomass can make a large contribution. And when you know it can be done, this strengthens your resolve to do it.

Another basis for my optimism is the rapid progress in research that is occurring in biotechnology. I have been so impressed with this that I have arranged for a special issue on biotechnology in *Science*. I believe that biotechnology is going to be a development rivaling the development of computers. What is happening is happening fast. There has been a good deal of overblown comment in the newspapers, but there is real, solid science behind it. Just as a tiny example, one of the things that has happened is improvement in the understanding of the mechanisms for production of biogas (methane). Previously what happened was that one pushed some pig manure into the fermenter, and dependent on the particular flora in that pig manure, sometimes the fermenter worked fine and sometimes it did not work. But now one understands better mechanisms for the fermentation. It is a two-step process. In a first step, biomass is converted into organic acids. The optimum condition for this step is an acidic medium—one with a low pH. In the second step, the acids are converted to methane. The optimum condition for this is a neutral pH. Thus, the two steps require different conditions, and the process is best carried out in two separate vessels. When this requirement is broadly understood and met, the usefulness of biogas production around the world will be substantially increased.

There also have already been substantial improvements in alcohol production: better organisms for the fermentation, organisms that can withstand a higher concentration of alcohol, organisms that can operate at higher temperatures. Today the production of industrial alcohol in this country is cheaper when it is derived from grain than when it comes from petroleum. In principle, 90 percent of the petrochemicals obtained from petroleum can be produced by fermentation of biomass. Transition to biomass as a source is a matter of time, economics, and working out some of the bioengineering. Ultimately, we will stop producing most of our petrochemicals from oil and instead use biomass.

In the United States, the very brightest of our young people over the last decade have been attracted to the opportunities of recombinant DNA and other opportunities that could be found in molecular biological research. That group of people will produce marvelous breakthroughs and change the efficiency of conversion of biomass into useful things.

I have mentioned the developments in Mexico, Brazil, and the Philippines. One could describe things happening in other countries, but these examples must suffice. I have also mentioned a relentless push in research in biotechnology in the United States. A desirable achievement coming out of this conference would be a thrust toward establishing the kind of international institutes for research on biomass that have been so successful in changing prospects for food around the world. I hope that seeds planted in these Symposia will lead to better transfer of technology in this important field.

ISHRAT H. USMANI

Statement Following Presentation of Technical Paper
Parts A and B

I will be very brief, because I will be dealing with a very limited aspect of rural development.

I am happy to say that as a result of the UN Conference on New and Renewable Sources of Energy held in Nairobi in August of 1981, the developing countries in the entire Third World have started buzzing with activity concerning the role, the problems, and the prospects of renewable energy sources in the energy mix of each country, as well as the importance of reorganizing the institutional structures within and outside of the government agencies dealing with energy issues.

You will be pleased to know that as a follow-up to the Nairobi conference, we, at the invitation of the Italian government, are now going to Rome to consider what concrete steps should be taken at the local, regional, and global levels to implement what is called the Nairobi Programme of Action (NAP). The NAP is particularly concerned with the energy problems facing millions of people living in the rural areas of Asian, African, and Latin American developing countries.

The point which I have been personally advocating in the United Nations is that for the Third World countries to have any meaningful socioeconomic development, development must begin at the base rather than the top of the pyramid. The base, of course, comprises the remote and small villages where—in Asia, for example—nearly 75 percent of the people live. Those villages are far removed from the national power grids and other centers of economic activity.

Take the case of India, where I went in 1977 at the government's invitation. There I met several colleagues who had been working in the Atomic Energy Commission at Trombay. A very smart, energetic group approached me and said, "Sir, you would be very pleased to know that we have designed India's first radio telescope at a cost of only a couple of million dollars, which is negligible compared with the cost of an imported one. It is entirely the effort of the Indian physicists, engineers, and electronic technicians." I was very impressed and knew that the Indian scientists were brilliant and dedicated, but I was a little disappointed that their talents should not have been devoted instead to combating the poverty that blights the lives of millions in the rural and urban areas of India. As it was a clear case of distorted priorities, I asked them, "What use will India make of this radio telescope?" They said, "Well, we will record messages from outer space." And I said, "Have you first recorded the messages from the streets of Calcutta?" They obviously did not like that question—it was, of course, very pungent—but I wanted to drive some sense of priorities into their minds.

I am happy to say that the philosophy of "first things first" is beginning to take hold in many developing countries. For example, the Indian government has now appointed a very high-powered commission for the promotion of alternative energy sources, and Bangladesh has established an autonomous Rural Electrification Board.

One of the main reasons for the economic stagnation of the developing countries' rural areas is that the village economy—mostly agriculture—has depended only on the muscle power of humans and their animals. Therefore, unless there are energy inputs from other sources, there is no hope of improving the quality of life in the vast majority of the rural communities.

The whole edifice of industrialized and prosperous countries in the East and the West was built on one principal source of energy—namely, oil, which was cheap and abundant, selling at $2–3 per barrel. Today, when it is the Third World countries' turn to industrialize and develop, we find that oil is priced at $30–35 per barrel! The industrialized countries feel relieved these days, because there has been an oil glut and the price of oil has exhibited a downward trend toward $28 or even $25 per barrel. But this price movement means nothing to the poor living in the Third World's rural areas—people who hardly can afford to burn oil even at $2–3 per barrel.

What should be done for or by the people living in rural areas? The only alternative for them is to harness the locally available renewable energy sources—the sun, the wind, biomass, and in some cases, depending on the location, mini hydro. But the two sources most universally available to every Third World village are the sun and biomass. The technological levels of remote villages are so poor that no engine converting one energy form into another can work—be it a solar engine, a diesel engine, a petrol engine, or a coal engine. Such engines may work for some time, but the lack of transport facilities, the unavailability of spare parts, and so on makes their continued operation and maintenance extremely difficult if not impossible.

Therefore, we have to think of a technology that does not require any engine of conversion at all. Fortunately, such technology is available. It is the technology of the photovoltaic (PV) cells which convert the sun's light (not its heat) directly into electric power. The PV cells offer an ideal solution to the power needs of the Third World's rural areas because most of them are located in the solar belt, from 35° north to 35° south of the equator. As someone has said, "The price of oil rises every day, but so does the sun!"

Unfortunately, the prevailing price of PV cells is exorbitantly high. There are two reasons for this. One is that the total energy now produced by PV cells is only about 7 or 8 MW, and 50 percent of that is produced in the United States. The second is that the cells are made from silicon that has an impurity level of only one part per million (although silicon in its raw form is abundantly available in the earth's crust). Such ultrapure silicon is actually intended for the sophisticated electronic industries making integrated circuits, computers, and calculators, and so on. It is priced at about $85–100 per kilogram. Studies show that PV cells with a net conversion efficiency of 10 percent (which is good enough) can be produced from silicon that has an impurity of one part per ten thousand and that this "solar-grade" silicon would cost about $12–14 per kilogram, since it can be derived from the commercially available metallurgical-grade silicon sold in the world markets at $1 per kilogram. "Solar-grade" silicon, however, is not being produced by industry, because no market exists for such a grade!

It is clear that the price of PV cells could be brought down through economies of scale if the cells were mass-produced for Third World rural areas out of "solar-grade" silicon. And this would be possible if the decisionmakers and energy planners of the Third World countries were to undertake an extensive rural electrification program on a decentralized, village-to-village basis—starting with the small and remote villages—with the help of PV cells and other appropriate technologies that could harness the locally available renewable energy sources (such as mini hydro, wind, biomass) to produce power and integrate their outputs with that generated by PV cells.

Rural electrifiation has proved to be a great instrument of change resulting in accelerated socioeconomic growth. It took a great US president, Franklin Roosevelt, to create not only the Tennessee Valley Authority, to generate power, but also the Rural Electrification Administration, to advance low-interest loans to rural areas for electrification. Since then, the impact of rural electrification in many countries such as India, the Philippines, Sri Lanka, and others has been astounding, both in the increased GNP and in the improved quality of life.

Electrification of millions of remote Third World villages by grid extensions is virtually impossible because of the high cost of transmission and distribution lines over long distances and the low load factors in the villages. Isolated diesel power generators are feasible, but the high cost of oil and difficulties of operation and maintenance make this option also unattractive. The alternative that has the brightest prospects is power from PV cells, supplemented wherever possible by mini hydro, wind power, or power from biomass.

I am pleased to report that many countries, realizing the importance of silicon as a raw material available from quartz and sand deposits and of radiation as a fuel available from the sun, are taking to PV technology and are looking for the transfer of know-how from advanced regions such as the United States, Europe, and Japan on terms that may be mutually advantageous. For example, India has decided to set up two silicon-cell manufacturing plants of 10-MW capacity each with a goal of producing them at about $1 per watt. Whether they will succeed or not I do not know, but there are good chances of success. The United Nations is helping Pakistan to set up an R&D facility for a silicon technology center, and there is interest in other countries such as Egypt and Brazil.

I am absolutely certain that with the sun, the water, and the sand, the problems of energy—at least the small, decentralized village level—can be solved. I might also add that those who think that electricity would be a luxury in the villages since it would be used only for lighting, television, radio, and so on—things which would not add materially to the productivity sector—that those skeptics are wrong. Experience has shown that more than 60 percent of the power supplied to a village is utilized for productivity purposes, mainly in the agricultural sector. Pumping water for irrigation not only helps the villages to acquire "food security"; it also augments their incomes. Only 20–30 percent of total rural power consumption is attributable to lighting, running the community TV set, or operating the medical refrigerator used for storing lifesaving drugs and medicines at the rural dispensary—and incidentally, surveys conducted after rural electrification show that lighting helps to improve the literacy rate among children and, oddly enough, reduces birth rates!

KEICHI OSHIMA

Statement Following Presentation of Technical Paper
Parts A and B

I will be very brief, because the content of Sympcsium II's discussions and summaries is already printed in the very thick second volume of the Symposia Series' *Proceedings.*

I am very much impressed by the parts of the technical paper that were presented by Professor Rose and Dr. Gibbons. I would say that it is more than a technical paper; it is a very philosophical paper. So, from my point of view, I would like to mention how the present energy situation was discussed in the Symposium II work session on the industrialized market-economy nations and refer to the point raised in the presentations by Professor Rose and Dr. Gibbons about what actions we should take.

The present situation in the industrialized market-economy nations is quite different from what we had after the oil crisis. In these countries, the issue is no longer energy conservation or less use of oil, because there has been a tremendous development in conservation—almost a 12 percent decrease in the energy intensity-to-GDP ratio mentioned in the paper—and also, dependence on oil has decreased by 20 percent. This has had a modifying effect on the approach to thinking about energy in the industrialized market-economy countries. First, the sense of the energy problem's urgency is diminishing: people feel that they have almost achieved a major part of their goals. Second, industries are now experiencing some negative effects of energy conservation: the oil industry is suffering from excess capacity; the demand for electricity is decreasing; and there are energy-intensive industries such as petrochemicals and electrochemicals that want some change in government policies. What I am saying is that, exactly as was mentioned in the paper, we are no longer in a period of crisis where the people agree upon a common goal and objective; we are now in a transition period where different interest groups have different viewpoints.

There is also now some discussion that the allocation of financial resources should be changed: instead of using these resources to further increase energy productivity, they should be used to assist energy-intensive industries. This means changing priorities from energy to social considerations, even though the result may be a decrease in the nation's energy productivity as a total.

There is another problem: as was pointed out by several participants in Symposium II, the issue lies not within the industrialized market-economy nations but rather at their interface with developing countries and oil-producing countries. But because of adverse economic situations, most of the industrialized market-economy governments have deficits in their budgets. And also, there are constraints on future investments in the private sector. Together, this creates a tendency in the industrialized countries to look inward rather than toward global issues and results in there being less drive to look at problems in their global rather than their domestic context. Thus, there is a tendency for the energy policies of the industrialized nations to become more short-sighted, more domestic, and more inward-looking.

Under such conditions, I want to raise a few points. In spite of the present tendency toward relaxation, I think the uncertainty about the energy future is still the same. Namely, there remains the possibility of a substantial increase in the total global energy demand, if the economies of the developing countries are to be improved. Also, the possibility of abrupt increases in the price of oil with some political disturbances still exists. And recognizing that the largest energy consumers in proportion to the rest of the world are the industrialized countries, and that the power of technology, capability of research and development, and financial resources exist in these countries, I think that there should be some initiative taken to change the present attitude of industrialized countries to one which looks more toward the benefit of all mankind—for this would benefit not only the developing countries but also, eventually, the industrialized countries themselves, by activating the whole world economy through management of these energy problems.

Thus, the transition to high-priced energy is not only the concern of the industrialized market economies; it is the concern of the whole world. If this concern is not successfully met globally,

I am afraid that the repercussions will in the long term be felt by the industrialized countries. One thing that should be included in the communiqué of this Symposium, therefore, is that there should be more dialogues and trialogues—with the developing countries and the oil-producing countries—and with the initiative or leadership of the industrialized countries.

Finally, it has to be recognized that the major alternative energy sources in the industrialized market economies are nuclear, coal, and natural gas—sources which, according to Part A of the technical paper, will be less negotiable than oil has been, and whose production will become increasingly technology-intensive (a situation that is true even with solar and biomass). Therefore, the industrialized countries with technological expertise should make major contributions in developing future energy resources and should not ignore the energy problems of the developing countries. In this regard what Dr. Usmani said is very important: if there is at present no market for a new technology especially adapted to a developing country's conditions, I am afraid that without some intellectual or political will, the private enterprises in the industrialized countries will have little interest in developing that technology, because their prospects are likely to be better in an industrialized country's market. So, this kind of complex issue should be identified and discussed in the dialogue between industrialized and developing countries to create a political will to go beyond the market mechanism.

I think that is one important point which was discussed at the last Symposium's work session on the industrialized market economies: we must go beyond the short-term economic interest of the industrialized market economies and promote some mechanism to look into global issues from the viewpoint of the benefit of the whole world, what is the interest of the whole world's benefit—a viewpoint that is also in the interest of the industrialized countries in the long term.

Statement Following Presentation of Technical Paper Part C

I fully agree with what Mr. Landsberg said: that this is not a crisis; it is a process of transition, and there is a need for continuous wise management. Also, as I stated previously, the whole matter is very much interrelated on the global scene.

But when we refer to the policies and actions of the market economies, the basic problem is really "Who is the actor?" I think there are two things to be considered. One is that technology transfer or the creation of new technologies, both of which may have to depend on the capabilities of the market economies, raises the question of who is going to do this: Is the government? Or is industry? In the case of industry, there must be economic incentives or something that attracts the market forces. On the other hand, if you say government . . . Now, as I mentioned, every government of the industrialized market economies is faced with increasing financial difficulty and has fewer financial resources available. So, one point we have to think through at this Symposium is how some incentives for industries or political will for governments can be created in the market economies in order to promote technological cooperation on energy problems.

The second thing to be considered is the relationship of energy and economic policy. Specifically, this means that energy is not a separate issue; it is part of the whole complex issue of world economic development. (Of course, we also have to take into account the environmental issue, but I think the major one is the economic issue.) Again, this raises the question of determining how market-economy industrialized countries can contribute to the future. For example, there is some proposal to have a trialogue of oil-producing countries, industrialized countries, and developing countries to discuss future oil pricing policies. I do not know whether this is a realistic proposal or not, but I believe it is worth pursuing.

Furthermore, we should see energy in the context of future world development, for the energy issue is not just an issue of the balance of supply and demand. It really has to be considered in a broader context of the industrialized market economies' whole program of economic aid to developing countries. What I am saying is that the energy issue is closely interrelated with the development programs of developing countries, and consequently, this has a crucial impact on the world economy and its activation. I think this point was also mentioned in Mrs. Marcos's keynote address.

IOAN URSU*

Statement Following Presentation of Technical Paper
Parts A and B

In November of last year, we left Symposium II with a deep sense of having achieved something of real consequence: we were a *team*. We started it divided, through a canonical exercise that discriminated among market and nonmarket, industrialized and industrializing, energy-surplus and energy-deficit nations. It took us a couple of days to end united, to realize how close we either are or could be in sharing the energy challenge—its burdens, frustrations, promises, and expectations.

Let us not deceive ourselves and those here at Symposium III: we *were* political in our approach, if only by the mere fact of talking about energy in terms of human needs, goals, and values. The proper management of people's lives—defusing, overtaking, confronting conflicts and converting them into solutions—is what the Greek "politikos" was invented for. We should instead be proud of reaffirming the original meaning of politics in the midst of a world of violence, uncomprehension, shortsighted behavior, poor perception, and lack of responsibility with regard to many of the critical dangers we all face.

The "spirit of Knoxville"—if one may call it that—that was carefully nurtured during Symposia I and II is indeed within us. One can see it duly acknowledged in the technical paper worked out so remarkably by David Rose, John Gibbons, and Hans Landsberg. Beyond the intellectual reflex of criticizing this or that opinion, factual discrepancy (from one's own standpoint, of course), and selective inattention toward or subjective evaluation of a pertinent issue, we must feel sincere reverence and gratitude for what the authors did for us all: they made it possible to pull ourselves from the pressures of our daily lives, work, and problems—to reestablish the team and make possible a fruitful outcome of the International Energy Symposia Series.

Of course, no formal analytic reaction to the intellectual excitement created by this paper can possibly be given in either five pages or five minutes. As chairman/integrator of Symposium II's work session on industrialized nonmarket-economy nations, I want to state, first, that I am satisfied with the coverage given in

---

*The two statements which follow were delivered orally in slightly different form by Dan V. Vamanu of the Romanian National Council for Science and Technology, who served in Ioan Ursu's stead at Symposium III.

the paper to the results of our session. The tradeoff between concision and completeness is fair enough. The message gets through.

It is true: the energy clash of the seventies and its epiphenomena caught the industrialized nonmarket-economy countries in the middle of a forceful and taxing thrust for economic growth, and these exigencies, along with a host of other pressures and constraints, are threatening our well-deserved dream of socially shared decent prosperity, our economic security, and the prospects of our participation in the international division of labor—the most positive side, in our opinion, of today's interdependence.

It is also true that among the overwhelming majority of the countries in our session's group with the "energy-deficit" tag, unfortunately, there is an acute awareness of the multidimensional nature of the energy issue. I can only hope that our session's work at Symposium II brought about enough evidence along this line. The centralized approach to economic and social management in our group's nations—as widely diverse as that approach really is—still leaves us with a keen and often painful sense of the externalities inherent in almost any major decision, from the overall strategy of preserving economic integrity and development down to tidying-up measures in our national households. We enjoy the resilience which comes with the endogenous generation of growth through our ultimate, proven resource—our people. All costs of actions taken—sectoral adjustments; technology substitutions; facing the pressures of the energy and financial markets; and reevaluating domestic investment, credit, and pricing policies—have traditionally been heavily internalized by our societies, which are organized so as to absorb as uniformly as possible all additional efforts, shakeups, as well their spillover effects. How resilient and sustainable our economic defense lines and development paths can be made under the pressure of energy and raw material shortages, credit markets, and the increased stiffness of the world technology pools is—right now and presumably in the years to come—one of the hottest issues of debate and determined work in our countries. It might be true that getting bogged down in the morass of the *total* problem leaves little room for partial but effective action. Yet in our societies, and I fear in many others, one cannot help but face the whole mélange of problems that stick inextricably together and stubbornly resist academic disaggregation, precisely because they are *born* aggregated and are nurtured by the same world order, with its precedents, routines, and inertia.

"What do people want?" That is the question with which we are time and again confronted. Well, we know for ourselves that people want a decent and *dignified* life. Not just recently but for many centuries, on the old continent and elsewhere, this difficult match has been sought after, dreamed of, fought for. That is why I am particularly happy that the question of values was brought up in the technical paper. It takes a connoisseur of history—of facts, myths, and civilizations—to understand that for many nations, independence (in energy and in all other contexts, for that matter) is not merely a possible strategy but a deep-rooted, unquestioned *value.* Semantics has, certainly, a lot to do with the acceptability of this concept. Energy security, the basic sustainability of systems, energy/economy potential self-sufficiency, sound supply/demand tailoring, and balanced energy trade—all these and other concepts do approximate the idea of energy independence, in my view, although they do not encompass it completely. Apart from inconceivable autarchies, the selfish satisfaction of the haves at the expense of the have lesses, or have nots, the desperate practices of *complete* self-sufficiency at all costs, and other misconceptions of this kind, many nations know and *feel* great merit in the attempt to stand on their own feet as far as their endogenous capacities to supply their societies with all the basic inputs required *for both subsistence and development* are concerned.

An interdependence between cripples might work, but it is a poor one; an interdependence between the handicapped and the champs is witnessed, in desolation, today. Why not indulge in dreaming, and working for an interdependence among sane partners, each at its own will and choice?

At this point, I cannot help seeing the profound degree to which countries of different Symposia II categories fall within the same pattern of needs and constraints. The need for technology, for fair access to foreign markets, for energy planning that incorporates multiple approaches, for capital and cash, for better infrastructures and management—to quote only few of the features given in technical paper—are striking commonalities of the so-called industrialized, nonmarket-economy countries and energy-deficit industrializing countries. The more criteria scanned, the more basic and irreducible the classification of "developed" and "developing" countries appears, with its frequently resented although, alas, unavoidable connotation of the rich and the poor. In this connection, it seems proper that the technical paper's authors also recognize the difficulties of the oil-endowed countries and the legitimacy of their search for a true and equitable development based not on fate's ephemeral fortune but on dedicated, productive labor.

I share the general feeling that today we increasingly experience the revelation that questions of economic efficiency quickly become questions of equity. It stands true for domestic economies of labor, and it stands true for the international cooperative effort to attain mutual improvement. While historical bitterness may for some time ahead deter awareness of this fact, one must get used to the idea—the sooner, the better.

That we can no longer separate our scientific analysis of the problem from our values and beliefs seems to be a pervasive mood in the technical paper. That's right, and that's good. In fact, it might well be the only way out of the morass bogging down the energy debate, too heavily biased by the conventional litanies of the economics of the affluent, cheap-energy age—an age which is definitely over. No roses for the positive sciences in this respect. No doubt, we need them in the future, and we had better hurry to improve them. Instead, this development provides for "minimizing divergence"—a nicely put term in the paper—by bringing values and beliefs into the open, on a common and meaningful ground. Allow me to see our Symposia Series as a true paradigm of this new attitude. Those who fear the danger of a single-focus "convergence" should be reassured. There is no need for it and, in fact, no chance of it. United in our efforts, understanding, will, and good will, we may well be heading wherever our values—in the broadest sense—call us.

Statement Following Presentation of Technical Paper Part C

Nuclear power. We all recognize it as a complex issue. But let us be frank about it: the mere fact that we are debating whether it's good or bad, whether we should want it or not, and whether we should give it the green light for further maturation (e.g., through fast breeder reactors, closed fuel cycles, and safeguarded expansion) proves patently that nuclear power *is* one solution at hand, as real as its drawbacks may be, to appease the hunger for energy. But this one solution happens to be under the control of the few who simply *have* it. This is, certainly, a one-of-a-kind situation in the history of energy and technology, and mankind must cope with it by an unprecedented effort of comprehension and originality. To put it perhaps a little too blatantly, in order to better capture the idea, the wisdom that some countries should exercise restraint in making what some think are hasty commitments to only a partial solution—to an unforgiving and not yet entirely consolidated energy technology—should be properly balanced by the wisdom of proving our determination to take gradual action in order to adopt this technology in a way consistent with our, again, unforgiving needs, world security included, and limited major options (or, as the technical paper put it, "many, but none that are easy").

I believe that no sound and lasting solution to the problems raised by nuclear power can be achieved unless each nation is permitted to decide for itself. It takes ample assistance and fair access to adequate knowledge and pertinent technology in order to go the right way on demand analysis, planning, investment, grid integration, and so on. As many of us know, it was eventually proved that prohibition is a pitiful way to withhold the forbidden apple, regardless of how sweet or how rotten that apple is. On the other hand, people *can* learn to wisely meet many of life's difficult challenges, and without doing so at the expense of others.

There is a steadily increasing number of people who admit plainly today that the solution to nuclear weapons nonproliferation is *not* found in stopping nuclear power, and among these people, one may find real authorities in the field. The relationship between nonproliferation and international security goes both ways. The question of which comes first—proliferation or lack of security—makes sense. The solution to nonproliferation is definitely much more political and complex than it is technical. Therefore, a curtailment of peaceful, safeguarded uses of nuclear energy because of nuclear weapons proliferation would be, in my opinion, utterly unfair, particularly as long as unsafeguarded military reactors, devised as such, are unrestrainedly doing so well all over the world.

Given enough time and will power, those who have nuclear power *can* make it an appropriate technology—at some cost, of course, but also with great benefit—for all sorts of countries. The emerging interest of the International Atomic Energy Agency in alternative reactor types—smaller, more versatile in terms of the potential end uses of the energy produced, easier to handle, and cheaper, one hopes—is a good example of the straightforward actions so badly needed in our times. For, if I may quote from the Executive Summary of the "Overview and Strategy 1982–1986, Research and Development Plan" of the Electric Power Research Institute here in the United States, "The issue is not a choice of conservation *or* coal *or* nuclear *or* renewable resources; rather, it is our willingness to use conservation *and* coal *and* nuclear *and* renewable resources. We do not enjoy the luxury of selecting from these alternatives; we must utilize all of them." [P2156-SR-SY, prepared by EPRI Planning and Evaluation Division, February 1982, p. 19]

The less developed countries. I have already touched on this crucial issue in my work session summary at Symposium II [*Improving World Energy Production and Productivity*, chap. 18]. I can only reiterate my profound conviction that all action programs in the energy field must have as their mottoes, "There cannot be peace in a hungry world." The developing countries are at the center of the energy issue. Because of demography, but also because of vitality and resources, it is their advent in the world arena which will shape our *common* future. It is therefore utterly important and, in fact, encouraging that here, in Knoxville, Tennessee, in the United States, an unambiguous, straightforward recognition is being given to the fact that it is in the interest of *all* countries, developed and developing, to embark together on the endeavor of erecting a better, mutually satisfactory energy order. Discovering one difficulty after another in the North/South dialogue is, certainly, an integral part of a serious analytic attempt to approach the issue, but we should be well aware that this is only a warm-up time preliminary to a real commitment to solving it. A personal view: without discarding affordable oil, foreign aid, and open foreign markets as relevant to the needs of many, it is, nevertheless, true cooperation in the creation of comprehensive, endogenously generated—and thus adequate—infrastructures which can really help the developing countries out of their problems in the long run.

Technology transfer and other inputs, including those in the fields of education and training, are unavoidable parts of the answer. These must be channelled both North/South *and* South/South. The latter interchange is of immense consequence for adequately revealing different resource choices, technological choices, and lifestyle alternatives available to developing societies as they evolve, thereby helping them to avoid mere model replications and blind alleys that just end in other sorts of painful dependency.

Efficient energy use. Although the conservation potential of a given developmental strategy may be limited—especially when life habits, capital stocks and technology substitution, lead and pay-back times, and side effects are considered—I believe there is not much to be gained by overemphasizing such limitations, as eventually occurs in most debates on energy. Efficient energy use is by far the soundest investment that can be made in the transition to more sustainable energy/economy systems. It can be achieved largely with present-day technologies; it pays back, sooner or later; it is both demand and supply oriented; it is environmentally advantageous, because it reduces the environmental costs incurred from ecosystem conversions; it can help institute nonconventional new and renewable energy resources and their technologies as meaningful substitutes in real life systems; it is affordable in both centralized and decentralized, market and nonmarket approaches; it can go "hard path" or "soft path." When wisely done, it can make comfort proud of its energy consciousness, and austerity a meaningful discipline of life. Last but not least, it is a living symbol of the new approach to energy in our times. Its educational value can greatly help succeeding generations to feel less frustrated by their inheritance.

Being relatively site specific, there are innumerable sound ways in which more efficient energy use can be attained. In our Symposium II work session, we scanned a substantive sampling. The point is that, taken as a whole, conservation is probably one of the least risky endeavors an energy policy can undertake to accomplish change. If head-on actions are to be recommended, this is *the* one.

The environmental issue. I will not comment on this issue here—I expanded on it in my comments at Symposium II, where, incidentally, the fuelwood crisis fit quite well into the picture.

Governmental and political intervention in the energy realm. It seems obvious that while in operational terms the desirability of government intervention is system and country specific, in societal and moral terms the responsibility of governments regarding their actions in the energy field—whether and how to do what—is conspicuously equal for all governments, anytime, anywhere.

Saying that government intervention could eventually hinder domestic markets and increase their unpredictability is to postulate the universal validity and desirability of the market's taking the leading role in the energy drama. However, it seems that this particular wisdom is not only site specific but also, time and again, reconsidered, even in the same place. Indeed, as witnessed since the late seventies, an ominous swing of opinion and consequent action on the relative merits of various issues—regulation versus deregulation, public versus private responsibilities, centralized versus decentralized approaches—prevails in various places.

All this is only to say that, in this Symposia Series' outcome, an emphasis on any one economic approach should be pondered carefully, and this approach should in any event be made as independent of any biased preconception as possible.

The elusive solution and cross-national management policies. I join the technical paper's authors in many of their conclusions. In fact, if one cares to compare the conclusions in my Symposium II summary with the ones at hand, their convergencies are pleasantly striking.

However, a caveat may be worth attention: the paper's discrimination between *intra*national and *inter*national issues in determining management policies seems to me, from my present vantage point, downright radical. Market/government relationships, the needs of less developed countries, environmental issues, nuclear power, conservation—all these and other issues, no matter how *inter*national in their expression, action, and effects, are nevertheless, *national* in that their roots and motivating forces are found in national behaviors, habits, constraints, and policies. (In that regard, the acid rain problem is a striking example.) From the standpoint of an action-oriented conclusion, the situation is even more disturbing: Who is supposed to handle the "transnational" issues mentioned, and how? I would resent being told that, first and foremost, "transnational" entities should (and, as a matter of fact, would object to the wording, because of its possible far reaching connotations.

I believe that the solution—*international cooperation among sovereign nations*—comes with the issue in a truly horizontal fashion. In fact, this is *the* issue in the energy problem and, as I see it, one of the central issues of our Symposia Series and of The 1982 World's Fair.

Now, this conclusion is *not* elusive—for example, it was saliently evidenced in the address of the Symposium III chairman, Dr. Armand Hammer [chap. 2]. Rather, we have to admit that unfortunately the *concept* of international cooperation is sometimes perceived in international dialogues as an elusive one. On subjects such as *technology transfer, access to markets, and so on,* it may need further and better definition before everybody accepts it and makes commitments to it. Well, let us help this process to the best of our ability. And, first, let us have international cooperation—its problématique included—spelled out more clearly in the other horizontal issues under consideration.

The long way to the best of all possible worlds. I agree: we are all on the way from an unsustainable to a more sustainable energy management system. As Nicolae Titulescu, a Romanian whose centenary is being celebrated by the United Nations this year, once argued, peace is something to be endlessly erected.* So is a better, more sustainable energy future. We should be prepared to go together along this endless way to betterment, always dreaming of perfection.

Finally, what next? Some things to be kept in mind as we conclude this Symposia Series:

- Address the established international fora in the UN system, including the nongovernmental organizations—make them aware of our achievement here; properly link this remarkable action with their ongoing process in order to gradually solve, by means of aiding endogenous efforts and boosting international cooperation, one issue after another in the global energy problem.
- Take home the spirit and the highlights of this event.
- Maintain communication.
- Be earnest in action and confident in our common chance of success.

For although "Energy Turns the World," *we* turn the energy—remember?

JAMES E. AKINS

Statement Following Presentation of Technical Paper
Parts A and B

What we're talking about is OPEC. When the first oil cartel—that is, the international oil industry—dominated the oil scene, there was a period of stability and adequate supplies and the prices remained low; in fact, they declined. Although OPEC was set up in 1960, the oil industry dominated the scene for another ten years. When we talk about the turbulence in the oil scene, as the technical paper did, we are talking about the last ten years. But we have to understand exactly what this turbulence was. During the Mideast war of 1973 and the oil embargo, the world lost only about 5 percent of its oil supplies. That was not generally recognized at the

---

*See, e.g., N. Titulescu, "Dynamics of Peace" (Berlin: May 6, 1929) and "Advances in the Concept of Peace" (Cambridge: November 19, 1930) in *Nicolae Titulescu: Diplomatic Documents* (Bucharest: Political Publishing House, 1967), pp. 287–303 and 337–55. Also refer to *Romanian Review* 1, 1982.

time; there was panic in the world oil markets, and the price of oil was bid up very substantially. Then again, the second big oil shock was caused by the Iranian revolution and the Iraq/Iran war; here there was almost no shortage at all. But because it was *believed* that there was a shortage, the price again doubled. That doubling of price resulted in declining consumption and the restored balance of supply and demand.

I suppose there never really can be a shortage of oil; at least this particular American administration has concluded that there cannot be; it has done away with its rationing plans. Even in the worst political case—closing the Strait of Hormuz—I suppose there would be no shortage; the price of oil would go up to $100 per barrel; a lot of nations could not afford to pay; and supply would be back into balance with the new lower demand.

The turbulence we have talked about is continuing during the so-called oil glut. As the shortages were grossly exaggerated, so is the glut. *The Wall Street Journal*, perhaps one of our most famous business publications, has been writing for the last year about the permanence of the oil glut and the decline in oil price; it refers to $20 oil or even $10 oil. The demise of OPEC is trumpeted by this newspaper in biweekly articles.

The "glut" is not a true glut; this is not a word that should be used in connection with oil. We do have a certain amount of surplus production capacity in the world, but the important thing to remember is that today, right now, 4 to 5 million barrels per day of OPEC oil are being used that are not being produced. In other words, we are drawing down stocks. Theoretically, stocks can be drawn down to zero, but long before that happens, the companies that have been drawing down their stocks will stop. References have been made here today about the price of oil going to $28 per barrel or even lower. However, the price decline stopped; it dipped down briefly below $28 per barrel, but the price of oil in the spot market is already higher than the marker crude in the Persian Gulf.

I suppose there is a lot that we can learn from this so-called turbulence—and there has been turbulence. Unfortunately, however, as Toynbee said, "The only thing we learn from history is that we do not learn from history." We panic during shortages, but during shortages we also stockpile oil—we did this in the United States during the last crisis. But during periods of relative comfort we convince ourselves that there is a glut, that there is a permanent end to the crisis. We are going through this now. We are buying bigger cars. Our president has done away with the standby transfer rationing. And, of course, we in the United States now know that in Alaska we have more oil than Saudi Arabia has; we know that we have a trillion barrels of conventional oil to be produced at present-day prices. We know all this because our president has told us it is true, and American presidents speaking *ex cathedra* are infallible. There are other myths, of course, that we tend to believe. We heard in the last political campaign that we did not "conserve ourselves to greatness"; conservation is no longer an "in" word. In fact, one prominent Republican said that conservation is "not the Republican ethic."

OPEC has been dominated for quite some time by Saudi Arabia, but not nearly to the extent that most people believe. The experience of the last few years has been atypical. Saudi Arabia has a small population, it has extremely large oil reserves, and it has been willing to serve as the swing producer among the exporting nations.

The technical paper this morning referred to oil as the "swing fuel": when we need more energy we will turn to oil; when we need less we will cut back on oil. Saudi Arabia has played the narrow role inside OPEC of being its swing producer. How much longer it will continue doing this is debatable. Saudi Arabia has done this, largely for political reasons—there were some economic reasons—but everything is changing now. That will be a subject for pursuing this afternoon.

Another point that was mentioned this morning was the interest in technology transfer. This is one of the things that OPEC talks about constantly. They say, "If you want our oil, there must be a transfer of technology from you, the industrialized nations, to us, the industrializing nations." But they never spell out what this means. It is always thrown out in conferences such as this—OPEC always mentions it—but when you try to pin them down—What do you mean? Where do you think you are being held back? What is being deprived?—then they come up with almost nothing.

Interdependence in energy has also been referred to. Very few nations can be totally independent in energy, all forms of energy. And part of that, I suppose implicitly, is a discussion of a consumer/producer dialogue. This is also something in which OPEC has been quite interested. In fact, the idea of a conversation between the main OPEC countries and the main oil-consuming nations was raised by Saudi Arabia in 1974 and was rejected by the man who was then the US Secretary of State. Subsequently, we entered the North/South dialogue with bad faith. The OPEC countries and some European countries, notably France, decided that they had to talk about a broader group of issues—not just energy but all of the issues that affected the underdeveloped world. Energy was exceptional, because the OPEC countries, they thought, had the upper hand. And why should they talk just about energy, where OPEC had a strong position, when there were a number of other issues—such as finance, the development of other resources, loans, aid—that the other underdeveloped countries wanted to talk about?

We went into the conference in Paris with the avowed goal of talking it to death, and that is, of course, exactly what we did. I hope that will not continue; I suppose one of the things that could come out of this Symposium would be a real determination to talk about other related issues, not only about energy. We will also have to talk about a number of the other issues that affect the underdeveloped countries and, notably, OPEC countries.

Statement Following Presentation of Technical Paper Part C

I would like to say a few more words about OPEC. In the paper it was pointed out that OPEC is not a true cartel; that they had never done any of the things that the cartel had done. All quite correct. In 1979 Saudi Arabia actually increased production dramatically in order to keep a lid on oil prices, again not the action of a cartel. Saudi Arabia has been the dominant force in OPEC, a role that it has more or less enjoyed.

What I want to raise now is that this situation has changed. In fact, we may be right at the edge of a dramatic change in the world oil scene. Those who talk about the world "oil glut" ignore the fact that OPEC oil has been drawn out of stocks. These optimists also say that in the future when the Iraq/Iran war ends we will have each of these countries producing 3 or 4 million barrels per day. This would be a tremendous amount of oil and would have a further depressant effect on oil prices. We have seen the actions in the last two OPEC meetings, when the Iranian delegate said that he would not abide by the limits set by OPEC for Iran. This was widely interpreted as a good sign for the consumers, but I venture that this was totally misunderstood by almost everybody. The Iranian delegate has no desire to break OPEC prices. He thinks the price is far too low today, but he says that it is totally unacceptable arrogance of OPEC, particularly of the Saudis, to suggest that Iran should produce 1.3 million barrels per day when the Saudis are producing 7 or 8 million, particularly since Iran has a population which is eight times as big as Saudi Arabia's.

If the Iraq/Iran war ends soon, and it could, with Iran as the victor, I guarantee that the world oil scene would change and Saudi

Arabia's position would be totally transformed. Not that the Saudis are going to want this, but the Saudis will have no choice except to adapt to the new realities of the Persian Gulf. Sheik Ahmad Zaki Yamani has just said at the last OPEC meeting that if the oil price rises above $34 per barrel, the Saudis will increase their production to keep the price in line. If Iran wins this war, Saudi Arabia will not be in a position to do this.

We know that Khomeini has called for the execution of Saddam Hussein of Iraq. That has been published. That is, after all, the reason for the Iraq/Iran war. But what we generally don't know is that Khomeini has also called for the execution of King Khalid and Prince Fahd of Saudi Arabia, because they are cooperating with the great Satan—that is, us. He says that King Khalid has done nothing to secure the liberation of Jerusalem; therefore, how can he be trusted to protect Mecca itself? The population of eastern Saudi Arabia is at least 50 percent Shi'a. If the Shi'a win a victory against Iraq, it will have a tremendous effect on the Shi'a throughout the Middle East. The Iranians then will say, "Please, can we increase our production? We are going to have to sell our oil at a lower price in order to increase our exports." No, they will say to Saudi Arabia, "By God, you cut your production. You can produce no more than we can produce; if we can produce 2 million barrels per day, you produce 2 million barrels per day." Then, the price of oil does not stay at $34 per barrel. It goes much higher.

GUY J. PAUKER

Statement Following Presentation of Technical Paper
Parts A and B

Like Professor Oshima, I feel that it is not necessary to reproduce orally for you what has been well presented in Symposium II's *Proceedings*, which is available to all of us. I would instead like to supplement what was said at the Symposium last November with what would be useful for our deliberations during the next couple of days.

I just came, as did my colleagues Professor David Rose and Dr. Fereidun Fesharaki, from the fifth annual meeting of the Asia-Pacific Energy Studies Consultative Group in Honolulu, concluded last Thursday, where thirteen countries from the Asia-Pacific region were represented by senior government officials, academic participants, and representatives from industry. And we looked this year at the theme, or the problem, of the transition from oil to other energy sources. Now, this is highly relevant to the oil-importing industrializing countries, whose problems our work session group discussed here last November. I would like, within the very few minutes available to me, to inform you about the conclusions of the Honolulu workshop.

First of all, we concluded that, despite very substantial and to some extent successful efforts to manage the transition from oil, petroleum will remain a major, if not *the* major, energy source for the balance of this century. Oil production and consumption will probably be roughly in balance, at current or normally increasing prices, until toward the end of the century, but by the year 2000 there probably will be a shortfall of roughly 6.5 million barrels per day—again, assuming the validity of extrapolations from present circumstances.

There was a surprising consensus that coal will play an increasingly important role in the energy transition. That makes it even more important for us to discuss at this Symposium the issue that was raised before us yesterday by Mrs. Imelda Marcos concerning the possibility of a program of concessional sales of coal from the United States, Australia, perhaps Canada, and other coal-producing countries to those industrializing oil-importing countries on whom the present need to import oil places such a heavy burden, especially on their balances of payments. To take as an example the country represented by Mrs. Marcos yesterday, the Philippines has recently spent about 2.5 to 3 billion dollars per year on oil imports. If they instead were able to import coal on concessional terms, a very substantial amount of foreign exchange would be liberated for capital investments, while the peso counterpart for the coal imports could again be applied to development, as was done with PL 480.

Other conclusions of the workshop in Honolulu last week were that natural gas will represent an increasingly important primary energy source and that, as an energy source of last resort, nuclear power will unavoidably become more important in the developing countries, as it is today in the energy plans of industrializing or highly industrialized countries in northeast Asia, such as Japan, South Korea, and Taiwan.

The point was made repeatedly at the Honolulu meeting that rather than acquiring the technological capability for the 600- to 1000-MW reactors that are now prevalent, there is a need for industrializing countries to avail themselves of improved technologies for small-scale nuclear reactors in the 200- to 300-MW range, because of the quasi-decentralized needs of their economic structures, the fact that their power grids are not fully developed, the fact that archipelago countries such as Indonesia or the Philippines have problems with linking various parts of their countries by grids, and other reasons which time will not permit me to go into now.

There was a noticeable decrease in the emotionalism with which in the past nuclear energy had been rejected by some and solar energy had been proposed by others—while everybody was in agreement that solar energy is a very attractive source of energy, very few saw substantial solutions to their current and foreseeable future problems from that source.

Hydro power was seen, of course, as a very important energy source, but, for reasons that are beyond our comprehension, Providence in many instances placed hydroelectric power sources in very remote and inaccessible areas. Therefore, using such hydro power remains problematic, except in the instances of micro and mini hydroelectric sources, whose development is considered very promising.

On balance we agreed that the solution to the problem of oil-importing industrializing countries definitely lies in a very sophisticated, very complex management of a whole spectrum of energy sources rather than an excessive commitment to any one source. Even so, the problem is seen as an extremely difficult one, especially as—and there was substantial agreement on this—the demand for energy in these developing countries will probably exceed simple extrapolations from present rates of growth, which are already very high, sometimes reaching 14 percent per year, which results in a doubling time of five years.

I am increasingly convinced that the political pressure from the populations of these developing countries demanding electricity will become very, very great. You may recall that at the first and second Symposia, we were given figures originating from the monumental study done at IIASA. Their extrapolations for the year 2030, or fifty years from now, were seen by some as quite manageable. However, I disagreed with this, because of the nonlinearity that will be caused, I believe, by the increasing demand for commercial energy sources—especially in the form of electricity—from those populations which are now still outside the commercial energy market. The reason for this belief is that it seems inconceivable that the present young adult population's grandchildren—those who will be the politically important population fifty years from now—will accept living in villages that have no electricity and where they therefore cannot obtain a miminum of light, information and entertainment in the form of television, and sanitary refrigerated food for their children. It thus seems that the figures on which the present calculations are based should be reviewed and revised.

It also appears that the pressure will be less intensive with regard to those fuels that are needed for transportation—liquid fuels. There has been a lot of discussion about the various sources of alternative liquid fuels, or synfuels. However, the pattern of the most advanced industrialized countries of today will not necessarily be emulated by countries that have not yet entered the age of the private automobile. There will not be one car or one Moped available to each Chinese or each Indian or each Indonesian; probably the pressure will be for more thoughtful means of mass transit.

The problem of providing energy for the oil-importing industrializing countries should be a source of continuous examination by groups such as ours, because we are concerned about the future of the overwhelming majority of the 6 billion people who will live on this planet by the end of this century and the 8 billion people who will live here fifty years from now.

Statement Following Presentation of Technical Paper Part C

It is not for me to decide whether Hans Landsberg is a good guy or a bad guy. I have been told that he is a bad guy, and therefore if one gets him into the sight of one's gun, one should shoot.

I do not quite understand how the points that Mr. Landsberg raised, which are very elegant conceptually, fit the problem that we have been given here of coming up with some policies concerning the energy problems of the world. I was trying to run through his five major points—market and government supply/demand issues, needs of less developed countries, environmental issues, nuclear power and nuclear weapons, technologies for efficient use and for sustainable energy systems—and asked myself, "What would I do with these questions if I had to be the policymaker or planner for an oil-importing developing country?"—which was the work session that I had been asked to chair at Symposium II last November and on which I was asked to report briefly this morning.

There are so many varieties. There is a country like the Philippines, about which we heard both last night from our keynote speaker and a little bit today, a country which is blessed with a wide range of policy options because they have geothermal power, they have fertile land—I won't detail all this. What about a country like Pakistan, which has about 3-percent forest on its almost desert territory and which has no oil, or almost none; very little coal; very little gas; and so on? How does one handle the concrete problems from this elegant conceptual formulation that Hans Landsberg gave us? I think he owes it to us to go back to his five points and give us a very brief application of this to any developing country of his choice, so that we could really move from this to the next stage, which would be to complete suggestions for policy.

CHAPTER FIVE

Symposium III
Participants' Comments

DAVID LE B. JONES

We have just over two hours until five o'clock. I think it would probably be fair at the end to give David Rose, Jack Gibbons, and Hans Landsberg a chance to reply to the discussion, if they wish to do so. I would therefore propose to limit comments initially to four minutes, so as to allow everybody a reasonable chance to get into the debate.

I think it would also be helpful if comments could concentrate on the international aspects which this Symposium is about, rather than on national programs, although I realize well that the two are closely linked. And it might also be useful if participants in the discussion kept in mind some of the key points which have been raised by the Symposium II chairman/integrators—for example, Ambassador Akins's opening statement about the prospects for oil prices. But also, for example, three other questions which have come up: from Dr. Pauker's statement in which he compared the Philippines and Pakistan, the question of whether these energy problems can be tackled on a worldwide basis or whether they must be looked at more in national terms and what the balance is between the two; from Professor Oshima's statement and also that presented by Dr. Vamanu for Professor Ursu, the question of the balance between government action and the operation of the market, internationally as well as domestically; and finally, of course, from both Drs. Alonso and Vamanu, the international problems to which the development of nuclear power gives rise.

AMORY B. LOVINS

I should like to question three assumptions made by several earlier speakers in remarks which I felt didn't take economics quite seriously enough.

The first is the assumption that global energy demand must and will increase perhaps by two- to sixfold over the next fifty to one hundred years. Of course, the demand for energy *services* can be expected to increase, especially in the developing countries, but whether this means that the demand for *energy* will also rise depends on how much more energy productivity is worth buying and how much will actually be bought.

Hunter and I, with Florentin Krause and Wilfrid Bach, have examined this question in some detail in a study for the federal German government, published by Brick House (Andover, Massachusetts) as *Least-Cost Energy—Solving the CO_2 Problem*. It shows that the systematic use of currently available, currently cost-effective efficiency improvements would more than quintuple the primary energy efficiency of the 1973 West German economy—the most heavily industrialized and one of the most efficient in the world. We then used that case study to construct regional and global scenarios which assumed doubled world population, complete heavy industrialization of all developing countries, increases of economic activity by fivefold for the world and tenfold for developing countries, and using energy in a way that saves money. The result of these combined assumptions was a two- to threefold decrease in projected global energy demand. That result, we feel, is technically conservative. It is based on up-to-date empirical data from a dozen countries. We did assume that developing countries can ultimately become just as energy efficient as the most industrialized countries, but can do so faster and cheaper because they can build their infrastructures right the first time rather than having to go back and retrofit them later. This tacitly assumes that developing countries will not meanwhile spend their money on obsolete technologies like burning coal into which they might be led by coal subsidies.

We were encouraged to note that since 1979 the United States, for example, has actually gotten more than one hundred times as much new energy from energy savings as from all expansions of energy supply combined, and that of those expansions we have had more new energy from renewables than from any or all nonrenewables. So we are now getting, for example, about twice as much delivered energy from wood as from nuclear power; we've had more megawatts of new generating capacity ordered as small hydro and wind than as coal or nuclear plants or both together. And all this is happening because efficiency and appropriate renewables are simply the cheapest marginal investments. They are in particular so much cheaper than Dr. Hammer's preferred but uncompetitive options that the United States could more than eliminate its oil imports in this decade just by improving the efficiency of its buildings and cars, and could do so before a synfuel plant or power plant ordered now could deliver any energy, and at a tenth the cost.

Second, several speakers have tacitly assumed that electrification will become an even more important part of the energy picture. I'm glad that Dr. Alonso refocused our attention on whether that's so. His figures showed upwards of a quarter of energy being electrical demand. I believe that was actually primary energy which went to make electricity. In fact, in the industrialized countries only 7 or 8 percent of delivered energy is needed and can be economically justified in the form of electricity, and that limited demand is saturated about twice over by present supply. With the kind of highly efficient use I cited a moment ago in the German example, the *fraction* of delivered energy required in the form of electricity may indeed double, but at the same time the *amount* of electrical demand would fall by about threefold, assuming constant economic output. Dr. Usmani's correct call for rural electrification also helps to focus our attention on the lack of economic rationale for centralizing electrical supply in most circumstances. Scale is therefore a very important economic question here.

Third, and finally, Dr. Alonso's summary of necessary but not sufficient conditions for the expansion of nuclear power assumed that the institutions which are to buy the reactors can afford to build them and are certain to be able to sell their output. I'm not aware of any market economy today in which those conditions can be assumed with confidence. This ought to be added to a list of uncertainties. And in the otherwise excellent summary of nuclear issues, Dr. Alonso assumed that nuclear power can be decoupled from nuclear bombs. Some of us have argued in detail that that is not possible, much as we would like it to be possible. It became clear in the nuclear panel of Symposium II that some countries don't want it to be possible: at least one and possibly two of the developing countries represented in that panel explicitly stated that they wanted reactors partly in order to have the option of building bombs.

ALVIN M. WEINBERG

Once more I find myself having to respond to Amory Lovins. Professor Lovins continues to insist that electricity is bad, whereas Dr. Alonso and I insist that he has it backwards, that electricity is good. And the fact is that the fraction of energy supplied as electricity in the United States has increased from 21 percent in the late 1960s to 34 percent today, and I notice that the same thing is happening in Australia and certainly to a tremendous extent in France—and this is occurring largely for economic reasons. It's not that people have a doctrinaire attachment to the idea of electricity; it's rather that electricity turns out to be economical.

During the past year, we at the Institute for Energy Analysis have been examining what we call the rediscovery of electricity, which carries with it the idea that a highly electrified world is a world we want rather than one we don't want. We want it not only because it makes economic sense but because, as Dr. Alonso pointed out, it offers one of the surest ways of responding to the dismal news such as that conveyed earlier today by Ambassador Akins, about oil—electricity can displace oil in many sectors where oil is now being used, and this electricity can be generated by nonoil sources: hydro power if you have it; biomass if you have it; coal if you have it; nuclear if you *can* have it.

I would like to say something about what we at the institute call the design of the second nuclear era. In many countries, the first nuclear era has all but ended. In the United States no new nuclear power plants have been ordered for a very long time. And there are those, and I dare say Amory Lovins is one, who would comment, "Well, it's about time." My response would be very different.

I would at this point invoke the position that was expressed by Helmut Schmidt, at the Ottawa conference a couple of years ago, I believe, when he said that now that we have looked into the nonproliferation regime—the big International Fuel Cycle Evaluation, as it was called—we ought to launch an international effort to reexamine the technologies of nuclear energy. And this should be done with a view to eliminating at least some of the problems to which Hans Landsberg alluded in his technical paper presentation. I refer in particular to problems connected with the large amounts of radioactivity in reactors and the possibility of developing reactor systems that are much more forgiving than those we are now constrained to use. I am pleased to be able to report that, even at this early time, there are a number of technological ideas which appear to offer possibilities over the next ten, fifteen, twenty years of providing the world with nuclear energy systems that are much more forgiving than the current ones. Rather than figure out ways of conveniently giving up on nuclear energy, the world—the international community—should look very, very hard at these possibilities.

MARCELO ALONSO

I have a very brief remark, if I might.

First, in my statement I didn't indicate at any moment that nuclear power and nuclear weapons can be separated. I want to emphasize that this is an issue which must be examined very thoroughly, very carefully. Some people believe nuclear power and nuclear weapons can be separated; others believe they cannot. Well, I have my opinion, of course, but I think it is appropriate to note here that if we are going to continue to use nuclear power, this issue must be resolved in a satisfactory way. That is one point.

The other point is the problem of capital investment. To me, this is one of the most serious problems right now. For example, the Interamerican Development Bank has calculated that if all the energy expansion foreseen—or all the electricity projects foreseen—for Latin America for the next twenty years are carried out, it will require, I believe, about 130 billion dollars. Of course, those in the Interamerican Development Bank might say, "Well, that is not beyond the financial possibilities of Latin America." I doubt that very much. I think it will pose a tremendous drain on the financing available, because in addition to funds for electric energy development, these countries will need a great deal of financing to satisfy the requirements of other economic and social sectors. So, I think that this problem of financing the supply of energy—of finding not only the most efficient approach, not only the most acceptable approach, but also the most economic approach—is another issue which we cannot resolve here but on which we can indicate that something must be done.

DAVID LE B. JONES

Thank you, Dr. Alonso. If I may say so, I think that was a particularly valuable comment, because it points to one of the practical questions coming out of Hans Landsberg's presentation: What sort of new international institutions do we need, and how is the western world going to help the developing countries to make investments on the scale needed to develop their energy resources?

AMORY B. LOVINS

I want to clarify my good friend Alvin Weinberg's impression of what I said. Hunter and I did not say that electricity is good or bad, but that it is economic for some uses and not for others. Our criterion is not to accept or reject any particular technology in any doctrinaire fashion, but to try to figure out the amount, type, and source of energy that will provide each end-use service at least economic cost. The electrification now going on is not driven by real market competition; it is driven by policy and implemented through subsidies, rolled-in pricing, and promotional tariffs.

Now as to the capital question. We recently looked at the investment required in this country to implement the so-called Sawhill Report—that is, over the next twenty years, to more than double national end-use efficiency and to make energy supplies by the year 2000 at least one-third renewable, at a gross capital investment of about 0.8 trillion 1980 dollars. That sounds like a lot, except that one thing it displaces is 1 trillion dollars' investment in new power plants that would no longer be required. Another thing it displaces is 2 or 3 trillion dollars' worth of direct fuel combustion. We looked at the cashflow required to finance the 0.8 trillion dollars' investment. We found that about nine-tenths of it could be covered directly from savings in electricity bills and from loans which electric utilities could give out of a revolving fund financed only by their cash retained earnings of about 2 billion dollars per year. The other tenth or so of the investment required would amount to a total of less than a hundred billion dollars, to be taken out of several trillion dollars of direct fuel savings. Therefore, the net economic effect of the program would be to export over 2 trillion constant dollars back into the capital marketplace, where that sum would be available for other purposes. The key, therefore, is not only the lower capital intensity of the alternative investments but also that they produce a much higher velocity of cashflow. You get your money back sooner to be available to be spent on something else. Therefore, the amount of investment capital required is very much smaller than if sunk into devices with very long lead times.

DAVID J. ROSE

I hope that the authors of the paper presented this morning are not precluded from talking until the end, because I want to say something now. Several points have been raised on which there is considerable disagreement—constructive disagreement, because it allows debates to be generated which help show where things lie.

One thing that struck me was the difference between the views expressed this morning by Dr. Abelson and Dr. Hammer. Dr. Abelson said that food is going to be very plentiful; Dr. Hammer said it is not. That is a subject for a food conference and probably can't be resolved here, but I personally feel somewhat spooky about the business of developing enough food to feed 8 billion people in the year 2030, especially since many of the new food technologies are less than perfect. For example, the short-stem fast-growing rice is very good if the conditions are right, but since it has a much shorter growing cycle than other types of rice, it is rather more susceptible to short droughts and things of that kind. Some fields in the Philippines planted with the new super rice are actually doing worse than some planted with the old varieties. That is not to say that much improvement could not be made in the food problem.

Also, Dr. Hammer seemed to greatly favor mining for more coal, getting more oil from Mexico, processing more oil shale, and so on which is a very different approach toward getting energy from that supported by others and in my opinion, an approach that would lead to a very substantial disaster for our civilization. First, we would get stuck with some new technological options which, once adopted, would be very hard to divest, as history has shown; second, we would be ignoring such long-term problems as the global carbon dioxide problem, which I believe is real—the bullet would be on its way and it would be too late to duck before it hit. So I am underwhelmed, so to speak, at that particular option.

That is not to say that I find myself totally enamored with some of the views expressed last night and today on biomass fuel. If you look at the basis of the figures given, you will find that they presume that there will be 30 tons per hectare-year of dry material produced, and that leads to monocultures—of leucaena, for example—with the difficulties associated with all monocultures. Also, at present prices, you end up with something like $.50 per hectare-hour of gross income for labor even after the crops have been cut down by mechanical means. This may be all right in some circumstances, but not in others. Regarding Dr. Hammer's proposition that the Sasol process is good—it may be good if you pay South African miners' wages, but not otherwise. So I find some difficulty with some of these approaches.

Regarding electricity—there has been a lot said about electricity—the conventional charts show energy derived from coal, oil, hydro, electricity. But then they only show conversion losses for electricity, and they show those as being equal to approximately twice the electric energy produced. That represents a crummy calculation of thermodynamic availability since it includes the availability argument for electricity but discards it entirely for all the other fuels. If you actually calculated the effectiveness rates of the other fuels in their usual uses, you find that these rates are very low. This is not to argue that we should have an all-electric world. What I am saying is that most other fuels are used even less effectively than electricity—for example, fuels burnt in home furnaces. It is interesting that on the island of Hawaii, where I spend some part of the year, it is usually better in most places to buy an electric heat pump than a solar hot water heater, because they make better heat pumps these days, and also, even at the price of electricity in Hawaii, it turns out to be a pretty good deal. Now, heat pumps actually tend to preserve the so-called thermodynamic availability. We notice also, as Alvin Weinberg says, that electricity use is rising, not only in the United States but around the world—as total energy use goes up, electricity use goes up even faster. Part of the increasing use of electricity has to do with its increased thermodynamic availability, and also with an availability of another sort: electric energy tends to be delivered exactly at the point of use.

Now, regarding the question of nuclear power, I agree with those who say the first nuclear age is ending. It is time for a second age; time to rethink. Is there something to rethink? The tattered shreds of my engineering recollections suggest that there is; the opportunity grows for having new fuel cycles in which there may not be the need for reprocessing uranium or producing plutonium, and also the possibilities increase for developing small reactors, factory-built and very much safer. In order to explore these things, the East-West Center in Honolulu is conducting a week-long workshop next January for all the Asia-Pacific nations that wish to be involved. We will cover everything from nuclear weapons proliferation to nuclear waste to the use of small reactors to the possibilities of breeder reactors, other kinds of fuel cycles, legal and institutional matters—and training, of which a great deal is needed, will also be covered. The first nuclear age showed that the electrical utilities were not really ready to handle these issues satisfactorily, but I do believe that nuclear power is going to have a resurgence. In fact, it never had a *de*surgence in many countries. Korea and Taiwan spend a larger fraction of their Gross National Products on nuclear plants than any other two countries in the world. Not far behind them are Japan and France. The Soviet Union has made more identical reactors (their model vver-440) than of any other kind in the world—over forty of them. So I think there will be new things.

Solar power: I am all for it. If it comes along, fine. That is another topic mentioned this morning in passing.

But finally, I would like to say that there has been little attention to the very long-term future, which will be a nonfossil one. Not absolutely nonfossil—but relatively—one in which the preponderance of energy resources will be supplied by either renewable or relatively inexhaustible forms. This means it's solar power in one form or another and/or nuclear—most probably a combination of those two. And all of this requires much better technology, much more sophisticated technology, much more international collaboration in training, education, and mutually cooperative effort, in order to ensure that this world we live in will last for the long term.

H. G. MACPHERSON

I have been wondering a bit about how we can achieve some practical solutions, some practical actions, based on the great wisdom developed here. In this connection, I note that Mr. Jones suggests that we try to stick to international matters, but I would suggest that the problems inevitably are somewhat national. For example, the coal in the United States: To whom does it belong?— does it belong to the people who dug up the earth and put it down there in past times, or does it belong to the people who own it? To whom does the sulfur dioxide that comes from burning it belong? Now, I am not going to be so impractical as to suggest that the energy resources of every country belong equally to all the people of the world, but this does point out that each country has its own problems to which it must find solutions for itself, and in keeping with many of the sentiments expressed here, these solutions should take into consideration the needs and interests of others and the harm that can be done to them.

I find a good deal of inspiration in the countries that have faced problems; they have decided on a problem that is important to them, and they have done something about it. I could cite, for example, Brazil in its fuel program, or, as we have heard, the Philippines. I suggest that there is a lot internationally that we can obtain from these national solutions or national attempts, and as Phil Abelson mentioned in his statement this morning, the examples that these countries provide of successful solutions or at least partially successful attempts, using different technologies in different parts of the world, should be sources of inspiration and knowledge on which other people throughout the world can draw.

M. Y. SHANA'A

I come from the Gulf Organization for Industrial Consulting in Doha, Qatar, which was established by the seven Arab gulf states to promote industrial development, including, of course, energy.

Not having been here before but judging from the discussion today, it seems to me that all the suggestions being discussed here focus on long-term future effects. But regarding one point that was raised by Ambassador Akins—and somehow, I felt that there were no comments on it—I wonder if Ambassador Akins was trying to tell us that the problem we are dealing with now is not solely a long-term one but may occur in the near future. These issues involving the long-term future—whether we go to electrical, nuclear, solar, or what have you—definitely must be considered. But I would like to hear from Ambassador Akins again, if he would be kind enough. Is he trying to tell us that we may have a problem tomorrow with which we must be concerned at this meeting, or shall we continue to concentrate on long-range prospects?

JAMES E. AKINS

We tend to relax during periods of relatively large energy supplies. We certainly didn't do anything in the 1960s, although the handwriting was on the wall. We said that the Arabs could never cooperate, that there could never be an oil embargo, that the price of oil was going to go down to a dollar per barrel. This was the received wisdom in many of our major universities and was rarely questioned. After we got through the 1973–74 crisis, we relaxed again and did very, very little. The real price of oil continued to decline from 1974 to 1978, and then we had another shock. Now we have what the *Wall Street Journal* and other publications call the "permanent glut"—the end of OPEC, the decline in oil prices, the fact that we have nothing to do in energy matters except relax and enjoy the discomfiture of OPEC and other oil producers or exporters.

I said, about the beginning of 1980, that I thought we probably had seen a peak in oil prices: there was enough oil available in the world to meet global demands in this century, and even through the first couple of decades of the next century. That statement has been enlarged on and accepted quite widely. But that wasn't the end of my statement. What I said was that this economic projection was based on a number of political assumptions. Those who talk about the comfortable energy position we are in today make these assumptions, whether they know they are doing so or not.

The first assumption is the one that I referred to this morning: that the Iraq/Iran war will not spread, that we will have a continued impasse in this war. That is ending right now. The Iranians know very well that Iraq is being supported financially by the countries of the gulf: Qatar, the United Arab Emirates, Kuwait, and, most particularly, Saudi Arabia. The gulf ports are being used to supply Iraq with military equipment—that is scarcely a secret; all who open their eyes in the gulf see this happening. The Iranians have a functioning air force, thanks largely to the supply of spare parts that Israel is giving them, and they have a fairly large number of air to ground missiles. These missiles have not been used against Iraqi troop concentrations but could be used against the ultimate suppliers of Iraq—namely, Saudi Arabia and Kuwait. Blow up the Kuwait electricity plants and water distillation plants, and Kuwait is no longer a functioning country; blow up the loading facilities at Ras Tanura, and the so-called world oil glut ends very dramatically.

We are making a few other assumptions, too, when we talk about how comfortable we are in oil supply. One is that Saudi Arabia will not change its oil policy. I referred to that this morning; I think Saudi Arabia has already changed its oil policy. I doubt very much if it would be politically feasible in Saudi Arabia to go back to 10 million barrels per day of oil production, even if that level is needed by the end of this decade.

We are assuming, of course, political tranquility throughout the Arabian Peninsula, and, most importantly, we are assuming no wider Middle Eastern war. And all of these assumptions have to obtain, every single one of them—and maybe other assumptions as well—if we are going to have a comfortable oil supply situation in the short run.

We could have a real energy problem tomorrow. We have to talk about the long range—that is what we are doing here. But we don't have a lot of time. We have relaxed much too long. Every time there is a comfortable position, we listen to people like Professor Adelman of MIT and we listen to the *Wall Street Journal* and its current guru, Professor Fred Singer from Virginia, who tells us, "No problem, relax, OPEC is disintegrating. There is nothing you have to do except enjoy this wonderful brave new future." In other words, they tell us that we have lots and lots of time to carry out all the alternatives we have talked about today. I am suggesting that we do not have much time. The entire political scene in the Middle East could alter at any time, and with it the disappearance of the "oil glut."

L. HUNTER LOVINS

Ambassador Akins's comments are most interesting. The usual reaction—if one takes it seriously, as I believe one should—is, "Then we must increase domestic supplies of energy so as to relieve that foreign vulnerability." That has been done in the past, however, in such a way that we have walked ourselves into a trap. We have tended to build facilities which can be turned off much more easily than oil from Arabia can be turned off. For example, a handful of people could shut off three-quarters of the oil and gas supply to the eastern United States in an evening without leaving Louisiana. They could do it in such a way that it would be down for a years.

These concerns are the subject of an analysis we have done for the Pentagon*, in which we looked at how vulnerable this country is to energy shut-offs. It turns out we are frighteningly vulnerable. But it is also possible to design energy systems which could not be turned off: a system which relies on efficient use of energy, because that gives us the "most bounce per buck," and on more dispersed, diverse, renewable sources.

We tell the story of a fellow named Joe Jodduck who lives in the northern Great Plains and powers his farm with wind power. He was watching the television news one night and saw that his whole area was blacked out. So he went outside and looked, and

---

*A. B. and L. H. Lovins, *Brittle Power: Energy Strategy for National Security* (Andover, MA: Brick House, 1982).

indeed, all of his neighbors' lights were out—so he went back inside and watched his wind-powered tube to see when his neighbors' lights would come back on.

A lot of us would like to be in that position, but the only way we can be, individually or as nations, is to look very seriously at the vulnerability of energy systems, and to design systems that cannot be turned off by terrorists, national disasters, or technical accidents. Happily the systems that give the most resilience are also those which are the best buy in a free market—one without subsidies, one in which new electricity isn't sold at less than half its marginal cost. We must soon realize that the renewable future— solar, wind, bioconversion, micro hyro—all sized appropriately to the task that we want done—is really the only future that we can count on, for economic reasons and for security.

DENIS J. IVES

I would like to take this opportunity to come back to the international question. There have been a number of comments over the last day or so about the concept of international cooperation, particularly with the developing countries, but I personally have been a bit disappointed that we have not delved into that concept in more detail, and I hope that we still have time for discussion on its aspects. For this purpose, I would like to cover the ground briefly and see if I can attract some additional comments or debate.

First of all, I tend to look at the question of cooperation with developing countries as something that can be categorized—not too sharply, but to some extent—between conventional energy resources and appropriate alternative technologies.

In the conventional resource category, commenting first on oil and gas: I would like to suggest that beyond contributing to resource assessment, the most obvious way to cooperate with developing countries is through normal private-sector activity in exploration and development, and I think the important point to bring out is that there are ways in which that activity can be executed without a loss of national sovereignty or national equity. There are sharing arrangements that are on the public record. I thought Dr. Hammer's remarks this morning about oil and gas and the ways his own company has devised of sharing and working with developing countries was an important example of this.

Now, beyond that, I come to the area of coal. Similarly, I think, we could look to private-sector cooperation for the development and application of coal, and I want to take a moment or two to suggest fairly strongly that I hope the idea of coal subsidies which has been propounded in a couple of this Symposium's addresses is not gaining much momentum or support here. I'd say that would be the wrong direction in which to move: it would change the market signals very dramatically; it would introduce distortions and move energy economies in the wrong direction. For instance, just to take one country that has been mentioned, the Philippines, I find it hard to see what internal reason there would be to pursue the difficult area of dendrothermal energy—and it is difficult—if one of the alternatives was to use highly subsidized coal in large power stations. In addition, we are all aware of the budget deficits which many of our more advanced countries are facing. It would be very difficult to conceive of a practical way in which such a very large-scale financing scheme could be arranged.

As far as governments are concerned, I think there is probably more scope for cooperation on appropriate alternative technologies. We have to be careful that these are not too sophisticated and that we don't too quickly start seeking exotic technological variants, but in the area of, for example, fuelwood replenishment, there are many countries with quite extensive reforestation experience so I find it hard to see why we can't have early progress in that area. Similarly, I think rural electrification is an area where additional moves can be made, to the extent that electrical capacity is available.

As far as Australia is concerned, in dealing with its neighbors on some specific alternative technologies it is trying to give assistance on mini and micro hydro, practical small-scale solar heating, and practical applications of wind energy.

Australia is disinclined to look for the bigger fix in these technological areas and believes that it must be patient and, as has been suggested earlier today, prepared to engage in a process that will lead to a change in the response to the problems. For it, as for other countries, I think there are a variety of possibilities. But this must be a gradual process, and I think that our countries at the government level will have to look for some good and useful demonstration projects on an appropriate scale.

Finally, I think we also have to further develop our information and communication processes with developing countries. We have to be careful that more advanced countries don't appear to be trying to impose solutions to problems that they perhaps have only studied at a distance.

NAIM AFGAN

Two speakers whom we heard today—this morning and afternoon—have thrown some doubt on the meaning of technology transfer. It strikes me that we have a difference of opinion on this subject, and I would like to have some discussion on it. It is my impression that the meaning of technology transfer for those who need technology is very clear, and even the United Nations has paid attention to that, organizing the UN Conference on Technology and Development (UNCTAD).

I would like to point to just a few of the technologies that are relevant for the developing countries and that are needed to increase their energy sources—for example, modern technologies in exploring for different energy sources such as oil, coal, uranium, and other energy sources. Modern technologies such as these are not available in developing countries, and they are not even available in the marketplace. I hesitate to mention that in the field of nuclear energy the situation is even worse. There are certain restrictions which have political ramifications. For the transfer of technology or even the use of some materials, a country has to sign a special contract, thereby limiting its sovereignty.

Thus, there is a strong need today for technology transfer in many of the developing countries, in order for them to feel free and sovereign.

HANS H. LANDSBERG

I want to reply to Professor Afgan's point on technology transfer, because I was very brief.

My question is this: Is not the test one of whether you can, in fact, buy or be licensed to use the technology when you want it? If you can, I see no problem. Now, if you can neither buy it nor be licensed to use it, one or the other, then you have to ask further: Is it a proprietary problem, and is it discriminatory?—Does Company A not license it to anybody, or does it simply not license it to Country A or B or not at all for foreign use? If that is true, is there some kind of a military or security problem associated with the technology, such as a restriction on some part of the fuel cycle?

You have to run down the hierarchy of problems. If it is in a sense a discriminatory action, the question arises of what you are going to do about it. If it is internally discriminatory, you can do something about it by law in most countries. If it is domestic versus foreign, it gets much harder. Do you ask the government to do anything about it? It is a real problem in that sense, because it looms very large in discussions. As you no doubt know, in the Law of the Sea negotiations the provision that the consortia which would be formed must, under the Law of the Sea provisions, make the technology available to the seabed authority was one of the large stumbling blocks and has not been resolved so far.

This is therefore a real issue, and all I am saying is that we should not simply talk rhetoric, saying, "We need to transfer technology." We should say exactly what we need. Is there a block, is there an impediment? Let's look at the various points I have made to test where the problem is.

FEREIDUN FESHARAKI

I would like to follow up on an earlier comment [omitted by speaker]. I think that history will disprove the prognosis that the real price of synthetic fuels will stay the same while the price of oil catches up. As we have seen, the price of synfuels to the price of oil has remained at a 2:1 ratio for the last eight or nine years, and there is no particular reason to believe the ratio will change. So, even if the real price of oil goes up to $50 or so, which you would think at this time may be necessary for bringing the synfuels in, by that time the synfuels may be $100.

In addition, perhaps because we are at a world's fair and the mood is very much a private-sector mood, I think that perhaps the government is being given too much of a bashing. I think the government role is important. Insofar as synfuels are concerned, the events of the last month—the folding of the major synfuels projects—signify that it is hard to imagine that synfuels will survive without government intervention, without taxpayers' money. The Sasol case to which Dr. Hammer referred is a case which is highly subsidized by the government. The fact that the Germans were able to make petroleum out of coal during World War II was very much due to government subsidization. And if there is a little more success in France than in other places, it has been because of government subsidies.

Government subsidies must be part and parcel of synfuels if we want to maintain a synfuels industry. The investments are too big. I'll give you an example. At 400,000 barrels per day of synfuels or liquid from coal, it would cost about 7 or 8 billion dollars in capital investments—the cost of a large company like Conoco, which was bought for 8 billion dollars. And if you have 8 billion dollars, you might put it in Conoco rather than putting it into a 400,000-barrels-per-day synfuels industry.

Another point on subsidies for coal or subsidies for exports of other energy sources for developing countries. We must realize that we are not only talking about subsidization of the price of fuel. If you do subsidize fuel prices, you must also think of subsidizing the capital stock, because these things will not change overnight. The oil-burning capital stock must be converted or thrown away; new things must be bought. A great deal of money is involved. Small-scale renewable sources will not help us with this problem, and it is not only the fuel itself in the large-scale energy systems that I am talking about. On large-scale energy systems, if we want to provide subsidies for the fuel, we should also think of providing subsidies for capital stock, because without changing the capital stock they will not be able to use the subsidized fuels.

GIACOMO ELIAS

Coming back to the renewable sources like solar, I think that when we speak about cost, we know very well what the cost of conventional power production is, but we do not know so well the cost of nonconventional power production. And regarding nuclear power production: I am very familiar with the Adrano and the Almeria power stations in Italy—both are 1000-MW stations—and they seem to me not sufficiently cheap and flexible to be suitable for developing countries. They are very, very sophisticated, and I think they could create a lot of problems for countries that are not technologically well developed.

PETER S. VAN NORT

I have spent my career in energy production, and I would like to comment on the suggestions made by the Lovinses. I think that, as someone—I believe it was William Stratten—has said, the future can be seen most clearly at the edge of what is going on today, if you can see the edge. In that sense I would like to believe in what the Lovinses have said ought to happen, and I have spent some amount of time trying to make it happen.

I worked for a utility in Wisconsin, and we worked on alcohol fuels and low-head hydro and solar power and windmills. I would like to share our experience there, because we tried very hard to make those things work. In Wisconsin, the farmers finally decided that alcohol fuels were not at that point economic, and several cooperatives which were planning to pursue this pulled out even though they were subsidized. We had two companies that were going to put low-head hydro, of which the state has a great deal, back in operation. The company I worked for had shut down over one hundred fifty low-head hydros in the early 1950s. In one case, the company's owner said that what he was doing was playing, because he had the money to play, and that maybe the low-head hydros would be economic by the 2010 era. In the other case, the company said that the low-head hydros were not even covering their own costs, and the only reason that the company had them was to get the consulting contracts that would come from being in the low-head hydro business.

The utility I worked for subsidized solar water heating, and the only people we could find to take it were those who had $3000 sitting around. It didn't make any difference who you were—a farmer or a rich man or an out-of-work school teacher—if you had $3000 and were interested in energy conservation, the utility would put in solar water heating. And when we talked to other people who ought to have been interested in it, they could not justify a pay-back period of ten to twenty years even though the solar water heating was subsidized.

The utility had lots of windmills in its system, and we encouraged windmills; we even paid people for the excess energy generated and given to us—we paid for that at a price higher than the replacement power cost. And yet those people were unwilling to make a commitment not to ask for power when their windmills did not work. So even if every one of our customers had windmills, without that commitment, we would still need to have the power plants to supply them with electricity when their windmills didn't work.

I believe that there are tremendous inroads to be made with conservation and alternative energy sources. I can't even comprehend the numbers that Amory Lovins stated—he said them so fast that I could not write them down, so I can't comment on the size of the numbers—but the numbers are mind-boggling, and from my Wisconsin experience I can't believe that they are achievable. I believe we will make inroads.

Wisconsin had a program to do an energy plan. The governor finally got fed up with the federal government and said that we would do one of our own. Wisconsin is—I guess you would have to call it in the context of this meeting—an energy poor industrialized area, with no energy resources whatsoever except biomass. We asked, "How will we deal with the rest of the United States— the states that produce coal or oil or gas?" And while we looked at scenarios where we could achieve a 46-percent conservation of our energy between 1980 and the year 2000, nobody was willing to say that should be the State's plan, because of the changes which would be necessitated. Everybody agreed that the principal plan, or focal point, should be conservation—and when I say "conservation" I include renewable resources and things of that sort. But nobody was willing to say that that was the ultimate solution.

Therefore, I think it would be wrong for a symposium of this magnitude to say that we should choose one path over another path. I believe that one of the speakers earlier today commented that there are unique solutions for unique situations, and we consequently must have all technologies available. Thus, based on my practical experience of trying to make some of these technologies work, to conclude that we should go one way to the exclusion of all other ways would be wrong.

DAVID LE B. JONES

Thank you, Mr. Van Nort, for a very valuable comment. With your last remark you have brought us back to the key point which Hans Landsberg posed at the start. You've said very forcefully, and I think most people here would agree—perhaps Amory and Hunter Lovins wouldn't—that we are not going down one clear path or another clear path; we are, as Hans Landsberg described it, managing a process.

What I feel has been missing to some extent in this discussion so far is an examination of the following questions: How does one, in fact, manage that process? Who manages it?—the hidden hand of the market?—the government?—firms, consumers, and the government working together? And what sort of policies does one have to carry out the process of management? How far can those policies be international? How far can they be national policies on the same basis under different political systems (a point which we touched on at the second Symposium, when some of us were very struck with the emphasis on the role of prices and the marketplace in both the centrally planned economies and in the nonplanned industrialized economies)?

Perhaps, in the time that is left to us—and it is getting short— it would be helpful to those preparing the communiqué if we could concentrate the discussion on those sorts of questions.

ROBERT W. KIERNAN

I am Director of Energy at the National Association of Manufacturers, and I would like to address the question of who should manage the energy problem—the government or the market?

I think one of the best things the United States, as the world's largest energy consumer, could do to contribute to worldwide energy stability is to bring its own energy house in order. One giant step that could be taken in that direction is to continue to deregulate US energy markets. I think that by doing so we could solve the problems posed by both Ambassador Akins and the Lovinses; that is, we could both reduce our vulnerability to an unstable world oil market and enhance the development of alternative energy supplies.

In the United States, the natural gas market is primary among those that should be deregulated. By deregulating it, I think we can displace a great deal of the oil that we currently import, develop alternative technologies, and increase conservation. Federal subsidization of gas use in this country is certainly not the economic way to go, and I think it inhibits the US goal—and the worldwide goal—of increased energy stability.

PETER S. VAN NORT

Commenting again from my experience in the utility industry and building on my prior remark that there is no single solution, the most troubling thing relative to management of the energy problem is inconsistency of direction as opposed to lack of direction. It would be difficult for me to comment about this on an international scale, although I assume that it would hold true there as well.

Given the assumption that there is no single solution, it is important to establish a set of ground rules—whatever they may be—and then proceed on those ground rules until an end is achieved, rather than establish a set of ground rules, go halfway down the road and change the rules, start over on another path and go halfway or a third of the way down *that* path, and then change directions yet again. Based on my experience, again, I think the utility industry can go to solar power or nuclear power or coal or hydro or whatever you like, as long as someone sets the ground rules and leaves them alone until something gets done, rather than going halfway and then changing, and so on.

So, regarding your point, I am not sure it is as important to decide *who* is to manage as it is to adopt the principle that whoever manages should leave the direction alone—or constant; I don't mean "alone" in the sense of walking away—but leave the direction constant long enough to achieve a solution, before that direction is changed.

L. HUNTER LOVINS

Mr. Van Nort would perhaps like to have outlined for him a clear-cut direction that we can all follow to the end. Unfortunately, in a democracy things don't work that way. It is going to continue to be a very messy evolution—there are going to be many different interest groups bashing heads over this issue for many years to come. And I, for one, am very grateful that it is that way, because none of us has the wisdom to dictate the answer. We cannot get there by mandate, even by the laying of ground rules by which the game will be played. We simply don't know enough.

The answer that Amory and I find as we travel around is that individuals and communities, provided with information on what is possible and opportunities to act on the incentives that are already manifest, are solving their energy problems for themselves. They need help, largely in the form of information and removal of barriers: clearing away of subsidies that distort the apparent price of energy, clearing away of such things as obsolete building codes that in many areas will not let you build a state-of-the-art solar house, getting information out to architects so that they will know how to build a house that requires no energy to keep it comfortable year round (as Amory and I are now doing).

I am sorry if Mr. Van Nort does not know the full range of technical possibilities for energy efficiency and renewables. We can cite chapter and verse of where people are grabbing these opportunities and making good money in the market as entrepreneurs. I would strongly urge this group to resist any proposed uniform direction. Let it all work itself out in the messy way of a real democracy. Let's identify where institutions are holding up the process and oughtn't to be. Let's identify where information is needed, where technology transfer is needed. But to the greatest extent possible let's give individuals and communities the chance to solve their own problems, because they will surely do it far better than we.

DAVID LE B. JONES

That was a very interesting and important point that Hunter Lovins made. It sounded very familiar, very similar to what a lot of ministers were saying at the International Energy Agency meeting yesterday. I am not sure if you would like to be in that faction. I wonder if any of the participants who come from the centrally planned economies could comment on what Hunter Lovins has said and how that fits into the way in which they run their energy policies.

[Comment which followed omitted by speaker.]

G. WAYNE MEYERS

As a new participant in this Symposia Series, one of the things that I have heard here are projections about what the world's population and its energy requirements will be. My experience with projections is that they are usually wrong.

From an international perspective, perhaps one thing to consider is what we want to achieve—political stability?—an eradication of hunger?—energy stability? But these goals probably differ depending on whether a nation is industrialized or developing. Perhaps one way to achieve international cooperation is to have each country determine what its long-range goals and priorities are and which technologies should be developed to support these goals and priorities. In the developing nations, one should then see which countries have the same goals and priorities and use this as a basis for cooperative technical exchanges. This way, there would not be so much debate about solar, biomass, and so on, because each nation would have its own goals and objectives. But there would be a way to establish an international basis for technical cooperation, and that might lead to an exchange of goods and services.

M. Y. SHANA'A

Regarding whether government should be involved in planning or ground rules and so on, I recall that one of the Symposium participants has predicted that the price of oil will stay at about $35–$40, even in the 1990s, while the price of synthetic fuel will go up to $50 or $60—whatever the numbers are. First, I think the price of oil will not stay at $35–40 unless the rate of inflation drops to zero or lower. Otherwise, the price of oil will have to keep up with inflation. But if oil is at $35–$40, synthetic fuel is at $60; if oil goes up to $60; then synthetic fuel goes up to $80. I think synthetic fuel can survive if—and only if—the oil supply is completely depleted. That is when we will have no other choice.

I'm mentioning this now because the difference in the operating modes of various countries is remarkable. Take the United States: it is being operated mainly by the private sector. Take the centrally controlled countries: they are being operated by government. Take the OPEC countries: oil in those countries is operated or supervised by the governments. Coming back to the United States: unless there is an incentive to develop synthetic fuels, the private sector—because it is private, because it is profit-oriented—is not going to do so. And the United States may end up wishing it had. Well, this means that government must step in and some crash programs not necessarily profit making ones—must be undertaken now, in the United States and internationally, to provide for the future situation.

We talk about international cooperation. The remark has been made that we should enlarge the concept of internationalism and think about it in expanded terms—for example, in terms of coal, alternative technology, rural electrification, information and communication, technology transfer, and so on. But I hope that before this assembly comes up with such recommendations, it will recall the so-called priorities. The people in some countries may not be interested in electrification—they may be interested in finding a few grains of rice to feed their stomachs. Instead of giving them electricity when they have nothing to eat, it may be better to think of giving them a few kilos of fertilizer to improve their grain production, even though they have to keep on using kerosene lamps. So I hope we don't forget the priorities when we talk about international cooperation.

I also hope that, even at a Symposium such as this, we will not only talk about solutions but will address the questions of who is going to implement them. This is really the crux of the matter—not to say that people need electrification; that they need this; that they need that. I hope that this Symposium will come up with definite suggestions regarding the problems and their solutions—solutions which will necessarily result from cooperation between the industrial countries and the developing countries. And it is not enough for us to say there should be cooperation; we must say how the cooperation should take place. What are the steps recommended? Who is going to carry them out? That is really the international cooperation we should seek. It is not sufficient to say that there is an international need to go to the least developed countries and do one, two, three, four—we must decide *how* it is going to be done, and *that* is where the ground rules should be stipulated.

Finally, I hope that whatever has been or will be said here will stay far away from politics. We should think of ourselves as only technical people, far away from politics, and then simply state what must be done for the interest of the human race in the future.

DONALD L. KLASS

I am with the Institute of Gas Technology (IGT) in Chicago and have been involved in oil, gas, and biomass research for quite a few years. I have heard many issues mentioned this afternoon. I would like to comment on two of them.

The first is the last subject which was discussed; namely, government intervention versus nongovernment intervention, or perhaps competitive free pricing as a determinant of the development of new energy sources, particularly in the United States. The example that I think is outstanding the terms of government intervention concerns Brazil. Phil Abelson mentioned this morning the course of action Brazil has been taking in its alcohol fuels markets, and I am sure almost all of you are aware of the excellent progress it has made. But I would like to suggest that the only reason for this progess is government intervention. By legal mandate in Brazil, one can purchase only gasohol for an automobile; one cannot buy unleaded gasoline. This is required by law. If we in the United States had government mandates of that type, our alcohol fuels program would also be a sterling success. Yet, in this country we rely on tax incentive, tax forgiveness, and also on the sale of gasohol in limited marketing areas at a maximum price differential of about 4–5¢ over unleaded gasoline. If competitive free pricing continues to determine the progress of synthetic fuels in the United States, I submit that government intervention will be essential. Gasohol has been a big success in Brazil only because of government intervention.

My other comment concerns technology transfer. I have heard this referred to many times this afternoon. By definition, it is the sharing of information, perhaps on an international basis. If Company X isn't willing to share its information with Company Y, or if one country isn't willing to share its information with another country, then we are not going to have technology transfer on any scale. I was involved in a technology transfer project with a group in Brazil. The Brazilian group was interested in the transfer of biological gasification or biogas research information, techniques and data that we at IGT had developed over a long period of time. We were willing to share this with sixteen engineers who spent a year with us in Chicago learning about what we had done. If we hadn't been willing to share this information, there would have been no technology transfer out of our organization. So, sharing should be kept in the forefront in capital letters. If there isn't any willingness to share, there isn't any technology transfer.

ISHAG BASHIR

Since energy is a global issue and I believe that no country can solve its energy problems in isolation, I would like to go back to the question of international cooperation. This was also a subject of debate at the 1981 Nairobi conference, but at that time no suitable resolution was achieved. So, I would like to request this Symposium to better define international cooperation, stating how it can best be effected—whether by international institutions or by encouraging bilateral relations. The government of my country, Sudan, already has bilateral technical cooperation with the United States, with Australia, with the Federal Republic of Germany—but most of the time this has been left to the initiative of the two countries. It thus would be good if international cooperation could be put in more realistic terms.

P. RAGHAVENDRAN

I am from India and am participating in this Symposium in a personal capacity. Regarding the question of international technology transfer, I would like to share an experience we had in India with an oil conservation program.

Through surveys we determined that replacing inefficient burners in small furnaces and boilers offered considerable scope for industrial fuel oil conservation. We then tried to find burners which would suit our purposes. There were three or four burner manufacturers in India, and we threw it open to them to collaborate with foreign manufacturers of burners. However, even after four years there was hardly any progress, because the advanced technology of industrialized nations was not appropriate for our country. The operating conditions of our boilers and furnaces are different: they are subject to frequent load fluctuations, to over-loading because of inadequate capacities, and so on. Ultimately, we had to fall back on indigenous research and development to arrive at a burner which was appropriate for India's needs.

I think that the lesson for developing countries from this experience is that sole reliance on technology transfer from de-veloped nations may be inappropriate. There is as large a scope for bilateral transfer between developing countries whose experiences and situations are similar, as there is between developed nations. For example, I think India could share a lot of its know-how with other developing countries, particularly in the use of small-scale energy. We have developed more efficient kerosene stoves, gas stoves, and low-air-pressure industrial burners—and such tech-nologies may be more appropriate for other developing countries than some of the technologies available from developed nations.

EDWARD LUMSDAINE

I would first like to respond to Don Klass's comment. I think that the government intervention and subsidies question has been overemphasized. You know, of course, that Brazil has a military government and we don't, so there is a basic difference in the two governments.

I also want to give a minute or two of personal testimony about solar energy. I have been involved in solar energy for the last twenty years, on and off. I spent three and a half years as a director of the Solar Energy Institute in New Mexico, and I have built a number of passive solar houses. I think that government subsidies have not been particularly good for solar energy. For example, in the area of solar industrial process heat, where the us government provided 100-percent subsidies, the program has been a failure. I visited almost every solar industrial process heat plant built in the United States and subsidized 100 percent by the government. All the government wanted to do was turn these plants over to indus-try to operate. And many of the facilities—most of them in fact—are not operating, because the operation and maintenance costs are several times the cost of conventional fuel at the moment. It costs roughly $15–$16 per million btu to operate and maintain some of those facilities, whereas the cost of natural gas is about $5 per million btu.

Now, photovoltaics and other areas like passive solar are doing very well without government subsidies. Passive solar, for example, has never received much in terms of government subsidies. The government didn't even recognize that passive solar existed until about a year ago. Expensive active systems were supported for quite some time, but passive solar systems were not recognized in terms of tax credits until very recently, and then only imperfectly. And yet, tens of thousands of passive solar homes are going up. I can tell you from my own experience: I have built several; my wife has designed them; we have been able to sell them; we have been able to make a profit. They consume about 25 percent of the energy used by an average house, and we have just finished another house here in Knoxville and are living in it. It consumes probably 20–25 percent of the energy used by a regular house here in Knoxville. So it can be done, and it does not require large or even any government subsidies.

I think the government ought to be involved in research and development, but not in subsidies through tax credits. Recently, when I was in Australia, I found that a Solarhart solar water heating system costs $800—800 Australian dollars, which is roughly 1,000 us dollars. When that system arrives in the United States (with some modifications)—and I don't know what the transportation costs and taxes are—but by the time it is installed in San Diego, the cost has risen to over $2,000. Now, California has a 55-percent tax credit. You think about that.

I thus am not sure that government subsidies and so on have been very good for solar energy or for the taxpayer. For example, it still costs $3,500–$4,000 to buy an active solar hot water system. If I invest that money, even at 10 percent, I could pay for all the gas and electricity I need. So the active systems that have been heavily subsidized by the government have just not panned out economically at least in comparison with conventional (also heavily subsidized) energy sources. Of course, environmental considerations present a different story, but these have been of least importance in government policy in the past.

J. ERICH EVERED

I endorse strongly many of the comments I have heard today. I feel that this group should avoid proposing a single path for the future.

What is desirable is the removal of artificial and institutional barriers to the flow of information and technology—the removal of barriers to the implementation of the vast array of energy technologies, both central and decentralized, that we have discussed. I think it is the responsibility of the industrialized countries to support energy development in the developing countries through technology transfer, however we might define it.

Another point: The market approach is the most effective manner in which to manage the energy problem—the energy processes about which we are deliberating—especially in these uncertain and unpredictable times in which we find ourselves. The unregulated market is the most efficient allocator of resources, and it provides the correct incentives for both renewable energy resources and synthetic fuels. We have heard today that renewables work in some places and not in others, work at some times and not at others. I think removal of any artificial barriers to the development of renewables is the best policy.

I also disagree with the comments made earlier that synthetic fuels will never be economic until conventional petroleum supplies are depleted. I think that long before then, as the total available production of conventional crude oil begins to shrink relative to total world demand, the market price of crude will surpass the level at which technologies can provide synthetic liquid hydrocarbons. But before that time, whether or not synthetic fuels should be subsidized or in some other way economically encouraged is a strategic question which can be answered only by individual countries based on their own needs and their individual perceptions of their countries' positions.

But, again, I would return to my first point. I think that we should avoid proposing a single technical path. Instead, open channels of communication and international cooperation are the appropriate approach.

KEICHI OSHIMA

I just want to give my thoughts on technology transfer, because, hearing all the comments, I think it is a rather complicated matter.

Different technologies have different characteristics. For example, consider time frames—if you are talking about the adoption of efficient burners, the development time is fairly short since this can be more or less achieved by applying present technology, but if you are talking about synfuels technology, the R&D will be long-term since technological breakthroughs will be needed. It is thus difficult or even dangerous to discuss all these technology transfers together as if they belong in the same category.

I think that in longer term technological developments there is a greater role for governments, especially if economic collaboration is involved. In that case, government must give incentives in order for industry to pursue a technology. The market mechanism predominates in the market-economy countries, but some priorities must also be set in technology transfer to meet the recipient countries' needs.

Furthermore, in order to achieve the goal shared by industrialized and less industrialized countries of attaining technology that will meet long-term future needs, a continuous flow of information—possibly through some kind of intellectual institution—is needed to establish a global context of mutual understanding. I greatly hope that this point—the importance of continuous discussion and information exchange—can be included in the communiqué.

I think that, as Mr. Landsberg said, energy problems should not be tackled on a one-shot basis but by some kind of continuous management. Perhaps continuation of this Symposia Series could be recommended in the communiqué.

ROBERT SADOVE

I would like to congratulate the authors on their excellent paper and comment on one aspect of it—that the transition from old energy production modes to new and more sustainable ones is going to be much slower and more difficult than people think. We in the World Bank have been involved in an expanded energy program which entails 25 percent of our lending this year—$3 billion for energy. We are also in the midst of a program of energy assessments being done in sixty countries with assistance from the United Nations Development Programme. We've now completed thirty assessments, fifteen of which have been processed through our board and discussed with the countries involved. The experience so far is encouraging but certainly underscores the difficulties ahead. What is needed, as stated in this morning's paper, is "good management" consisting of policies that meet short-run needs without creating long-run difficulties. The main points of consensus listed at the beginning of the paper should continue to be stressed, and we find they are very important in most of the countries we have studied. And certainly, also, what Mr. Landsberg has identified as points of tension are points where there obviously are potentially great difficulties. I think that you couldn't say it better than he has said it in the two lead paragraphs of the section entitled "The Elusive Solution and Cross-National Management Policies."

I think that there is a lot of confusion in discussions about renewable types of energy. Fuelwood is one problem where we can be optimistic about a solution, even in the relatively short run, if effective programs are carried out. Solar is quite another question. At its present state of development it is undoubtedly a long-term proposition for most of the developing countries. A thousand dollars has been mentioned as the cost of a solar heater, which may not sound like much here in the United States, but a thousand dollars is way beyond the per capita income levels in most of the developing countries. Similarly, the cost of a biogas unit, which sounds very modest, is often very high when considered from the perspective of most household income levels in developing countries.

There is not time to go into much detail here, except to reiterate my support for the paper. I would certainly question some of the observations made by its critics. It appears to me that many experts on nuclear power emphasize the problems with its development, often giving the impression that other forms of energy—for example, micro hydro or hydro—look a lot better. And those who know coal also think that hydro is okay, but those who know hydro say, "Well, micro hydro is awfully difficult." Our friend from Australia mentioned the support that his government is giving to Nepal, and I surely would emphasize the difficulties the Nepalese are having in developing their substantial hydro resources. It seems as though every one of the areas we study has a unique set of problems and difficulties, and this has been noted well in the paper. I think most of us feel humble in the face of the various "energy crises" as reflected in the statement that these three gentlemen have prepared—a little more humility on the part of those of us who argue for one approach rather than another would probably be a good thing.

HYO JOON HAHM

I have some comments on technology transfer as embodied in developed and developing countries. I don't think that technology transfer is a simple problem or that a developing country can readily apply technologies from developed countries to its own purposes, such as economic development or industrialization. We should consider several facts about the technologies that come from developed countries.

First, as you well know, these technologies are not necessarily appropriate to developing countries. Second, these technologies are usually developed by private industrial organizations, and when they transfer them to a developing country, their main goal is to maximize the attainment of their own aims, such as increasing their market shares or getting a kind of monopolistic advantage. These are two main reasons why a developing country should not think that its purposes, such as economic development, as I mentioned, will necessarily be met by a developed country's technologies.

Another aspect of technology transfer is the lack of appropriate infrastructures in most developing countries. This means that they cannot easily digest foreign technologies, including technologies for energy conservation—not only those for alternative energy sources such as solar, wind, and so on, but also those for energy conservation.

JOHN H. GIBBONS

I want to make three points.

First of all, the complexity of the process of change and the time required for change has reiterated itself many times today—whether it be for energy development or energy consumption patterns or food production or changes in population growth rates or economic growth. Even without surprises, an enormous amount of time is required to do the essential things that we have been talking about today, things that are all interconnected. Now, to me, this implies a universal need, sustained by a great mutual self-interest, for worldwide participation in improving methods of analysis of where we are, how we are moving, and how we might shape our futures. There are some embryonic approaches to this kind of analysis that have emerged in the past decade, but it seems to me that it's time to give much more concerted worldwide attention to this. Such an activity could be materially aided by periodic forums such as this Symposium to explore how well we're doing in understanding the state and direction of things—and how the future can be shaped by present actions.

As a footnote to that, it also strikes me that the major changes that have affected the world since long before man came on the scene have occurred *not* gradually at all but suddenly and by great surprise. Evidence extends from the late Cretaceous period, when apparently we were zapped by an asteroid, to the Irish potato famine caused by a virus, combined with an agriculture overly dependent upon a single commodity, which grossly changed the history of a nation, to Jim Akins's commentaries about what may happen in this decade in the Mideast. If, in fact, we have to deal with a world in which we must think and plan in terms of a no-surprise future and yet at the same time must be prepared for surprises, this underscores the imperative to think about resilience. Resilience, at least in my mind, means diversity as well as efficiency.

A second point—a couple of comments about nuclear energy. I was trained in nuclear physics and had a great and joyful time as a researcher at Oak Ridge National Laboratory for nearly two decades. I therefore have a more than average interest in following that subject. Nuclear energy carries the promises of heaven and the perils of hell. Dr. Alonso said this morning that we probably would be better off without it—at this point, at least, in our world history. And I keep asking, "Why the intense, repeated confrontations between proponents of energy productivity and decentralized energy on the one hand and the proponents of major centralized energy, particularly nuclear energy, on the other?" One answer is, I believe, implicit but not as explicit as perhaps it should be, and that's the concern about the degree of subsidy that is embedded in the development of nuclear energy, coal, synthetic fuels, and other centralized major supply side options. That concern appears as a push either to see such subsidies removed so that alternatives can have a chance to compete fairly; or alternatively, to provide similar subsidies to decentralized and conservation options. Otherwise, even without thinking about externalities, we have great difficulty in identifying least cost paths toward desired futures, and we start focusing on energy as an end to itself rather than as a *means* to social ends. Of course, social cost in nuclear energy is a factor that is so different depending upon the individual sense of value that its incorporation in the nuclear equation makes it a most difficult thing to wrestle with.

Also implied in this confrontation is the degree and level of necessary central governance that must, perforce, accompany some of these technologies. You might say that Amory Lovins is the most avid apostle of the free market. He is John Locke's disciple, because he believes that big government as necessitated by big and unforgiving technology may not be the best way to go if we have alternatives.

Third and finally, I recall the story of a white American talking with a black American about various economic problems the nation was facing. The black man said, "You know, you and I came over here in separate ships, but we're in the same boat now." I think we citizens of the world are in the "same boat" now in terms of mutual self-interest in facing our energy future in a more coherent way. I was struck by Phil Abelson's comments this morning, and by some of the Office of Technology Assessment's recent work in molecular biology—it led me to think of the enormous rate of change that particular science is undergoing and the enormous opportunities which the accompanying rapid progress in biotechnology gives to the goal of improving the human condition in the coming decade or two. If you think about combining the contribution of the science of molecular biology from the industrial countries with the contribution of the genetic stock of plants from around the world—many if not most of which come from developing nations, and many of which are threatened by species extinction—then you have an interesting set of mutual interests as a basis for collaboration, for meeting not only energy needs but also food, chemical, and other needs.

DAVID J. ROSE

I said most of my remarks before, but Dr. Sadove's comments on international programs of education, training, and so forth remind me to make one more.

About two weeks ago, I was speaking to one of Dr. Sadove's colleagues at the World Bank, Mr. James Fish, who remarked very wisely that many things in the energy area around this world need doing, and many of them involve appropriate technologies. They are relatively small—micro hydro in the right places; wind power, perhaps, here and there; biomass in the right places. And he remarked that one of the difficulties about the World Bank is that it is hard for it to distinguish good small projects—that is, really small ones—because to do good assessments of small projects takes much more effort proportionally, and it's a little easier to take the usual route of something large since the amount of assessment per dollar is lower. This led to a discussion of the need, then, for vastly increased indigenous expertise around the world on all of these issues, whether they be biomass or micro hydro or wind or assessing nuclear vis à vis something else, or using energy more appropriately and effectively—all of these things.

Something that seemed to come out loud and clear was the need for a cooperative venture on education and training, by which I do not mean forcing things down people's throats or into their heads, but an exchange of experience about what the option space is (if I may use that term once more). Here is an area where the industrialized countries and the less industrialized ones can work together. Jack Gibbons just remarked about the proper use of biomass for food, energy, and other purposes. With genetic engineering and with many species, especially in tropical regions—regions that look sturdy but are in fact fragile—much needs to be done.

So the need for a global education program on a much better, more organized scale than we have now seems indisputable. I'm not prepared to say just how we should go about it—classes where and professors moving where—but it's something that we could work on very productively and that would find very little opposition.

HANS H. LANDSBERG

I'd like to clarify a few things that I said in my presentation that have come up repeatedly in this discussion. One is, and Ambassador Akins picked it up, that I talked about the process. I think I ought to be a little bit more specific, so let me go from the domestic to the international and be specific.

I think the process that I'm talking about domestically, at least in this country and in a good many others, consists of, as far as I see it, four elements. One is to adjust to higher energy prices; one is to move to a different energy mix (these two elements are not quite disconnected, but they are separate); the third is to move in those directions with the least harm to the environment, to economic growth, to economic and social equity, and to world peace; and the fourth is to provide some protection for contingencies. I call this a process. The parameters change and the approaches change, but I think it is a fairly clearly defined one.

Now, when you move this to the international arena it gets much more difficult. To nail down what one means by this: it does include a great many innocuous, noncontroversial, but very useful things—information, education, sharing experience, and so on. I think that is easy that far. It then gets to somewhat more difficult pieces of that process that include financial assistance and technological assistance beyond education, information, and so forth. It gets even more difficult when we come to the problem of the common property resources—that is, environmental resources—to questions of nuclear safety and so on. And then even further, it becomes really sort of sticky—for example, any moves toward reaching "stability," orderly markets, a compact between consumers and producers, et cetera that are sort of the ultimate, way in the distance. And it's interesting how it's not only problematic but very ephemeral. If you now think back to what use to be called the Yamani plan by which the OPEC price would move in consonance with a growth in the GNPs of the developed countries, adjusted for inflation, et cetera—I think if that plan had ever been put into effect, it would have long been cancelled by the OPEC countries, because things have gone very differently than it was thought they would go. So that, I think is a very faraway stage, raising substantial doubt in my mind.

This reminds me of what one of my British friends once said—that the British always had arrangements for buying sugar at an agreed price, but when the price of sugar was low they had to pay the higher price fixed in the agreement, and when the price of sugar was high the exporting countries would break the agreement, so the British had the worst in both cases. These agreements are simply very hard to maintain in the face of changing conditions. That's what I have in mind by a process that has to be watched and managed.

Which brings me to the second point. Mr. Jones threw out the question: "Who manages?" In my own mind, the only thing I could imagine by "managing" is public policy in setting the framework and passing laws and giving the incentives that are or are not wisely set and applied. Again, in terms of this country, our oil price control program was a very unwise one—certainly in retrospect, and, I think many of us believed, even at the time. That is a piece of management; it's public management. If I named two others that are very current, they would fall in the area (in this country, again) of government budgeting. One is the general drift of the R&D budget in the Department of Energy; the other, that department's conservation budget. The latter is being practically wiped out, even though—taking me to my third point—a great many things are in fact not being picked up by anybody outside of government; if government drops the ball, it will just lie there. That is what I mean by management. I can't think of any other management in that sense except public policy, both in the market economies and in the nonmarket economies.

Which takes me to the next point. By government intervention, I had a much narrower thing in mind when I first mentioned it; namely, the emergence of government as an actor. I mentioned government as buyer and seller, rather than in the conventional sense of government intervening in a daily or continuing way in market dealings. I think the emergence of government as buyer and seller is recent—in oil it is certainly overwhelming—and it creates a number of problems that we have not faced in the past. That is in the narrow sense. In the broad sense, the question really, and I think someone said it, boils down to the appropriate roles of government versus the private sector in the market economies and the different political systems. This is a vast subject which we can't possibly deal with adequately. I alluded to it when I said that, in the current budgeting in this country, for instance, the idea that the government has no place in promoting greater energy efficiency is, I think, wholly mistaken. For instance, many of the industries or activities in which there is an enormous potential for conservation, such as building and construction, have simply no capacity for doing any research and development. They are not organized this way. And so there is a role for government, and the government pulling out of it will simply leave a large number of fields unattended. Of course the appropriateness of the role of government and the private sector respectively will vary from subject to subject.

Next, Guy Pauker was one of the first to raise a question about these five areas. That was merely, Guy, a didactic device. That is, we were trying to channel the discussion into some kind of structure under some headings so we wouldn't jump from A to Z and back to K and forward and so on and so forth. It has not worked too well, but it may have given some sense that certain clusters of issues can be dealt with together. It was not done with the idea that these would provide guidance to Pakistan about what to do about its water system, or another country about what to do about its forests. But each cluster had some coherence. Undoubtedly, this was not necessarily the best structure, not necessarily even a good one, but it had a very narrow focus.

The last point is really a point of clarification. Amory Lovins made the remark which I have heard many times before, not from him but from others, that this country now uses twice as much wood as nuclear. He's got many answers; maybe he's got this one too—but I have never come across anything to support this statement, with this exception: that most of the wood in this country is, of course, used by the forestry products industry; they use their own stuff. Once you eliminate that portion, which has never been in the energy statistics, the remaining amount is relatively small. It is an item that needs clarification. Perhaps by counting wood refuse used in the wood industry and by some heroic assumptions, you can get the result that Amory Lovins presents. I have never seen it done convincingly. Interestingly, this issue is again a sort of a testimony to the "package" approach. If you are for wood, you are good; if you are for nuclear, you are bad—or vice versa; it works both ways. I hope to God we can stay away from that kind of categorizing.

DAVID LE B. JONES

In the United Kingdom, we had a public inquiry recently into a major new coal mining development. It went on for several months and moved the National Union of Mine Workers to comment at the end of it that the evidence had ranged from the mating habits of the mayfly to the possibility of a revolution in Saudi Arabia. We've done even better this afternoon and have ranged from the end of the Cretaceous period to the possibility of a revolution in Saudi Arabia. Fortunately, I don't have to try to sum up the discussion—it falls to others to draw the wisdom which has been expressed here into the communiqué which the symposium will be issuing. But perhaps I could mention three or four points that particularly struck me.

The first is the question of the short-term risks in relation to oil which were so vividly highlighted by Jim Akins. But short-term risks on energy of course are not confined to oil. There is always the possibility, I suppose, of a repetition of Three Mile Island in a form which might lead to every pressurized water reactor being closed down. There is always the possibility of industrial action in some of the other energy supply industries. These are risks which, for the moment at least, we have to live with and deal with as best we can by contingency planning.

The second point, brought out very forcefully by Jack Gibbons, is that the energy future is unpredictable and is getting more so. The easy and glib answer is keep your options open. But keeping options open is a very expensive process in terms of resources. If you put resources into synfuels against the possibility of an oil price of $100 per barrel by 1990 and the oil price is in fact $30, then you have fewer resources for schools or hospitals or homes or just letting the citizens live it up and enjoy themselves. So there is the enormously difficult problem of devising a policy framework which at reasonable cost is reasonably robust against the unpredictabilities which we face.

Third, on the question of government intervention, I thought our Hungarian colleague put it very well when he said that the question was one of the division of responsibility between government and companies. In all our countries, governments are and have for many years been deeply involved in the energy sector. The question is not whether government should be involved but just how it should be involved. That will vary from country to country. But it is my personal view, and I suspect many would share it, that the government's job is to set a framework which will help individuals to make decisions that, working together, will produce patterns of energy production and energy use that are broadly reasonable—one cannot be more precise than that—from the national point of view.

Last, there is the question of energy cooperation. David Rose emphasized the importance of exchanging information about how we do things, about better education on an international scale. But on top of that, there is the problem which was talked about a lot—of helping the energy-poor developing countries, encouraging the transfer of technology. I was immensely struck by what our Indian and Sudanese colleagues said about making sure you are transferring the right technology. The technologies that the less industrialized countries need are often very different from those which are being developed to meet the needs of the industrialized countries, and we will not help anybody if we try to thrust the latter's technologies down other people's throats, whether through trade or aid or in some other way.

Those were the points that particularly struck me. It is now a little after five o'clock, and I should draw this meeting to a close and again thank Jack Gibbons, David Rose, and Hans Landsberg for their paper and presentations. They have provided the basis for what I think we agree has been an excellent discussion.

AMORY B. LOVINS

[The following two comments were submitted in writing after the close of the discussion. The first responds to Hans Landsberg's last comment; the second to the comments of Peter Van Nort and Edward Lumsdaine.]

1. The us Domestic Policy Review of solar energy (TID-22834, February 1979, p. iv) estimated 1978 us primary wood use at 1.3–1.8 q, almost all by pulp mills with a nominal efficiency of at least 70 percent. Delivered energy to the mills was thus 0.9–1.3 q; the higher figure is conservative for 1980, and by 1981 the forest products industry got over half its energy from wastes. In addition, an estimated 1–2 q of primary wood was burned in 1980 in domestic stoves—up 2–3 since 1977–78 and 5–6 since 1972–73. Given the prevalence of unrecorded, nonmarket wood harvesting for private use (a term seriously undercounted in the 1979 Gallup/Wood Energy Institute poll showing private wood use totaling 1 q), even 2 q may be conservative: there are by now about 10 million iron woodstoves in the United States, increasing by nearly 1 million annually. I conservatively assume an average efficiency of 40 percent for private woodburning (most stoves do 60–70 percent or better, fireplaces much worse, but the fireplaces have a very low duty factor). Thus, delivered energy from the stoves in 1980 was of order 0.4–0.8 q, and the total delivered from wood was a bare minimum of 1.3 q, perhaps 2.1 q, and possibly even higher. In contrast, us nuclear power in 1980 delivered (net of grid losses) of order 240 TWh with a heat value of 0.8 q, or, as I stated, about half the total delivered by wood.

2. The unhappy experiences Mr. Van Nort describes are not typical of well-designed programs in the United States or elsewhere. For example, if solar water heaters are such a bad deal, it is hard to see why, by the end of 1982, 11 percent of Japanese houses will have them. Likewise, while the Department of Energy's demonstrations of solar process heat were indeed turkeys, entrepreneurs are successfully supplying solar heat to industry on a shared-savings basis; modern high-temperature collectors compete handily with oil and will cross under coal costs in the next five years, depending on us location.

If small hydro is uneconomic, why were there, in 1980, 10–20 GWe of it under construction and another 20 GWe in permitting? If wind power is uncompetitive, how come the United States currently has wind farms competing on utility grids in at least three states, with over $10 billion in wind contracts outstanding in several more?

Of course Mr. Van Nort will not find wind generators that can provide continuous power without storage or backup. What he fails to mention is that the central power stations he favors have the same problem of intermittency, only *worse;* and that a grid reliant on *diverse* renewable sources, such as wind, small hydro, and photovoltaics, is *more* reliable than one reliant on central thermal plants*.

We would like to see diverse solutions reflecting the multiplicity of tasks and options—options that should compete on economic merit. But we also firmly believe in doing the cheapest things first—starting at the bottom of the supply curve and working up. The empirical data we have collected (which Mr. Van Nort will find are fully documented*) lead us to suspect that almost any efficiency improvements, and most of the dozens of kinds of well-designed appropriate renewables, are already the best buys at the margin. Though not cheap or easy, they are cheaper and easier than their competitors, such as central power plants and synfuel plants. Thus the diverse mix we envisage should not include Mr. Van Nort's (or, for that matter, our own) favorite technologies unless they can really compete without subsidy. Our economic analysis shows that low oil prices (say, $20–30 in 1982 $) eliminate synfuels, do not hurt most appropriate renewables, and have no effect on the benefits of dramatic efficiency improvements. Despite its manifest imperfections, the market has done an astonishingly good job of weeding out silly options like synfuels (which save less oil, slower, at higher cost, than *giving* people free 40 + -mile-per-gallon cars provided they scrap their gas-guzzlers).

As for the role of government action in saving oil, consider five ways to invest $100,000, and how much oil each saves in its first decade:

- Weatherize houses, as in Fitchburg, Massachusetts, in 1979. Saving in the first ten years: 170,000 barrels at 60¢/bbl.
- Make forty-four new cars get 60 miles per gallon instead of 16 mpg. Ten-year saving (at the highest published marginal cost): 5,800 barrels at $19/bbl.
- Buy about 3,000 barrels from OPEC, stick it in a hole in the ground, and call it a Strategic Petroleum Reserve. After ten years it's still there, can probably be recovered, and has incurred an irrecoverable carrying and storage charge of order $60–70/bbl.

*A. B. and L. H. Lovins, *Brittle Power: Energy Strategy for National Security* (Andover, MA: Brick House, 1982); see also —, F. Krause and W. Bach, *Least-Cost Energy: Solving the CO_2 Problem, id.*

- Buy a little piece of a synfuel plant. After ten years it will have produced nothing. After that, if it works, it will provide up to 2½ bbl/d retailing at about $60–90/bbl (1980 $).
- Buy a tiny piece of the Clinch River Breeder Reactor. After ten years it will have produced nothing. After that, if it works, it will deliver electricity at a rate (in terms of heat content) of 1/7 bbl/d at a price upwards of $370/bbl.

The current US federal policy—taking these and similar options in exactly the reverse order, worst buys first—is a kind of involvement we can ill afford, for such misallocations *slow down* oil replacement by sinking capital which then cannot be used for other measures that would save more oil faster and cheaper, such as fixing up buildings and cars.

Special Papers

Editors' Note

At Symposium II, particular interest had been expressed in integrated approaches to energy technology transfer and in multilateral institutions for energy policy—interests to which the two papers in this section were directed. Due to scheduling logistics, the first was presented the afternoon of May 26 and the second at the closing session the following morning. However, they are grouped together here because they both are considered special papers of Symposium III.

CHAPTER SIX

Case Study: Italy's Public/Private Cooperation in Energy Technology Transfer

Giacomo Elias
Director of the Energy Project
Italian National Research Council

The increases and, above all, the lively fluctuations in the price of crude oil following 1973-74 provoked a grave crisis in the economies of those industrialized countries heavily dependent on oil imports. The reaction of those economies was not long in coming, and it has expressed itself in two ways: efforts have been made, on the one hand, to reduce petroleum product needs by promoting the rational use of and discrimination among energy resources and, on the other, to increase the export of products and know-how in order to counterbalance crude oil imports.

The contribution of research is fundamental to achieving success in these two efforts—above all, in the short term—but only if research results are very rapidly made available to the end users. What follows is an account of how Italy's energy problems have been tackled and the results obtained from research there.

THE ENERGY SITUATION IN ITALY

The reactions of countries to the economic crisis brought about by crude oil price increases and fluctuations since 1973-74 have been conditioned by their particular situations with regard to energy resource availability and needs.

Italy's situation is one of the least happy as far as availability is concerned: its level of dependency on oil imports is 83 percent, a level exceeded only by Japan's and Belgium's. Furthermore, oil is used to meet 69 percent of its total energy needs, a percentage surpassed only in Japan.

On the other hand, Italy's per capita energy consumption is not among the highest: at 2.55 toe per capita, it is considerably lower than the US level of 8.27 toe. The same can be said of the relationship of Italy's total energy consumption to its GNP: 0.655 MTOE per billion dollars (1975 US dollars), whereas the comparable figure for the United States is 1.017 MTOE.

However, industrial energy consumption as a percentage of total energy consumption is high in Italy, although it dropped from 45.68 percent in 1973 to 43.55 percent in 1979. In this respect Italy is in fourth place—exceeded only by Japan (53.01 percent), Spain (45.13 percent), and Holland (44.47 percent)—and is considerably above the United States (31.88 percent) and Canada (25.22 percent).

The contribution of the various energy sources to Italy's total energy supply between 1973 and 1980 is given in Table 6-1.

Table 6-1. **Italy's Energy Supply Distribution, 1973–80[a]**

Source	1973	1975	1979	1980
Oil	75.1	71.5	68.9	67.6
Natural gas	10.4	13.5	15.3	15.3
Coal	6.5	7.4	7.1	8.7
Hydro power	7.3	7.3	7.8	7.7
Nuclear energy	0.6	0.7	0.8	0.7

[a]As a percentage of annual total.

The Piano Energetico Nazionale (PEN), or National Energy Plan, which was approved in December of 1981 but had been under study since 1974, set the targets shown in Table 6-2 for Italy's energy resource distribution.

Table 6-2. **Italy's Energy Supply Distribution Targets for 1985 and 1990[a]**

Source	1985	1990
Oil	63.9	51.0
Natural gas	17.5	18.9
Coal	10.8	18.4
Hydro and geothermal energy	6.4	6.3
Nuclear energy	1.2	4.3
Renewable resources	0.2	1.1

[a]As a percentage of annual total.

Target total energy consumption levels are also set by the PEN. Total consumption was 146.9 mtoe in 1980; it should not exceed 165 mtoe in 1985 and 185 mtoe in 1990.

The above figures show that during the 1981-90 decade Italy is endeavoring to make a notable effort to diversify its energy resources and increase its energy use efficiency through massive investments (about $59 million*), incentives (about $7.1 million), and a Piano Nazionale di Ricerca per l'Energia (PNRE), or National Energy Research Plan, financed with $2.5 million during the first five years of the decade, from 1981 to 1985—but more about the PNRE later on.

Completing this picture of the Italian situation is the skewed balance of payments from technology imports and exports, which in 1980 was marked by a 3 to 1 ratio of outflows to receipts.

R&D IN ITALY'S ENERGY SECTOR

To redress the overall energy situation described in the preceding section by achieving planned supply diversity and drastic energy savings, a consistent and well-coordinated research program is necessary.

By 1975, the Italian government had already become aware of this need, and the following year the National Research Council's first Progetto Finalizzato Energetica (PFE)** was launched. The PFE formed part of a group of eighteen five-year research programs intended to produce rapid results in order to make definite progress possible in the most important economic and social sectors: energy, food resources, health, soil conservation, other environmental concerns, and so on.

Within this framework, the PFE in 1976 initiated a series of research activities in two broad areas: (1) the achievement of energy savings and (2) the exploitation of nonconventional energy resources (excluding nuclear energy, which is within the competence of the National Committee for Nuclear Energy). Subjects addressed included energy savings in automotive traction, in certain technological processes or components, and in the heating of buildings; they also included possible uses of solar, wind, and

*All figures are in 1982 us dollars unless otherwise indicated.

**This term is not readily translated. As explained by the author, the PFE, or "Finite Energy Project," entails short-term applied research efforts to solve problems deemed of high importance to the Italian community. To qualify under the PFE program, a project must be fiscally accountable and must be structured to achieve its purpose within a defined period. [eds.]

geothermal energy as well as the use of waste products. Furthermore, studies and research on normative and juridical issues were initiated to give the lawmaker help—through scientific data and information—in choosing incentives that could be adopted if necessary to spur private or public efforts in the energy field. Such research also developed and organized data on Italy's changing energy picture. A breakdown of the PFE's budget is given in Figure 6-1.

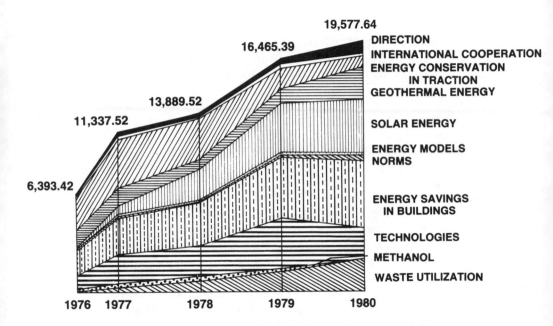

Figure 6-1. **PFE Budget Breakdown, 1976-80** (lire x 10^6)

The entire first PFE program, concluded in 1981 and costing about $80 million, involved some two thousand people in universities, industries, and research bodies, organized in just under four hundred operating units dispersed around Italy. (See Figure 6-2 for a breakdown of these personnel.) The completion of the PFE research projects' final reports is still going on, together with the diffusion of the results obtained. Roughly forty volumes in more than 120,000 copies have been distributed so far, and it is expected that these figures will probably double during the rest of this year.

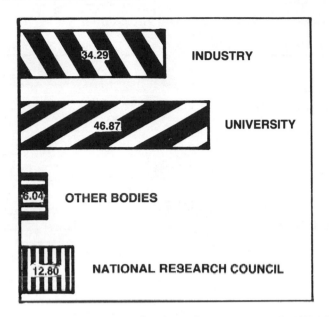

Figure 6 2. **Percentage Distribution of PFE Personnel, 1976-81**

The positive results obtained by the first five-year PFE on technical as well as organizational subjects have led to important developments in Italy's approach to energy research: the launching of the aforementioned PNRE (National Energy Research Plan) and the decision to finance a second PFE (PFE 2) for the next five years.

In particular, the first PFE was an experiment which made it possible to test the fruitfulness of daily collaboration among researchers from different backgrounds (universities, industries, research bodies) within the framework of research projects deemed of national interest and having predetermined objectives. When this experiment produced positive results within the restricted framework of a program coordinated by the National Research Council, the government decided that it was the right moment to move coordination to a high level and entrust a national energy research program (the PNRE) to the Ministry for the Coordination of Scientific and Technological Research, with the financing of PFE 2 as one of its essential components. All Italian research programs in the field of energy will, during the coming five years, have the PNRE as a common frame of reference, thereby placing them at the service of the aforementioned PEN (National Energy Plan), to aid its implementation. (For a breakdown of the PNRE research budget, see Table 6-3.)

Table 6-3. **PNRE Research Budget Breakdown**

Research subject	Budget as % of total	
Energy end uses	36.7	
Industry		37.8
Energy and territory		0.5
Building and community systems		23.1
Agriculture and zootechnics		1.4
Transportation		38
Fossil Fuels	18.1	
Coal		77.3
Other		22.7
Nuclear energy	17.0	
Other energy sources		
Solar		31
Biotechnology		1.2
Hydro		1.8
Fusion		25
Geothermal		13.3
Biomass		13.3
Wind		7.7
Waste		6.7
Energy carriers	9.2	
Electricity transport, storage, and distribution		46.7
Heat transport, storage and distribution		23.9
Electricity production		14.7
Hydrogen		14.7
Interdisciplinary activity	3.7	
Environment and health		45.9
Socioeconomic aspects		3.7
Legislation and norms		6.4
Energy models and data banks		44

NATIONAL RESEARCH AND BARRIERS TO INNOVATION

One of the more interesting aspects of the Italian experience based on finite research projects in general and on the PFE in particular is that this approach solves the problem of transferring research results to their users and, more specifically, to the production sector. This problem is to be found in all technologically advanced countries and is considered a difficult one, for the results of scientific research, usually achieved far from the production sites (except in some sectors such as the chemical and pharmaceutical industries), often do not find channels of rapid transfer. Thus, in most cases transfer takes longer than it might otherwise.

Evidence of this phenomenon has recently been given by Professor A. Piatier in his report written for the European Economic Community (EEC), "Barriers to Innovation in European Community Countries" (XIII (81) 04). This report makes it clear that if this problem continues, intermediate structures between research projects and production enterprises (above all, small and medium-sized enterprises) will be needed, together with significant financial and fiscal measures to break down the barriers to innovation.

But if, on the contrary, there is participation in research by future users from the very beginning, many obstacles to the transfer of research results—particularly research of a technical and sometimes of a psychological nature—disappear or become easier to overcome. This is what the first PFE achieved through its organization of the PFE's different research subjects into mixed operating units composed of (1) researchers coming from universities, private and public industries, and National Research Council laboratories; (2) technical staff working for local authorities; and (3) user personnel. In support of this assertion, let us look at a few of the sixty-two research subjects carried out over the PFE's five years.

One PFE research project was directed toward developing a new propulsion system for cars: a modular system which could maintain engine efficiency even under reduced load by regulating a fuel injection engine to run on two or four cylinders through a microprocessor control. Research on this subject was carried out by an operational unit of researchers from the Instituto Motori (Combustion Engines Institute) of the University of Genoa and Alfa Romeo Company. Thus, in this research, industry as well as possible users of the obtained results participated. Because of this, ten cars equipped with the new engine have already completed six-month test cycles in the city traffic of Milan, where they were used as taxis and where they achieved an average fuel savings of 24 percent below the usual consumption level—all in less than one year from the conclusion of the research project!

A second research project was directed toward reducing energy consumption in the heating of residential buildings. Some six hundred such buildings were monitored over a four-year period in order to understand their performance and assess the cost/benefit ratios of certain modifications. The monitoring instruments used were new "via radio" devices that made it possible to obtain data without disturbing the occupants, and today the devices are in normal use by Agip Petroli, a company operating in the housing sector, to obtain energy diagnoses of buildings.

An ultrasonic heat flow measuring device is now available for research purposes, and a patent on it will soon be pending. The intent is to market it as an instrument for measuring energy consumption rates. Mathematical models and data banks have also been completed which together make up a handbook, now being printed, for the energy-oriented planning and design of buildings.

All these research results, but particularly the rapidity of their application and distribution, are, without exception, due to the participation of operational units of researchers and technical staff representing possible industrial users or entities that are interested in exploiting the research results. To this end, for example, in sectors such as those involving renewable resources or waste utilization, representatives of state or local bodies have been included in scientific and industrial groups.

Obviously, the heterogeneity of such groups at the beginning created problems of technical and organizational coordination—problems not always easy to solve—together with problems of a psychological nature. There were clashes between different mentalities, different operational metabolisms, and administrative structures of differing agility, and there were conflicts between academic scruples and industrial approaches. But the collaboration, initially tolerated because it was a condition of obtaining financial support, has gradually been more and more accepted and welcomed, as the many advantages deriving from it and its concrete results have become evident to those directly interested.

CONCLUSION

After five years of activity under the first PFE and on the eve of a second five-year PFE, it may be concluded that this type of research organization—new for Italy and also, perhaps, for many other countries—has shown itself to be extremely valid. In addition to overcoming misunderstandings, it has enabled the merging of research and technical innovation by attracting again to the production community many researchers who appeared to have abandoned it.

CHAPTER SEVEN

International Energy Cooperation from a European Community Perspective

Michel Carpentier
Director General
Commission of the
European Communities

INTRODUCTION

The growing interdependence of the world economy has now become something of a cliché. But this does not make it any less of a reality. And it is as much a reality in the energy sector as it is in the other key elements of the world economy's development — trade, monetary affairs, and the general conduct of our macroeconomic policies. Indeed, energy is bound up closely with each of these elements. So it is a critically important issue on which to base the discussions at this Symposium.

I am representing here the European Commission and, through it, the European Communities.* My perspective on the question of international energy cooperation is inevitably that of a European. I intend, therefore, to dwell on the issues as they are seen from Europe. But let me first try to set them in a general context.

---

*Members of the European Community include Belgium, Denmark, France, Great Britain, Greece, Ireland, Italy, Luxembourg, the Netherlands, and the Federal Republic of Germany. [eds.]

THE WORLD ENERGY SCENE

A good deal has happened on the world energy scene since the first Symposium in October of 1980 set out to define the nature of the world energy problem.

That Symposium took place a few weeks after the outbreak of hostilities between Iran and Iraq. There was a background of widespread concern about the risk of oil supply shortfalls and of renewed pressure on oil prices—all that on top of the more than doubling in prices that had occurred during the previous eighteen months since the Iranian revolution.

Now the world scene looks rather different. Hostilities between Iran and Iraq continue, but there is no shortage of oil. Oil prices expressed in dollars have been falling and are continuing to do so, despite further production cutbacks by some of the oil-producing countries. The markets are softer than they have been since the mid 1970s. There has been dramatic change in the world's demand for "liquid gold," with OECD demand falling from 41.1 mbd in 1979 to 35.4 mbd last year, a drop of 14 percent over two years.

The background against which our discussions are taking place is therefore rather different from October of 1980. Concern about the risk of further price pressures has given way in the industrialized countries to *bewilderment* about the reasons for this remarkable turnaround on the oil markets and *uncertainty* about its implications for the future.

A review of what has happened over the last ten years on the energy markets suggests that any tendency toward high hopes would be misplaced. We must welcome and take advantage of the softening in the oil markets and the beneficial effects on our balances of payments that follow the fall in OECD oil imports, for these factors will help to reduce inflationary pressures and to improve the prospects for growth. But we should be wary of concluding that the risk of longer term energy constraints on growth have been removed, simply because of the changes of the past two years.

There are four main reasons for caution.

First, it would be foolhardy to bet on any particular level of *total world oil supply* over the decade or two ahead. There are immense uncertainties about recoverable reserves, about production and depletion policies of the major producers, about the economics of "difficult" fields under different oil price scenarios, about the scope for economic production of nonconventional oils.

But even under relatively optimistic assumptions, the total world oil supply in 1990 and 2000 is not likely to be much above its 1980 level of 49.5 mbd.*

Second, it is even more difficult to forecast likely levels of *total world oil demand*. Even if we in the industrialized countries succeed in economizing on the use of oil, the trend may be significantly different in the OPEC countries themselves and in many of the non-OPEC developing countries. Much depends on the developing countries' prospects for economic growth and on their success in mobilizing resources (financial, technical, and human) to increase domestic energy production and the efficiency of energy use. Major oil importers such as Brazil are already making significant efforts in this respect.

Third, none of us involved in analyzing the energy economy's trends and advising on their implications can satisfactorily explain why the demand for both energy generally and oil specifically have fallen so much more significantly in the recent past than anyone dared predict. It is difficult to tell on the one hand how much the fall is based on durable economics and durable changes in economic and industrial structure and, on the other hand, how much it is due quite simply to the recession.

Quite clearly there has been something of a break over the past ten years in the link between economic growth and the growth in energy demand. In the European Community our energy consumption in 1980 was virtually the same as in 1973, but GDP grew by around 17 percent over the same period. In 1980 a fall in our energy and oil demand occurred even though GDP grew by 1.4 percent. We have also experienced a steady fall in the share of oil in total energy consumption (from 62 percent in 1973 to around 50 percent last year), and there have been similar experiences elsewhere. But no one can be sure what will happen when growth picks up again.

Finally—and this is an issue for particular reflection—the present market situation could well *slow down* the process of structural change. The fall in oil prices, if it continues, could have important implications for the competitiveness of coal. It may also make much less attractive the economics of some new energy technologies and investment in energy saving.

All these uncertainties make the results of this Symposium more rather than less important.

---

*Excluding oil produced and consumed in centrally planned economies (CPES) but including CPE net exports.

THE EUROPEAN COMMUNITY'S POSITION

The need for a "long view" and the opaqueness of the glass through which we seek to see into the distance are felt especially keenly in the European Community.

Despite the fall in oil demand, the Community remains the largest single oil importer in the world, absorbing over 7 mbd in 1981 compared with fewer than 6 mbd in the United States and around 5 mbd in Japan. Seventy-eight percent of our crude oil imports came from OPEC countries in 1981, and some 60 percent from the Near and Middle East. And despite the fall in oil prices expressed in dollars, the Community's oil import bill was around $100 billion last year, equivalent to approximately 4 percent of our combined GNP. (The equivalent figure for the United States was about $60 billion, or less than 2 percent of its GDP.) The prospects for oil supplies and oil prices and for the transition away from oil are therefore of critical importance to us.

The nature of our transition is also conditioned by the fact that the Community does not possess indigenous energy resources (oil or nonoil) which are either on the same scale or as easy and cheap to exploit as those of some of our industrial partners, notably the United States. Most Community coal is deep mined and less competitive than imports. The oil resources in the North Sea are large, but even under optimistic assumptions, oil from the British sector is not likely to supply at its peak during this decade more than 25 percent of total Community oil consumption. The Community's production of natural gas has probably already passed its peak.

So even if we are able to expand efficient domestic coal production, even if there is a significant contribution from nuclear power (and that is constrained ultimately by outlets for electricity use), and even if there is a substantial improvement in energy efficiency, the Community's transition away from imported oil is bound to involve an increase in imports of other fuels. It is therefore only natural that our glass should be trained not only on the future but also, at the same time, on the rest of the world.

COMMUNITY ENERGY STRATEGY

The energy ministers of the European Community meet two or three times every year in Brussels to review the energy situaton in the Community and worldwide and to consider specific proposals put forward by the European Commission for common action to sustain the momentum of transition and to avoid new shocks to the system. They met last on March 16 of this year and underlined a common concern that the present oil market situation should not retard the transition away from oil and the progress toward the realization of common energy objectives.

These objectives and the energy strategy which embraces them have evolved in response, first, to the "oil shock" of 1973–74 and then, to the stimulus of the further dramatic upsurge in oil prices in 1979–80. The objectives focus on the need for increased energy efficiency and for the diversification of energy supplies, the stimulation of adequate levels of investment in the energy sector, a more coordinated approach to energy research and development and innovation, measures to improve the stability of the energy (and particularly oil) markets, and the development of a common line in external energy relations.

It would be misleading to suggest that the interests of all the members of the Community in every aspect of our strategy are always identical, or that common action and cooperation necessarily means organization, direction, and intervention from Brussels. The energy balances of the Community's member states vary widely and will continue to do so. In energy, as in other spheres, we are a diversified group of countries both in our resource endowments and in the emphasis which we give to different fuels. At one extreme is the relatively "energy-rich" United Kingdom; at the other is Italy, where indigenous hydrocarbons are unlikely to provide more than a limited share of total energy requirements. But the pressure of external events in the past and a recognition of the risks to *all* our economies in the future if the energy transition is mishandled have encouraged an increasing degree of communality of purpose.

First, each member state has seen the danger of renewed *instability* on the oil markets. All of us—including the United Kingdom—suffer if oil supply disruptions are allowed to put unreasonable pressure on oil prices. All of us will suffer if energy is allowed once again to stymie the prospects for economic growth.

Second, member states have seen the very positive advantages of cooperation in international energy matters. The Community's ability to agree in 1979 to set ceilings on net oil imports up to 1985 made it easier to secure a wider international agreement along similar lines at the Western Economic Summit in Tokyo later that year. Similarly, the energy transition program agreed upon at the Western Economic Summit in Venice in 1980 was facilitated by a prior Community agreement on long-term energy objectives.

More and more, it is becoming clear that the Community must speak with one voice and act jointly if it is to have the greatest impact possible in its relations with the producers of energy—whether oil, gas, coal, or nuclear fuels. And increasingly, we are doing so.

ISSUES FOR INTERNATIONAL COOPERATION

The emphasis of Community policy is not always identical to that of its partners in the industrialized world. Perceptions on opposite sides of the Atlantic do differ, and there are some understandable reasons why this should be so. Our degrees of external dependence differ; we have had differing approaches to the roles of public authorities (although, of course, this also varies among the Community's member states); we have had differing attitudes to the regulation of the energy markets. And differences of emphasis on other questions of international policy (e.g., East-West relations, the Middle East) may spill over into the energy field. But it is easy to exaggerate the differences and to forget the wider communality of interests to which I have already referred and which have been reflected in the outcomes of the major Western Economic Summits.

The picture has certainly been complicated a little in the last year or so by the divergence of views between Europe and the United States about the merits and risks of the new Soviet gas contracts into which some Community members have entered. These contracts for Soviet gas are an important element in our strategy of diversification. That they carry some risks is well understood. Equally, however, those risks have to be set against the alternatives, and the risks can and will be minimized.

At the end of the day, the success of Europe's policy of diversification is a fundamental common interest with the United States. Similarly, we in Europe will be critically affected by the success of the United States in constraining its own oil consumption and sustaining its oil production, by the speed at which US deregulation of natural gas prices occurs and the effect that has on both consumption and supply, by the pace of US nuclear construction and commissioning, and by the health of the US coal industry.

It is right that the European Community and the United States should consult on these issues, as we do; that we should cement our understanding of each other's policies; and that we should explore the scope for bilateral as well as multilateral cooperation through the International Energy Agency and the Western Economic Summits. And we are doing this not just with the United States but with each of our major partners in the Western Alliance.

The main areas in which the scope for such cooperation is greatest are those of coal and nuclear materials, where both the main producers and the main consumers lie in the industrialized world. We shall not succeed in opening up the markets for coal in Europe if we cannot rely on *growing* economic and secure supplies from overseas—from the United States, from Canada, from Australia. The coal chain is a long and complex one, and to make sure that all its links are complete will require the closest cooperation among private sector operators in consuming and producing countries within a framework of increasing intergovernmental contact. There is also scope for greater cooperation among the industrialized countries in the development of new energy technologies—nuclear fusion, coal gasification or liquefaction, new forms of energy transport and storage, and so on.

But cooperation among western nations is not enough if we are to fully meet the energy challenge of the 1980s and 1990s and make translucent the glass through which we see the future so darkly at present. We must explore two other avenues if we are to be assured of that energy security which is at the heart of our energy policies.

The first is for a greater meeting of minds with the *oil producers* themselves.

There are some who may be tempted by the present oil market situation to rub their hands with satisfaction about the difficulties facing OPEC and to suggest that we no longer have any interest in seeking better relations with the oil-producing countries. This is profoundly misguided. To sit back while the wind seems to be blowing our way is to fall into the same trap as the oil producers themselves, when oil prices were firm and they believed that they could call the shots. The wind can change direction all too suddenly.

Recent events have surely underlined the mutual interest of both oil producers and oil consumers in the developed and the developing worlds in attaining greater stability and predictability of oil price movements and supply levels. This stability and predictability would help those of us in the industrialized world to plan a steady progress away from oil dependence while avoiding severe shocks to our balances of payments; it would give the oil-importing developing countries a sounder basis on which to plan their own economies in the most rational long-term manner; and it would help the producers to plan more satisfactory depletion policies and the long-term financing of their development needs.

We should seize the present opportunity to encourage a recognition of this mutuality of interests. There are certainly reasons to doubt whether the time is ripe for successful formal multilateral discussions on energy of the kind we witnessed in the mid 1970s (e.g., the Paris conference). But there is a very strong case for exploring more informal and less structured ways to improve the meeting of minds.

The second important area of international cooperation is in our relations with the *oil-importing developing countries.*

The developing countries include about one hundred countries accounting for nearly 50 percent of the world's population, 25 percent of its economic output, and 15 percent of its commercial energy consumption. These countries differ widely in levels of per capita income and in levels of industrialization and urbanization. They span a wide range of economic bases with different prospects for future development: some depend predominantly on subsistence agriculture while others are based on commercial and export agriculture; some are predominantly mineral exporters; some are based on light industry; a number (the newly industrialized countries) are in a category apart.

It is therefore unreasonable to generalize too much about the nature of the developing countries' energy problems. But they do share certain characteristics:

- rapidly expanding populations engaged in a process of urbanization and industrialization,
- a shift of energy balances from noncommercial to commercial fuels, and
- a very high degree of dependence on oil as the key commercial energy source. (Oil provides nearly 65 percent of commercial energy supplies in developing countries as a whole, while coal is used to a considerable extent only in India and Korea, which have indigenous supplies.)

Furthermore, in many regions of the developing world the energy problem is compounded by the growing scarcity of firewood, the increasingly acute problem of deforestation, and the scarcity of fertilizers because of farm wastes being used as fuel. Potential shortages of both fuelwood and oil interact upon each other.

It is in the interests of the whole world to ensure that the potential energy constraints on growth in developing countries be removed. Developing countries are likely to be an increasingly important element in world trade in the years to come, and the industrialized countries' economic prosperity will depend heavily on the former's growth and development.

Our first duty toward the developing countries must be to allow them more room in the oil markets by continuing to constrain our own oil consumption. They will find it less easy than we do to shift to other fuels and to increase the efficiency of their energy use.

But the balance-of-payments difficulties of many developing countries and the evident need to ensure greater self-sufficiency in energy and to maximize the world availability of energy at economic cost means that we must go beyond that. We must consolidate and increase our efforts to stimulate domestic energy production in the developing countries and to encourage greater energy efficiency without, however, constraining their prospects for growth.

The Community and its member states have a good track record in the field of energy aid. Together, they are, after the World Bank, the largest source of total aid for energy investment in the developing countries, having committed in 1980 some $1,000 million, and they are the single largest source of aid in the form of grants. In 1980 the European Investment Bank alone committed close to $300 million for energy investment in developing countries, helping to finance purchases of equipment, construction of energy supply facilities, and so on; and the European Commission itself has been heavily involved in critical areas of technical aid, especially in the field of energy programming (helping to develop supply and demand balances and thereby identify rational policy options).

We have already done a good deal. But we can do a great deal more. And we can do it better as a Community by coordinating more closely among ourselves the help that we give by ensuring closer cooperation with the financial institutions of the oil-producing states, by establishing close liaisons with the multilateral institutions—notably the World Bank and the UN Development Programme—and by greater bilateral and multilateral cooperation with our industrial partners.

Ensuring the availability of finance from the public sector budgets in the West and from international institutions is, however, not all that is required. Sufficient resources will not be mobilized without an increased private sector effort. In this respect, the developing countries have their own responsibilities to ensure that the conditions are right to encourage both public and private investment from outside. And in the end it is they who must control their own destinies through sensible energy planning and management.

There is, I believe, a wide measure of agreement about the gravity of the developing world's energy problems and the need for a greater cooperative effort. This consensus was evident enough at last year's UN Conference on New and Renewable Sources of Energy in Nairobi.

The Nairobi conference was important both in itself and also as, for the moment, the only international forum for discussion of energy issues. It provided an opportunity to range beyond the specific issues of new and renewable energy sources into the wider problems of world energy supply and demand. It culminated in an agreed Action Programme. Next month in Rome there will be a follow-up meeting on the progress made with the Programme. We in the European Commission are determined to build upon what has been agreed so far.

CONCLUDING REMARKS

Let me say two things in conclusion.

First, to the energy forecaster and to the energy policy planner, there are very many uncertainties in the decade ahead. We may turn out to be guilty of excessive gloom and concern about the pace of change and the risks of a renewed energy constraint on growth. Equally, however, there are many dark scenarios that are perfectly plausible. Nobody likes to think too hard about what an economist might describe as exogenous political factors—a new Middle East war, a new Iranian upset, for example.

Second, while those of us involved in energy cannot presume to prevent the emergence of such exogenous political factors, we can try to ensure that their macroeconomic effects are minimized by rigorous pursuit of the goals that each of our countries has set for itself to attain more diversified energy supplies and more efficient energy use. These goals will not be successfully achieved without extended cooperation among those of us in the developed world and between us and both the oil-importing and the oil-producing developing countries.

It would help us all if this Symposium could contribute to an identification of appropriate guidelines for our common action.

National Energy Policy Presentations

Editors' Note

Prior to the Symposium, ministerial or cabinet-level participants were invited to make statements about their countries' energy strategies at the May 26 morning session. Not all chose to do so, and a few authorized representatives to speak on their behalf. Altogether, nine presentations were made, comprising the nine chapters of this section. Although general guidelines were given, the length and format of these presentations varied considerably. In addition, time limitations precluded discussion of the statements in all but one instance, where, due to special circumstances, the presentation was immediately discussed—a discussion of the others had been scheduled for the end of the session but had to be canceled for lack of time. Particularly in light of these constraints, the efforts of the session's chairman, Alejandro D. Melchor, deserves special recognition.

CHAPTER EIGHT

Energy Policy in the 1980s— The Risks of Success

Ulf Lantzke
Executive Director
International Energy Agency

INTRODUCTION

This is the third meeting of the International Energy Symposia Series in which the International Energy Agency (IEA) has participated. In Symposia I and II, we shared our views of possible paths for oil and alternative energy sources such as coal, nuclear, and gas. In this concluding Symposium, it is not the time to introduce new scenarios for the future. Rather, our collective task is to draw some conclusions from the papers presented over the past one and a half years.

Equally important is to ask ourselves what remains to be done. I think we would all agree that energy developments are unlikely to follow a smooth, predictable path. Indeed, if someone new to the energy business were to read the analyses of just the last few years of the leading energy analysts, that person could legitimately ask whether we know our field, so much have the analyses fluctuated between energy glut and scarcity. Thus, to temper the current vogue of seemingly relaxed confidence that energy is no longer a problem, I wish to point out a few issues which deserve serious attention.

ELEMENTS OF A CONSENSUS

First, though, where have we come to over the past eight years since the first oil shock? I believe we now have a fairly good base of common understanding of the energy problem as we are likely to see it in the twentieth century. All of us, whether major producers or consumers of energy, agree on several key elements:

- *First*, oil holds a special position as a limited and depletable energy resource which simply cannot meet incremental energy demands. This was stated most clearly by the first conference of the sovereigns and heads of state of the OPEC member countries. At their meeting in 1975, the heads of state declared that, while recognizing the vital role of oil supplies for the world economy, the conservation of petroleum resources was a fundamental requirement for the well-being of future generations. Thus, they urged the "adoption of policies aimed at optimizing the use of this essential, depletable, and nonrenewable resource." I think by now everyone has got this message— perhaps even more so than those heads of state imagined. Industrialized countries, by the policies on oil use and alternative energy sources they have adopted since 1974, have given basic support to this view expressed by the OPEC heads of state.
- *Second*, the structure of energy use must change in the coming years to achieve a better mix of energy resources. While oil will probably remain the dominant energy source for this century, greater emphasis must be given to coal, nuclear, gas, and renewables.
- *Third*, and perhaps most important, the availability of energy resources should not be a factor limiting economic development and social stability. All countries, regardless of their levels of development, regardless of their positions within various geographical, economic, or political groups, would agree that global energy resources should be used to promote economic development, not retard it.

If I am correct in my suppositions, why does this paper have a title which some may consider, if not provocative, at least contradictory? Let us consider objectively what is happening structurally in the world economy.

THE DRIVE FOR STRUCTURAL CHANGE

When referring to energy, and particularly to oil, it has become all too customary to think in terms of two principal groupings. One is the industrialized world, most of whose countries are members of the International Energy Agency. They are, of course, major consumers of energy. But they also *produce* large quantities of energy, including almost 36 percent of the free world's oil supply. The other group comprises oil-exporting countries, symbolized by OPEC but clearly a larger and very diverse group of countries. Obviously this image of two groups is simplistic and inadequate; it takes into account neither the very large number of oil-importing developing countries nor the nonmarket economies. Further, it ignores the legitimate differences of views among countries within any organization. However, the groups do serve to illustrate fundamental forces at work in the world economy, and both have been undergoing changes which very few would have considered possible even a few years ago.

The Industrialized Countries

As serious analysts of the oil industry know, the events of 1973-74 were not so much a sharp break with the past as they were the overt culmination of underlying trends that had been building for a number of years. However, the dominant role which oil had acquired in the economies of industrialized countries contributed to the sense of great unease with which they struggled to adjust to new energy realities. The scramble for oil supplies, while natural from the national point of view, did little to enhance a common understanding of the situation. The 1973-74 events—both the developments in the oil market and the industrialized countries' reaction to them—did, however, finally convince western political leaders that economic and energy security could best be attained by changing the energy supply mix. This implied reducing the key role that imported oil played in their economies, substituting instead indigenous resources of coal, gas, and nuclear as well as increased indigenous oil production where feasible.

The task of completing this changeover will still take time to accomplish. Oil will remain the dominant internationally traded energy source in this century. But substantial progress is being made to fulfill the goal, expressed in 1980 at the Venice Summit, to break, during this decade, the "link between economic growth and the consumption of oil."

The IEA member countries' oil requirements (including bunkers) are now lower than they were in 1973 and fell by about 4.8 MBD between 1979 and 1981. Their total energy requirements declined in 1980 and are estimated to have fallen again in 1981, notwithstanding real economic growth (admittedly at low rates) in both of these years. From 1973 to 1980, the following occurred in these countries, taken as a whole:

- Production of energy increased by the equivalent of 6.3 mbd of oil, with coal accounting for 37 percent of the total increase and nuclear power for 28 percent.
- The energy used to produce a unit of Gross Domestic Product (GDP) decreased by over 12 percent.
- Oil use per unit of GDP fell by almost 19 percent, reflecting both greater energy use efficiency and increased substitution of other fuels.

The IEA counties are just beginning to make progress, but the results to date indicate that their policy direction is essentially correct. Rapid increases in oil prices since 1973, the market reaction to these price increases, and government policies have all helped to reduce dependence on a single energy source, most of it imported.

However, we must be mindful of the high economic cost being paid for sharply reduced oil consumption. The higher prices have contributed to inflation, higher interest rates, sustained low growth, and massive increases in unemployment. Over the last three years, unemployment in member countries of the Organisation for Economic Co-operation and Development (OECD)* has increased by 11 million, reaching an estimated 30 million by the end of this year. The total real income of OECD member countries is estimated to be 1 trillion US dollars less than if the 1979-80 oil price increase had not taken place. These economic costs indicate the social and political dimension of adjustment problems forced on industrialized countries by oil price shocks of the 1970s.

The Oil-Exporting Countries

A similar process of structural change is under way among the major oil-exporting countries, whether members of OPEC or not. Whatever the rationale behind this structural change, it is clear that both market forces and government policies are supporting this natural development. I say "natural," because market economics dictate that the owner of a resource will try to extract the most value possible, consistent with the indulgence of the marketplace.

Thus, maximizing oil revenues to promote industrialization can be seen as a reasonable strategy to reduce dependence on a single export. Clearly, such a strategy, dependent as it is on exports to industrialized countries, cannot succeed in the long run if it

*The OECD is the parent organization of the IEA. As of 1981, all but three of the former's twenty-four member countries were also members of the latter. [eds.]

produces an essentially unbalanced reciprocal trading relationship. Nor can it succeed if it does not take into account the structural change under way in industrialized countries.

OIL—THE COMMON LINK

It is not easy to separate out the elements promoting structural change in industrialized countries and in oil-producing countries. They are essentially different ends of the same barrel. Oil is the common element in both processes of structural change. Had the events of 1973-74 and 1979-80 not taken place or had their magnitude been smaller, it is possible that the strong political and economic commitment to reducing oil imports would be lacking in industrialized countries. Similarly, without the revenues from these price increases, oil producers would have found it difficult to rapidly expand their economies.

Few would disagree that oil has been a central element in economic policies of the past decade. It is likely to remain the central element in coming years. This raises issues which demand careful consideration by all policymakers, whether in industrialized or industrializing countries.

First, will industrialized countries succeed in reducing oil imports to the extent that a supply disruption will no longer pose serious danger to their economic well-being, and thus indirectly to the economic well-being of the rest of the world? This implies a continuing reduction of imports from OPEC members. We already see a trend in this direction. In 1973, OPEC, the major oil producer outside Communist areas, accounted for 65 percent of the world's oil production; it now accounts for only about 45 percent. Moreover, because non-OPEC production is essentially at capacity, any swing in overall oil demand falls most heavily on OPEC countries. This has been evident on the downward side in the last six months or so. On the upward side, with a "technical" production capacity in the OPEC countries of around 34 mbd and a "willing" production capacity there of 25-26 mbd (taking into account production restrictions resulting from the Iran/Iraq conflict), it is evident that current OPEC sales could increase significantly if the demand was there.

The reduction in demand by industrialized countries may require that oil-exporting countries reassess their development plans. Where growing populations are encouraged to have rising expectations, a slowing down of development plans is not without political and social ramifications. Those who would base pricing strategy on maximizing revenues in the short term should review the oil demand trend that has evolved over the last two years. The obvious question, then, is: At what point does the increased price affect demand to the extent that lower overall revenues to producers could lead to social and political instability? Industrialized countries should not consider the latter possibility as benign, as they are unlikely to be able to isolate themselves from the results of any instability which arises in oil-producing countries.

A second issue is the reaction of oil-producing countries to the structural change taking place in industrialized countries. Will the former, to protect their market shares, modify their pricing structure to prevent further shrinkage of their export volumes? This would require OPEC, for the first time, to modify prices to conform with underlying market realities, rather than just defending a higher price level created by temporary turbulence in the oil market.

A new OPEC pricing strategy would bring mixed blessings to oil consumers, particularly those in industrialized countries. Lower oil prices, in real terms if not in nominal terms, would be a welcome help in moderating inflation, reducing unemployment, and promoting real economic growth. This would probably translate into a stimulus for other economies, such as those in the nonoil developing countries. But, if imaginative government initiatives were lacking, it might also result in a moderation of the structural change already under way in industrialized countries.

In the industrialized market economies, reduced real oil prices might increase demand for imported oil and might give a false sense of security to energy consumers. We are all familiar with the 1976-79 situation, but the facts bear repeating. In 1976, following the 1973-74 price rises and the ensuing world recession, world oil demand was low and there was significant spare OPEC production capacity. By 1978, in response to economic recovery, oil demand in industrialized countries had risen by 4.4 mbd from its 1975 low point. When the events in Iran in 1979 disrupted OPEC production, a further price explosion resulted. Some in industrialized countries had misinterpreted the message in 1976. As a result, efforts to reduce dependence on imported oil had slackened.

It is a human tendency to postpone, or even totally neglect, decisions on difficult issues, especially when things seem to be going right. The right strategy in energy is clearly one of the most difficult issues. The rapid changes in the oil market during the last eight years have not made it any easier for oil producers or consumers to formulate a strategy with confidence or apply it with consistency. From some energy analysts, we even hear statements which essentially advocate basing today's energy decisions on yesterday's headline.

A final issue I would highlight concerns the development of alternative energy sources. The short-term impetus for such an effort has been the price of oil. The long-term impetus is the general acceptance that oil is a depletable resource which will become less available as we move into the next century. While the short-term impetus may be subject to fluctuations, the long-term impetus is not. This argues strongly for a consistent policy, in both the private and public sectors, to develop alternative energy sources so that they will be available when needed in the 1990s.

CONCLUSION

It is far too early to see any clear answers to the issues I have described. That will depend on how clearly they are perceived by all concerned, and on what corresponding action will be possible under various political circumstances. Yet I would be derelict if I did not close by suggesting some way of encouraging those concerned to find acceptable answers.

In the past months, there have been public and private indications that some oil producing countries would be receptive to increased contacts with industrialized countries, possibly to gain greater mutual understanding of oil market developments. I personally would find this helpful, although I acknowledge that such exchanges of view have been difficult up to now. Past misunderstandings have perhaps not aided an exchange of views. In some instances, the use of easy rhetoric has tended to polarize issues unnecessarily. There has been a public perception of a group of rich oil consumers at loggerheads with a group of rich oil producers. This labeling credits no one and ignores basic facts. At the risk of sounding a bit theological, I believe I can fairly assert that there are no "sides" in energy; we are all producers and consumers of energy.

It seems clear that when energy, in industrialized countries and in developing countries, has become a major element of structural change, discussions among producers and consumers may be helpful to exchange views. Where mutually beneficial, it may be helpful to develop policies which are based on better knowledge of what is happening in the world and where it could be leading us.

The market conditions of today reinforce the need for stable energy relations among producers and consumers. The opportunities for working together, informally and without headlines, on issues of mutual, practical interest are many. We may be at a propitious juncture which it would behoove us not to ignore.

CHAPTER NINE

Italy's Energy Strategy

Giovanni Briganti
Administrative Counselor
Italian National Committee for
Research and Development on
Nuclear and Alternative Energy

I would like to present briefly the energy strategy currently in effect in Italy. As part of this, I will identify some of the main goals of the strategy—in particular, the targets set by the National Energy Plan which was approved by political authority in December of 1981.

BACKGROUND AND TARGETS OF THE NATIONAL ENERGY PLAN

As you may know, the Italian economy is highly dependent on imported oil. During recent years, our total level of dependence on imported energy sources has been greater than 80 percent: 98 percent of our oil, 85 percent of our coal, and 55 percent of our natural gas are imported. These percentages are much higher than the average corresponding figures for other European countries. Therefore, it is especially important for Italy to reduce its dependence on foreign oil.

Some salient figures from Italy's energy strategy are given in Table 9–1, which contrasts present energy consumption levels with those planned for 1985 and 1990. For example, according to those targets, coal use will increase from 8.5 percent currently to 18.4 percent in 1990; natural gas, from 15.5 percent to 18.9 percent. The intent of these targets—and the main goal of the strategy—is to reduce oil consumption from 67.2 percent to 51 percent during the ten-year period from 1980 to 1990.

Table 9-1. **Italy's Energy Consumption Strategy**

	1980[a]		1985[b]		1990[b]	
	Mtoe	*%*	*Mtoe*	*%*	*Mtoe*	*%*
Coal	12.4	8.5	17.7	10.7	34	18.4
Gas	23.0	15.5	28.9	17.5	35	18.9
Oil	98.8	67.2	105.4	63.9	94.4	51.0
Hydroelectric and geothermal	10.9	7.6	10.5	6.4	11.6	6.3
Nuclear	0.5	0.3	2.0	1.2	8.0	4.3
Biomass, solar, etc.	-	-	0.5	0.2	2.0	1.1
Total	147		165		185	

[a]Actual energy consumption levels.
[b]Energy consumption goals.

The actions required to achieve these goals will follow different patterns for the different sources. Some of the more important ones are summarized below.

Coal

Italy does not have any significant coal production—just a few mines in Sardinia. Thus, higher quantities of coal planned for use by 1985 and thereafter must be attained through international agreements with coal-producing countries such as Poland, South Africa, Australia, or the United States. One such agreement is that between Italy's energy agency (ENI) and Occidental Petroleum, leading to the foundation of a company called ENOXY.

Using large quantities of coal also requires sufficient transportation and distribution facilities. Accordingly, we are planning to build three coal centers in Italy by 1990: one in the northeast, one in the northwest, and one in the southwest.

Natural Gas

Italy's natural gas strategy is also based on international agreements. As you probably know, we have already built a pipeline from Algeria to Italy, and we are now trying to conclude negotiations with Algeria for a large quantity of imported gas based on a fair price. Another possible source of imported natural gas could result from an agreement with the Soviet Union for a pipeline that, crossing Europe, would arrive in Italy, but the political viability of this arrangement is not yet clear.

Nuclear Power

During the 1950s, Italy started an extensive program on the peaceful use of nuclear energy, but this program subsequently was stopped for political reasons that are not yet very well understood. In the last few years, Italy has built only one nuclear power plant— a plant located in the north of Italy, which is now contributing 850 MWe to the nation's electricity supply. In addition, a 2000-MWe plant is being constructed near Montalto di Castro to the north of Rome, and three more 2000-MWe plants are planned—one in the south and two in the north. Italy's nuclear power program also entails close cooperation with France and Germany in the field of fast breeder reactors. Italy has contributed a one-third share to the construction of Super Phoenix 1, and a decision about the construction of Super Phoenix 2 is under examination. The PEC experimental fast reactor being erected in Italy is part of the European nuclear power strategy, which includes specific objectives in the field of fuel performance evaluation for safety analysis.

CONCLUSION

These are, in general, the elements that make up our National Energy Plan. This afternoon, Professor Elias will present a paper reviewing Italy's approach to research in the field of renewable energy sources. In the meantime, I would just like to add a few words on two bills passed in 1981 and early 1982. The first bill provides the National Electricity Board with the funds necessary for the nuclear power plants and the coal power plants which, according to the National Energy Plan, are to be built in the next few years. The second bill (1) extends the role of the National Atomic Energy Authority (ENEA) to include RD&D on renewable energy sources (solar, biomass, wind, and so on); (2) authorizes ENEA to support the national industries in achieving efficient energy use; and (3) provides the funds with which ENEA can, by continuing its RD&D programs, improve the Italian industrial sector's ability in fields related to nuclear energy production.

Implementation of the National Energy Plan is now under way, but part of that implementation includes an assessment of the plan, since it was set up as a flexible tool. This will enable adjustment of the plan's goals and budget as needed.

In closing, I wish to thank the chairman of this session, and I hope that this brief presentation, although quite unofficial, is of some interest to the Symposium participants.

CHAPTER TEN

France's Energy Policy

Gaston Rimareix
Principal Private Secretary of
the French Minister for Energy

For a French civil servant responsible for energy, this third Symposium is an occasion to call to mind, in particular, our very definite and very much shared struggle to call a halt to the waste of the planet's oil resources by means of a quest to improve energy consumption control and develop alternative energy sources.

I therefore speak here in the name of a government and a country which has firmly set its sights on a policy of energy redeployment, characterized in particular by recourse to nuclear energy—that is to say, a policy designed to meet the challenge of the forces of nature and determined to assume, without falling short, its responsibilities toward the developing countries.

Countries like France, plunged deep in this struggle, find themselves in a very similar situation. We thus have three categories of common objectives:

- to reduce our countries' energy dependence (for many of us, a principal aim being to reduce the proportion of oil used),
- to decrease the "rate of elasticity" (that is to say, the relationship between growth in energy consumption and economic growth), and
- to increase the provision and use of the energy sources known as new and renewable.

The editors extend thanks to Dr. Ernest G. Silver, who provided the original French-English translation of M. Rimereix's paper, served as his translator during the Symposium, and reviewed the transcription of the discussion contained in the addendum to this chapter. All material in this chapter has been subsequently edited.

Although these objectives are largely identical, they are not implemented in the same way or at the same rate in all nations, for no one present can have any doubt that psychological contexts differ from one country to another. We are, nevertheless, dealing here with a problem that we all have to solve if we wish to preserve the long-term energy equilibrium of our planet, so it seems fitting, before such a well-informed audience, to inquire into this disparity.

INTRODUCTION: DEMOCRACY AND ENERGY IN FRANCE

After a major political change, now a year back, we in France have organized a large-scale collective examination of these subjects. If the "French experience" of the last months holds some interest for other countries, I would say that its secret lies in the quest for democracy: our energy program arose out of democracy and continues in democracy.

Democracy first: since the election of François Mitterrand as president of the Republic, the theme of energy, in particular the place of nuclear energy in France's total energy expenditure and more generally in French society, has been a central point of political discussion. Decisions made previously had created a public climate of disquiet and incomprehension, and this had to be dispelled. Therefore, immediately after the elections, one of the first decisions to be made by the new president of the Republic was to ask the government to prepare a program for energy independence and submit it to parliamentary vote.

Democracy once more: it has been a feature of the preparation of this new energy policy. On the one side, the reports prepared by experts in government departments under the authority of the Minister for Energy were preceded by wide consultation in which trade union representatives, professional organizations, conservationist associations, and representative bodies of energy producers and consumers took part. In parallel, the French deliberative assemblies on their side were preparing the debate: the Economic and Social Council, which is made up of representatives from French professional circles, devoted several meetings to the subject of energy, and in addition, the House of Representatives created its own ad hoc committee composed of six deputies with diverse interests which organized hearings and prepared information for Parliament members in this way.

Democracy continued: after all this preparatory work was

completed and published, it was then up to the government to propose to Parliament an energy program whose primary goal was to make energy a driving force for France's independence, growth, and development. This program was adopted by Parliament in October of 1981. It revolves around three main themes:

- energy and independence,
- energy and democracy, and
- energy and development.

I would like to briefly outline these main orientations for you.

ENERGY AND INDEPENDENCE

This is a crucial point. Energy independence, economic independence, and political independence are in fact closely linked.

The starting point is to lower to as great an extent as possible the *fraction of imported energy* in relation to total energy consumption. Our aim is to bring our level of energy independence, which was 25 percent in 1973 and is 35 percent today, up to about 50 percent in 1990. Clearly, such a development requires a very great redeployment effort.

The first method of attaining this objective is, naturally, to limit the energy intensiveness of the types of economic growth adopted. For this reason we have decided to launch a particularly determined and rigorous campaign for *energy saving*.

On the basis of a 5-percent growth rate, energy consumption in 1990 would be approximately 232 mtoe, corresponding to an increase of slightly more than 20 percent over current consumption (189 mtoe). To achieve its aim, France must make an effort to save an additional 40 mtoe in 1990 compared with 1980. For this purpose we must invest 40 billion francs per year over this period.

But this effort is also an opportunity: as a result of these investments, three hundred thousand jobs will be created between now and the end of this decade. To carry out this project, we have created a large-scale public utility, national and decentralized, which is called the French Agency for the Conquest of Energy. This body groups together existing organizations (the Agency for Energy Saving, the Solar Energy Commission, the Heat Mission, and the Geothermic Committee) and coordinates research, experimentation, and dissemination.

Alleviating France's dependence on foreign energy sources also means substituting, insofar as possible, *alternative energy sources* for oil. The proportion of oil should, in fact, go down from 48.5 percent today to about 32 percent in 1990. It is thus more important than ever to concentrate on the intensive development of all other possible primary energy resources.

Let us take first the case of *gas*, whose sources are more widely distributed geographically than those of oil. France has set as an objective increasing the share of gas in the nation's total energy supply picture from the current 13.2 percent to about 13.5–17 percent in 1990.

With regard to *new and renewable energy sources*, we expect to pay particular and significant attention to the development of biomass, solar energy, and geothermal energy. Their part in our overall energy program should reach 10–12 percent in 1990. Public activity on the decentralized utilization of new and renewable energy sources is mainly concentrated on research, development, and demonstration projects: we have thus decided to triple research expenditures in these areas over the period 1981–85. In addition, we intend to take measures to speed up the use of these energy resources.

Let us consider the case of *coal:* the large world coal reserves (particularly here in the United States), their relatively favorable geographic distribution, the fact that they are on the whole readily accessible, and the progress being made in utilization techniques—progress which should lead to increased recourse to this energy source. France is certainly not holding aloof from this movement toward coal, and the French nation has the will and the tools to play an important role in this regard within France's particular energy context. The nation is thus preparing for this role through an ambitious coal policy whose first priority is to obtain the optimum value for the nation's resources, and whose second priority is to enable coal to restrengthen its position in the energy market, especially in such applications as industrial use, heating systems, and collective boilers. But from production to utilization, coal needs people, and from research to marketing, coal needs dynamism and new ideas. We must reverse coal's image—from that of an energy resource in decline to that of an energy resource of the future.

Finally, I come to the energy source which is the most controversial: *nuclear energy.* This is an energy source which is relatively less dependent on its raw material, uranium (of which not inconsiderable reserves are to be found under French soil); it is also an energy source whose especially complex technological chain is well understood in France. Therefore, its position in an overall energy independence program is an important one for France.

For the French public in general and also for the new political majority elected last year, the issue of France's degree of recourse to nuclear energy has been controversial, and it was mainly on this point that last summer's debate on energy was concentrated. Two specific problems were carefully examined: (1) the annual number of units on which construction was to have begun in 1982 and 1983, and (2) the question of reprocessing fissionable material. On the first point, the previous government had intended to build nine units, the socialist deputies wished to reduce this number to four, and the new government and Parliament finally decided on six. Regarding reprocessing, a thorough study of this point has led the new government to decide to continue activities in this domain.

France's nuclear energy program requires some further comment on my part. On the one hand, the program adopted falls behind the previous one—six units instead of nine. But it is important to understand that this reduction corresponds to reduced energy needs linked both to the slowing down of economic growth that France has experienced in the last two years and to the energy saving effort that is being undertaken for the coming years. Thus, the moderation of the French nuclear power program does not reflect a lack of confidence but simply a general trend toward the control of consumption.

With this reservation, the French nuclear program is still sizable. If I compare the relative extent of this resource in the overall energy programs of the seven principal industrialized countries projected for 1990, I note that in France the proportion of nuclear to total will be the highest: between 26 and 28 percent, or over 60 мtoe. Also, it goes without saying that the French nuclear program aims to be complete; France has thus decided to continue all its activities relating to nuclear fuel reprocessing.

We have concluded that nuclear energy offers two essential qualities:

- it provides for electricity production at one-half the cost of coal and one-third the cost of oil, and
- of the principal energy sources which exist over the world, it is by far the safest.

In the latter respect, France has taken careful account of the fact that the risks specific to nuclear energy are 50-percent lower than the risks specific to coal in terms of accidents befalling workers and about ten times lower in terms of occupational diseases. In all of the countries represented here, we have to remember the dramatic accidents which have occurred in coal mines. We should also remember the other victims of mining who are never mentioned—the seven hundred annual victims of silicosis.

Speaking specifically about the continuation of nuclear fuel reprocessing, we in France are aware of another consideration which I feel will be of particular interest to you: our international commitments, which we wished to honor in their entirety. Thus, after a period of holding decisions in abeyance—a period which had, as is natural and reasonable, accompanied the aforementioned review of the French energy and nuclear program—and now that the orientations of French energy policy have been decided by parliamentary vote, it has once more become possible, as is also quite natural, to take up decisions that had been temporarily suspended.

ENERGY AND DEMOCRACY

The democratic debate of last summer did not result in an immutable position; the debate must be continual. It is, in fact, essential to seek the widest possible consensus around the issues of energy in general and the use of nuclear power in particular. To put this into practice, France has decided on a set of measures to improve the information transmitted about these issues, the confidence of the public in this information, and the responsibility of public opinion. These measures are concerned with information, decentralization, consultation, and control.

Information

Our feeling was that mutual information that develops confidence and responsibility cannot be the sole province of any organization or institution. Instead, such a mutual information system should permeate the entire institutional apparatus. We thus have decided (1) to create an energy information bank; and (2) to set up a local information commission on each energy site.

The task of the latter type of organization is to ensure, at the local level, the coordination of research and the dissemination of information. This commission should be formed in the preliminary phase of each project and should function as a pluralist, independent, and permanent body representative of all currents of opinion. Meetings of the local information commissions' presidents at national conferences should enable them to exchange experiences, thereby identifying obstacles and improving the administration of their commissions.

Decentralization

In a country like France, which is marked by a strong centralist tradition, energy offers an opportunity for decentralization. In addition, the latter offers an opportunity for improvement of the former, for decentralization presupposes new structures, new procedures, and a fresh distribution of expertise.

Regarding a fresh distribution of expertise, it is apparent that the proportion of new and renewable energy resources in the national energy program will not be able to grow unless the decentralized authorities are active in this area. Furthermore, policies for the rational use of energy, for energy economics, and for energy substitution require from these same authorities determination, power, and means. We are endeavoring to provide them with these capabilities.

Regarding new procedures, it has been decided that each region should establish an energy program which takes into account regional population and economic forecasts and which embraces national objectives for energy savings and the development of new energy resources. Policies concerning information, research, development, and incentives should be part of these programs.

Although the regions are the springboards from which decentralization can be put into effect and although they can express regional needs across the board, the individual town and village halls are the really practical, tangible places for the development of all these projects. These are the levels at which certain aspects of energy consumption can best be mastered, through planning for transport, traffic control, installations, and network management.

Regarding new structures, it has been decided to create a regional energy agency alongside each existing regional assembly. These regional energy agencies are seen as consultative and active instruments whose function is to provide advice and technical assistance on training, information, and the organization of special events to the regional assemblies and to local groups. As virtually permanent energy commissions working alongside the regional councils, the composition of these agencies must meet two criteria: representatives and competence. They thus should be composed of elected members and representatives of trade union organizations, public professional bodies, research associations, teachers' associations, and both public and private associations concerned with energy.

Consultation

In connection with the implementation of energy programs and the corresponding choices to be made, it is essential that local populations and communities should be closely involved and fully informed. Public support is a prerequisite of efficiency: the local information commissions and the regional energy agencies are organizations to be consulted just like municipal, general, and regional councils. Therefore, we felt that considerable progress could be made by reforming certain procedures, such as the public utility inquiry to be conducted at the time of the construction of a major energy installation. The question here is one of improving the information provided and ensuring fully informed debate on all sides during the discussions involved in this inquiry.

Control

But making a decision democratically at a utility installation's preparation stage is not sufficient; the installation's operation must also be overseen. We have thus been especially concerned with improving parliamentary and administrative controls.

To help achieve this, we have decided to create an office for the evaluation of technological options and a permanent parliamentary delegation for energy. Furthermore, to ensure better control of safety considerations, the following measures have been adopted:

- The role of the Atomic Energy High Commission has been reinforced and the independence of the Institute for Protection and Nuclear Safety has been guaranteed.
- A high official has been placed alongside the chief executive of the French Electricity Company in order to guarantee that questions involving the installations' safety are fully taken into account.
- A high-level special scientific commission has been created whose task is to follow up the progress of the La Hague power station, its extension, and, in a more general way, the technology of reprocessing.

Thus, our energy policy is not detached from the wishes of the nation.

The Importance of the Nuclear Energy Decision Process

Until recent months there was a veritable gulf between French energy policies and a French public that had been too systematically left in ignorance about the justifications for the decisions made. Clearly, this gulf was particularly wide in the area of nuclear energy, and the reasons for this were very natural: it is the energy resource with the most complicated production chain, and it is in this area that the tendency toward centralization is the greatest. Therefore, it is understandable that the whole process of decisions on nuclear energy has been badly understood by the public. We felt that it was imperative to put an end to this situation, for it is indeed true that as broad a consensus as possible is vital to the serene use of this precious energy resource.

Oh, how precious: from our viewpoint as French citizens, or from the standpoint of citizens of other countries at the same stage of industrialization and development, it is apparent that by continuing our nuclear energy efforts we shall be able to realize high levels of scientific, technical, and economic achievement. And precious also from the standpoint of global equity: I shall not tire of repeating that for countries such as ours, it is not possible to both favor the development of the less industrialized countries and oppose their recourse to nuclear energy.

ENERGY AND DEVELOPMENT

It is well known that the developing countries consume less than 20 percent of the world's available energy, whereas we—the developed countries—consume over 80 percent. Such a distribution cannot last: the progressive development of the world's less industrialized countries is bound to entail a high rate of increase in their energy requirements, including their oil requirements. In fact, oil offers numerous advantages for the developing countries: it is easy to use and cheap to transport and convert. To these factors must be added the consideration that the level of economic effort which the industrialized countries can devote to infrastructure retrofit and to the development of alternative energy sources represents a cost that is beyond the financing capabilities of the less industrialized countries.

For these reasons, the increase in the developing countries' oil consumption ineluctably implies a decrease in that of the developed countries. And, given the current nascent stage of the various alternative energy sources, we consider it out of the question to deprive ourselves of a recourse to nuclear energy. Thus, in the final analysis, we consider that to promote a more equitable sharing of world energy resources it is vital to work towards energy independence, and one tool in doing so is nuclear energy.

For France, a reapportionment of energy resources among developed and developing countries constitutes an economic necessity as well as a duty of solidarity by the former toward the latter—an economic necessity because of the spontaneous growth in the latter's energy requirements, and duty of solidarity because it is natural and right that the former, with high per capita energy consumption rates and with the financial means for energy redeployment at their disposal, should make the necessary effort to control their consumption rates and develop alternative energy sources in order to reduce their oil imports, thus leaving a higher proportion of conventional energy resources available for countries that have low per capita consumption rates and that obviously have neither the possibiliy of reducing this consumption nor the means of developing alternative energy resources on a large scale. This is why France believes that the role of the industrialized countries is to promote this new international energy-sharing concept rather than impede it or adapt to it in a passive way. France therefore places paramount importance on renewing the North/South dialogue.

The precedents which exist in this connection, created by the August 1981 UN conference at Nairobi and the October 1981 Cancún Summit, have demonstrated that such a dialogue is possible and have emphasized that extensive negotiations are both useful and urgent. The position of France on these subjects is clear: France is in favor of a broad dialogue between energy-producing and energy-consuming countries, particularly within the North/South framework and in the largest possible forum, that of the United Nations—a dialogue which would devote a considerable amount of time to energy.

To open such a dialogue could be fruitful if the objectives to be followed during the energy transition period were clearly defined in advance. France envisages, on its side, five points which seem essential:

• a more rational use of energy, particularly as far as the major energy-consuming countries are concerned;
• reinforced international cooperation for the development and utilization of alternative energy sources;

• more support for the exploration and development of energy sources in Third World oil-importing countries;
• greater energy supply security; and
• a reduction in price uncertainty.

Furthermore, France feels that general energy negotiations along these lines should take place within the framework of a broad dialogue: such a dialogue should be both universal and far-reaching and should not be exclusively concerned with initiatives taken at the regional or bilateral levels.

France has, in this respect, reaffirmed its commitment to arrive at an objective of 0.7 percent of its Gross National Product for public aid to development and 0.15 percent for aid to less advanced countries. Aid to development projects in the energy sector should be given priority, for this sector holds a position of priority in most developing countries.

For western countries, the way out of the energy crisis is not along the solitary road; on the other hand, there can be no collective way out unless we individually impose upon ourselves a tight and rigid discipline regarding energy: this is the philosophy which underlies the national and international energy policy carried out by France, and which France intends to reaffirm at the next Summit of Seven which is to take place at Versailles within the next few days.

CONCLUSION

Up until the 1970s, the economies of the industrialized countries developed in a context whose main features in terms of energy were abundance and price stability, or even a lowering of prices in real terms. Per capita energy consumption was sometimes even considered to be a criterion of economic development. Neither political leaders nor the best experts were able to foresee the 1973–74 oil crisis; responses to such a situation had not been prepared. We have all borne the consequences.

Over the last few years, and in particular since the second oil shock of 1979, an awareness of the world energy stakes has undeniably come about: considerable progress has been made on both economic analyses and scientific and technological research; and alternative policies, adapted to the world energy context and to the particular situations of individual countries, have been established and in some cases applied. But the difficulties are still great and the situation is delicate, in particular for developing countries that are not oil producers.

The détente situation which we have experienced over the last year must not lead us to let up our efforts. The reduction in the industrialized countries' energy consumption in industrialized countries, which is due largely to the current economic slowdown, and the reduction in the real price of oil, which is no doubt cyclic in nature, cannot be seen as justification to revise the energy strategies put into effect over the last few years. In any event, this is the French position.

Thus, we affirm the importance attached to the work of this third Symposium and to the reflections and recommendations of the organizations and experts who have been addressing this subject for many years and who have gathered together here. And we also affirm our hope that, at the end of the third Symposium, its work will be continued, for without doubt the question of energy will continue to be one of the most important and difficult economic and political problems we have to face from now until the end of the century.

ADDENDUM: DISCUSSION FOLLOWING PRESENTATION OF PAPER

P. Raghavendran

I'm from India, and I'm participating here in a personal capacity. It is quite encouraging to know that France plans to support energy use in developing countries, and it is also interesting to find that France places great emphasis on nuclear energy. I was wondering whether there was any element in France's plan which supports the development of nuclear energy in developing countries.

Gaston Rimareix

It will first be necessary for the developing countries themselves to define their energy policies, based on their own domestic resources and on the development models which they have chosen. The development of nuclear energy in these countries poses, without a doubt, difficult problems. But France is prepared to examine together with these countries the constraints and possibilities of nuclear power installations.

I would like to add two remarks. First, nuclear power is based on extremely complex technologies which require sophisticated scientific and technological infrastructures—infrastructures not always present in developing countries. Second, it is appropriate that attention be paid to the nuclear weapons proliferation problem. On this point, and in cooperation with the responsible international authorities, France intends to always ensure that all the appropriate safeguards are in effect.

Marcelo Alonso

I have two very simple questions. From your paper I see that France intends to reduce its dependence on oil from 48 percent currently to about 32 percent in 1990. But what about the total amount of oil you will be using—will that increase, remain the same, or perhaps decrease? That's my first question.

Gaston Rimareix

The latter, absolutely: the total consumption of oil, which was 90 million tons in 1981, will, according to our plans, decrease to 70–75 million tons in 1990.

Marcelo Alonso

I'm very glad to hear that, but now comes my second question: How are you going to do that?—How do you plan to decrease oil use? So, my second question is the following: How do you intend to decrease the rate of elasticity related to oil? This is the crucial point.

Gaston Rimareix

Our energy strategy is fundamentally based on dissociating economic growth from growth in energy use. We believe—and the results attained in France between 1973 and 1981 confirm this prediction—that we can reduce the rate of elasticity, which had been approximately 1 percent before 1973, to less than 0.5 percent. But this requires a voluntary policy of energy consumption control and of significant investments.

Hans H. Landsberg

I was interested in the observation in Monsieur Rimareix's paper that in France the cost of power generation from nuclear is about one-half that of power generation from coal. This is substantially different from what obtains in the United States. The US picture is not terribly clear, but in any event the comparable figure is nothing like one-half—some people would say there is a standoff, and some people would say that the cost of power from nuclear reactors built in the past is somewhat lower than that of power from coal. My first question is as follows: Is that figure of one-half a figure for the reactors now in operation, or for the six units to be built in the future? And the second question is this: The factors in the United States that result in high nuclear power costs are the high cost of capital, the long lead times, and the relatively low load factor—are any of these factors important in France?—and if not, how can one make a comparison between the cost of nuclear and the cost of coal in the two countries, since a significantly different relationship obtains?

Gaston Rimareix

The figures which I cited in my presentation are the costs, in 1982 francs, of a kilowatt-hour from nuclear, a kilowatt-hour from coal, and a kilowatt-hour from oil, which we estimate for power plants that will be in operation in 1990. (These calculations are based on an annual functioning level of 6,000 hours.) The cost of a kilowatt-hour from nuclear includes amortizations, financing expenses, operation costs, and fuel costs.

I am not very familiar with the American situation. Two remarks, however. The costs of coal are higher in France than in the United States, and this is one of the reasons for the difference between the cost of a kilowatt-hour from nuclear and a kilowatt-hour from coal in the United States and in France. In addition, according to the discussions that I had yesterday with your American colleagues, it appears that the construction time of a nuclear plant is very much shorter in France than in the United States. That also helps to explain the difference.

Richard L. Grant

In your paper I find it very interesting that there is an allusion to an objective of applying 0.7 percent of the Gross National Product to development of a public aid category and 0.15 percent to aid to developing nations. I'm curious, first of all, what the difference is between those two things: public aid versus aid to developing countries. Second, could you quantify that in some number such as francs or dollars—whatever is convenient for you? And third, how do you intend to implement that portion of it which is to be granted or somehow operated on in the developing nations?

Gaston Rimareix

The difference between the two numbers is the following: 0.7 percent of the GNP is the goal which France has set for all its public aid to developing countries, whereas 0.15 percent of the GNP is the figure which has been proposed by the Minister of Cooperation and Development concerning public aid only to the least advanced countries. Regarding the second part of your question, I do not have the exact numbers.

This aid may be distributed by diverse channels: either in a multilateral manner through an intermediary such as the United Nations or the European Economic Community, or through bilateral accords, especially between France and French-speaking countries with whom we have cultural relations and special economic agreements.

CHAPTER ELEVEN

Energy Policy in the Federal Republic of Germany

Ulrich Engelmann
Director General
Department of Energy
Ministry of Economics
Federal Republic of Germany

You know that the Federal Republic of Germany* is not a country with great energy riches—only hard coal, lignite, and to a certain extent natural gas deposits exist in our country on a mentionable scale. Along with our entire oil requirements, 70 percent of our natural gas needs and our entire need for uranium must be met from imports. Moreover, the doubling of the oil bill from 1978 to 1981, despite considerable conservation and substitution efforts, have clearly made us feel our dependence on the world energy market. In total our current dependence on imported primary energy stands at 60 percent. This means that the risks encountered in the world energy market are concrete risks to energy supplies in the Federal Republic.

Germany has to live with these facts, and against this background, German energy policy since 1973–74 has emphasized the following points: first, large-scale energy conservation; second, replacement of oil by all available alternative fuels; third, improvement of supply security by diversification; fourth, extension of emergency handling mechanisms; and, last but not least, international cooperation.

The key regulatory policy datum in Germany, also applicable to its energy policy, is the market-economy system. We are convinced that centralism, state control over the economy, governmental intervention, and liberal market-economy precepts are

*Or West Germany; hereinafter referred to as Germany or the Federal Republic for brevity's sake. [eds.]

inferior to free enterprise and the free play of market forces. Thus, an energy supply sufficient in quantity and competitive in price is a matter for industry in the first place and for government by way of support only. The main instrument is a free pricing system wherein the world market price of oil serves a steering function for Germany. As you know, free pricing is, in this time, not an easy undertaking for an energy policy. But it is successful. Only when market forces are ineffective or insufficient does the government enter the scene with a view toward enforcing or accelerating the necessary adjustment.

A glimpse at the core areas of German energy policy in recent years confirms that the road chosen back in 1973-74 was the right one. Namely, it shows us why Germany's real Gross National Product increased by 17 percent between 1973 and 1981, whereas its total primary energy consumption declined by 2 percent over the same period and its oil consumption came down by roughly 20 percent from 1979 to 1981 alone. Although the latter decline admittedly reflects cyclical influences, the share of oil in our primary energy consumption was about 55 percent in 1973 while the figure is now dropping to 45 percent, and a further reduction in the coming years is expected, for it is hoped that by the middle of the 1990s the share of oil in Germany's energy supply may be about 33 percent.

The success thus far has only been possible because industry and consumers have done their part to achieve energy savings. This has not been due solely to soaring oil prices: the German government has promoted this process through her intensive information campaign. The government thus has made its contribution to sharpen the German public's awareness of the need to save energy, and this awareness appears to continue since we have no market signals that investors and consumers are decreasing their conservation efforts, although we are alert to the possibility of complacency and agree that we should watch developments closely.

In addition to information, the German government has through some of its programs provided investment aid and tax relief for housing insulation and the development of new conservation technologies such as heat pumps and solar energy production (bearing in mind that solar in our country does not have the same possibilities as in parts of the United States or in other regions of the world). Such financial assistance and tax incentives have been supplemented by provisions setting minimum standards for space heating systems and the thermal insulation of buildings.

Let me turn to the supply side. By tradition, bituminous coal has played a prominent role in Germany, but German coal is uncompetitive due to its geological situation and the deep mining that is necessary. For this reason the German government, to assure the security of supplies, is supporting the production and sale of German coal in two big areas—namely, its sale to the utilities and to the German steel industry—with the rest of the demand to be filled by imported coal. Since the beginning of last year, the German border has been open to the import of coal, whether from the United States, Canada, South Africa, Poland, or Australia. However, it is difficult for German energy policy to convince consumers, especially industry, to shift back from oil (and, let me add, gas) to the dirty stuff of coal, and there is uncertainty in the international market, be it on the side of the consumers or of the producers, about how the relative price of coal will develop.

I should now like to address the problem area of German energy policy: nuclear energy. The German public still has reservations about nuclear power, yet it has been possible to make distinct progress in recent years. The share of nuclear energy in total primary energy consumption this year amounts to approximately 5 percent—compared with international figures, not a bad percentage. And 16 percent of the electricity in our country this year will be based on nuclear energy.

There have been optimistic forecasts by independent German economic research institutions that the share of nuclear in Germany's primary energy balance may triple by the middle of the 1990s, but this will not be the case even if the German energy policy is successful. Therefore, according to this policy, one of the priority tasks for the coming years is to raise the percentage of nuclear power not only in the interest of securing an adequate electric power supply in a period of rising consumption but also with a view toward producing electricity at low cost. For Germany, especially, since it is highly dependent on imported energy resources, it is indispensable to make use of nuclear power in the face of ever keener international competition for resources.

In our country, the realization of the nuclear power program is officially linked with a program outlining a coherent nuclear waste disposal concept. You know how difficult this is. In this context, it will, of course, be critical to give absolute priority over other goals to the protection of the people. The high safety standards of German-built nuclear facilities, which compare extremely well internationally, will therefore be maintained and developed further.

Based on the increased use of coal and nuclear energy, it has been possible to substantially reduce the use of oil in power stations. This year only 4 percent of Germany's electricity will be based on oil, and this figure is expected to go down in the coming years. Thus, this part of the utility sector is fairly secure from risks due to oil shortages. This is a success for the German energy policy, a policy which includes, for the utilities, advancing the use of coal, building up nuclear power, and having a stable market for gas. In this respect, Germany has therefore fulfilled its international obligations to find replacements for oil as quickly as possible in the utility sector.

Now I come to another interesting part of our supply: natural gas. Natural gas has a 16-percent share in Germany's primary energy consumption and is so far one of the leading supply possibilities for the German economy. The main continued aim will be to have households substitute gas for oil, because almost 40 percent of the oil consumed in Germany is used for residential heating. But German gas resources are limited, and this means that by roughly the end of this century, the domestic natural gas supply will meet only one-quarter of Germany's gas requirements, indicating that in future we will have to rely even more heavily on imported natural gas.

Diversifying foreign sources of natural gas will therefore remain a priority task of Germany's energy policy. And this involves a politically interesting figure: at the end of this century, the gas supply of Germany coming from Western sources—namely, the Netherlands, Germany, and Norway—will be about 60 percent. Import deals with the Soviet Union will therefore not result in any one-sided dependence for Germany. Supply shortfalls, if any, could be compensated by domestic production and other Western European sources, by interrupting gas deliveries to power stations and industrial consumers, and by drawing on stored gas.

This, then, is the national picture. I would like to conclude by adapting a remark made previously: It is obvious that Germany is fully dependent on the development of the international energy and oil market—"we are not the dog, we are the tail in this picture." And this means that Germany fully supports international cooperation in the area of energy and oil.

We are one of the founding members of the International Energy Agency, which has as a primary purpose the development of an international framework to help in crisis situations and to guarantee in the meantime solidarity in international terms. And the second purpose of the International Energy Agency is to monitor the energy policies of its member countries in order to ensure that their efforts are equal, keeping in mind their different starting points.

It also goes without saying that Germany has fairly good connections with the oil-producing countries. In the past year an increased economic connection with these countries has developed, and there has been a growth in understanding on both sides—those of the oil-producing and -consuming countries—about the international interdependence of the world's oil supply and its pricing. You can see this in the outcome of the last OPEC meeting. We fully support that international development; we are in favor of deepening our good existing bilateral contacts. We are cautious about entering into an international structure of organized dialogues—the experience of such exercises is not good—but that docs not mean that we do not favor a deepening international exchange on the interdependence of oil-producing countries and oil-consuming countries.

Finally, it is obvious that Germany fully understands the difficulties of the oil-importing developing countries, for we have doubled the sum spent for energy projects in the developing countries in the last year. And, needless to say, we support global negotiations along these lines within the framework of the United Nations.

CHAPTER TWELVE

The United Kingdom's Energy Policy

David le B. Jones
Deputy Secretary
United Kingdom Department of Energy

In making this statement, I will try to emulate the admirable brevity of Dr. Ulrich Engelmann, especially as there is a statement on United Kingdom policy in the published *Proceedings* of the second Symposium [see *Improving World Energy Production and Productivity*, chap. 14].

The United Kingdom is fortunate in the wealth of its energy resources: massive reserves of coal; at the moment, sufficient oil to meet our needs and to provide a net surplus for export; sufficient gas to produce 80 percent of our domestic consumption of gas. But because we are fortunate in being energy rich, it does not follow that we can insulate ourselves from international energy questions and international discussion.

There are two reasons for this. Our energy wealth in the hydrocarbons area is temporary. As far as we can see, unless there are massive new discoveries, we will again be becoming a net importer of oil on an increasing scale toward the end of the century. The second reason is a more general one. We have a very open economy, and if, as happened in 1978 and 1979, the rest of the world suffers from an explosion in oil prices, then the United Kingdom suffers along with the rest of the world. Our oil wealth insulates us from the direct balance of payments effects accompanying this price explosion, but we suffer, although slightly less than others, from its inflationary effects, and we suffer slightly more than the rest of the western world from the slowdown in economic growth and the increase in unemployment.

The UK energy economy has a very large and dominant public sector, although the present government is seeking to reduce it. Coal production is nationalized; electricity production and distribution is largely nationalized; so is gas distribution; and there is a substantial public interest in the North Sea, although development and production there are predominantly in the hands of the private sector.

Dr. Lantzke in his speech [see chap. 8] brought out sharply the problems of finding the right strategy for energy in view of the unpredictabilities and uncertainties which face us all. Like Germany, the United Kingdom under successive governments—and this has been true of labor as well as conservative governments—has basically adopted a market-oriented approach to energy policy, allowing the market to determine the best pattern of economic energy use and energy production. But we have not gone to the extreme of leaving everything to the market and hoping it will all come right on the day.

The British government is deeply involved in the energy sector—because of the special problems of nuclear power, because of the interrelationships and dependencies among the energy industries, because of our large public sector, but above all because of the sheer importance of the issues which arise in the energy sector in terms of security, in terms of regional and social policy, and in terms of the economic health of our country.

The key to the United Kingdom's market approach is the economic pricing of energy. We have had difficulties in this field in recent years. In particular, as part of the antiinflationary policies of the early 1970s, the prices of various energy resources to the domestic consumer, particularly the prices of gas and electricity, were held artificially low. Those difficulties are gradually being overcome. The present government has been increasing the price of gas to the domestic consumer by 10 percent per year more than the rate of inflation—in other words, a 10-percent per year increase in the real price of gas—and similarly, they have been increasing the price of electricity by 5 percent per year more than the rate of inflation. In the industrial sector, there have not been the same departures from economic pricing, and my government has been resisting fairly firmly heavy pressure from various sections of industry to reduce the price at which energy is supplied to them. Here, there is an international dimension: it is difficult for those national governments that wish to pursue a policy of economic pricing to stick to this policy if their industries are placed at a competitive disadvantage, because some other governments are artificially holding down the price of, shall we say hypothetically, natural gas.

The other key area of my government's energy policy is to remove obstacles to the proper functioning of the market. Legislation is before Parliament and should soon become law which will greatly weaken the British Gas Corporation's monopoly powers to buy the gas produced in the North Sea and to supply it to all consumers. Once this legislation is implemented, medium and large industrial consumers will be able to deal directly with the North Sea gas producers. This greater element of competition should give a substantial impetus to the further development of our gas resources, which have languished a little in recent years.

What, though, are the main policies which the British government pursues within this general market-oriented approach? First, to develop to the full and exploit our hydrocarbon wealth. Second, to create a viable and efficient coal industry that can hold its own on fair terms against imported coal, as broadly as it can at the moment. To that end, the United Kingdom is investing about £800 million per year of government money in coal development. Third, to further exploit nuclear power. At present about 12½ percent of public sector electricity is produced from nuclear power stations. That percentage should increase to 20 percent when three more stations which are close to completion come into operation. Our stations so far are gas-cooled reactors, but we will at the beginning of next year be starting a major public inquiry on the proposal for a pressurized water reactor. If that inquiry leads to a favorable outcome—one can not prejudge its results—then we will also have pressurized water reactors in our program. We are spending about £100 million per year on research and development into fast breeder reactors, and we are discussing with various governments represented around this table the possibility of cooperating in developing a full-scale commercial prototype.

For conservation, we rely primarily on the market price. We supplement it by government-financed publicity and advice, by government support for demonstration projects designed to show how new technologies can be effectively applied to more efficient energy use, and by certain mandatory standards—for example, about levels of insulation in buildings, energy labeling under European Community instruments, standards of efficiency for heat generation under European Community instruments.

As far as renewables are concerned, our research effort here, compared with some, is on a relatively small scale—about £10-15 million per year. Our work suggests that, with some exceptions, renewables under UK conditions are likely to be a less economic form of electricity than nuclear power. The exceptions are, possibly, (1) onshore wind power; (2) tidal power, where a major study of the case for a barrage across the Severn Estuary is under way; and (3) outside the area of electricity production, passive solar and some forms of geothermal energy.

That is a very brief account of some of the main features of the UK energy policy. It is a policy that relies primarily on the operation of market forces, but those forces are supplemented, as I hope I have shown, by measures of government action—measures which work with the market and move in the direction the market is moving, rather than attempting to overturn it and move in a different direction.

CHAPTER THIRTEEN

Japan's Energy Strategy

Toyoaki Ikuta
President
Institute of Energy Economics, Tokyo

The starting point of Japan's energy strategy is the nation's lack of self-sufficiency in energy supply and its consequent vulnerability to energy supply problems. In 1979, the rate of Japan's energy self-sufficiency was as low as 14 percent, the lowest among industrialized countries. This is because, despite its limited land area, Japan's population exceeds 100 million, and in addition, its indigenous energy resources are absolutely insufficient. Under these conditions, Japan is destined to face lower rates of energy self-sufficiency as its economy grows.

In other words, economic growth and energy self-sufficiency have in effect been making a tradeoff in Japan. This concept is supported by solid fact. During the ten years preceding the first oil crisis in 1973, Japan's economy exhibited a remarkable growth, but, as a result, its energy consumption doubled and its rate of energy self-sufficiency, shrinking in inverse proportion to growing consumption, deteriorated by half during the same period. If Japan's economy continues to grow in the coming years, its rate of energy self-sufficiency will inevitably decline further. I believe that this trend will probably last until the end of this century or the beginning of the next, when such alternative sources as solar energy and nuclear fusion are expected to come into the mainstream of energy supply.

In order to discuss Japan's vulnerability to energy supply problems, we have to pay the same attention to its high rate of dependence on imported oil, particularly Mideast oil, as is given to its poor rate of energy self-sufficiency. In 1979, oil accounted for 72 percent of Japan's total primary energy supply, and virtually 100 percent of this oil supply was imported. (Precisely put, Japan imports 99.7 percent of the oil it consumes.) As may be noted, this import level is much higher than that of other industrialized countries. Moreover, 70 percent of Japan's imported oil comes from the politically unstable Middle East, and Japan's level of dependence on Mideast oil is also the highest among industrialized countries.

These basic energy supply problems logically dictate that Japan adopt an energy strategy. First, Japan has to secure an adequate energy supply for the stable growth of its economy, and second, Japan has to reduce its vulnerability to energy supply problems as much as possible. In concrete terms, it is essential to minimize Japan's overall dependence on oil, and as for oil imports, efforts should be made to promote diversified supply sources, thus reducing the level of dependence on the Middle East. These energy strategy targets require a combination of several policy measures, all of which should be decisively implemented.

To begin with, energy conservation should be further promoted. In the past, Japan has made remarkable progress in the field of energy conservation. Over the seven years from 1973 to 1980, energy consumption per unit of GNP declined by 25 percent. In particular, energy consumption in the industrial sector decreased sharply by 34 percent. I believe Japan's performance in this field ranks as the world's highest.

Since Japan's economy is characterized by a scarcity of resources, progress in energy conservation can produce the same favorable effect as an increase in indigenous energy resources. For this reason, the Japanese government has been placing a special emphasis on policies to promote energy conservation and has enacted special laws which enable the government to adopt financial and tax incentive measures to encourage the introduction of energy-saving equipment. The Japanese government has also been providing energy-saving guidance and information to private firms and consumers. In a recently revised government outlook, a 15.5-percent increase in energy conservation by 1990 is planned.

The second subject of Japan's energy policy is expansion of its alternative energy supplies. In Japan, steeply increasing oil prices caused by the two oil crises, together with a deep distrust of oil supply reliability, have formed a strong incentive to shift from oil to alternative energy sources, and constant progress has been made. As a result, oil's share of Japan's total primary energy supply gradually declined to 66 percent in 1980, dropping below the 70-percent level for the first time since the 1973–74 oil crisis. This has contributed much to reducing Japan's vulnerability to energy supply disruptions.

The Japanese government has been giving top priority to expanding its alternative energy supplies and has adopted several policy measures to this purpose. To start with, a law designed to promote the introduction of alternative energy sources was enacted, based on which targets of alternative energy supplies have been set. According to a recently revised target, the Japanese government aims to achieve an alternative energy supply level of 5.2 million bpd of oil equivalent in 1990, representing a 210 percent increase over the 1980 level. By type of alternative energy source, coal accounts for 38.6 percent of the total supply; natural gas, 22.8 percent; nuclear power, 22.5 percent; hydro power, 10.1 percent; geothermal energy, 2 percent; and others, 4 percent.

Now, according to the government's outlook for energy demand, which was prepared concurrently with its supply target, Japan's energy consumption in 1990 is expected to be 10.17 million bpd of oil equivalent. If the predicted energy consumption level is achieved, Japan's level of dependence on oil would drop below 50 percent and its vulnerability to energy supply disruptions would be much improved.

To implement its energy policy measures, the Japanese government allocated 730 billion yen (approximately 3.2 billion dollars) to the Special Account for Energy Measures in fiscal year 1982, equal to some 1.5 percent of the Japanese government's total budget. Of the budget allocated to the Special Account, 23 percent, or 166 billion yen, is planned for expenditure on alternative energy measures. Government subsidies to support various types of oil substitutes are also covered by the Special Account.

Government subsidies to alternative energy sources are provided to promote not only such alternative sources as coal, nuclear power, and LNG, which have already been utilized commercially, but also the research and development of new sources, including solar energy and synthetic fuels, for the benefit of future utilization. At present, a comprehensive research and development program on new energy sources named the Sunshine Program is under way, to which the government has appropriated a budget of 42 billion yen (about 183 million dollars). In the Sunshine Program, priority is given to such fields as solar energy, geothermal energy, and coal liquefaction and gasification.

The third subject of Japan's energy strategy is its oil problem. Japan's proportional dependence on oil is expected to decline gradually in parallel with favorable results from its energy policies in the coming years. Nevertheless, it appears that the oil age, wherein oil continues to be the biggest single energy source, will last into the future. Hence, securing a stable oil supply forms the core of Japan's energy strategy.

To stabilize the oil supply, an adequate oil reserve is first required. Efforts must also be made to attain the maximum diversification of oil supply sources possible, including efforts to develop new oil resources.

As of the end of March 1982, Japan's oil reserves totaled a 118-day supply, including 101-day reserves held by oil companies and 17-day reserves held by the government. Although oil companies are required by a law to build up oil reserves totaling more than 90 days, the government is extending financial aid to these companies, including subsidization of interest rates. The government's reserves are currently stored in decommissioned oil tankers. By the end of 1988, the government plans to boost its oil reserves to 28 million tons—nearly three times over the present level—by constructing inland and/or offshore reserve terminals.

Government aid for the development of new oil sources has also been extended, primarily to the Japan Oil Corporation (a government corporation). Of the total energy budget, about 20 percent has been appropriated for this purpose.

As for the diversification of oil supply sources, a shift from the Middle East to such regions as Southeast Asia, the United States, and China is needed, but this involves a number of delicate problems to which solutions are not easy. At any rate, it is essential that Japan continue its utmost efforts in this field. For the time being, the foci of Japan's efforts seem to be on the development of offshore oil fields in China and on negotiations with the United States to realize imports of Alaskan crude oil.

As I have outlined, an effective energy strategy is critically needed for the stable growth of Japan's economy. In a broad sense, it can be said that Japan's survival depends on its energy strategy. To achieve this strategy, priority should be given to sophisticated political measures which, to be effective, should be carried out with the cooperative efforts of the public and private sectors.

In the meantime, considering that international economic relations, with trade as a central factor, are the most important foundation of Japan's economy, we should never forget that international cooperation in the field of energy policy has great significance. International cooperation is essential to establish stable supplies of not only oil but also alternative energy sources. In particular, large-scale projects to develop new energy sources seem to intensify the need for international cooperation. Thus, it is critically important for Japan to map out and implement its energy strategy within an international framework. In the coming years, there will be a growing need to strengthen the solidarity among friendly nations, which, I believe, will prove very significant for the prosperity of all of humankind.

CHAPTER FOURTEEN

Energy Policy in Australia

Denis J. Ives
Deputy Secretary
Australian Department of
National Development and Energy

INTRODUCTION

Since 1973, the energy policies of industrialized nations have been dominated by a concern for the availability and security of energy supplies, particularly oil, as essential ingredients for sustained economic growth. Prior to 1973, industrial economies had grown steadily on the basis of cheap, plentiful oil, but attitudes changed fundamentally as a result of the rapid 300–400 percent increases in OPEC oil prices in 1973–74. Further price rises in 1979–80 reinforced the need for change.

Oil-importing nations have therefore been alerted to their dependence on politically sensitive sources of supply and their vulnerability to future oil supply disruption, as well as to the increasing scarcity of world hydrocarbon energy resources, at least in the convenient liquid form we know as crude oil. The energy policies of industrialized countries are now generally based on assessments of higher future energy prices. The current plentiful supplies and easing of oil prices are seen by Australia as a temporary aberration from a trend that still points to increases in the real prices of crude oil and of all energy resources in the long term.

Despite a rich endowment with energy resources such as coal, gas, and uranium (see Table 14-1), Australia has not been insulated from the changing world energy situation. Indigenous oil supplies currently meet approximately two-thirds of Australia's oil needs, with the prospect that without further discoveries its level of self-sufficiency will decline during the late 1980s. The required remainder has to be obtained from world markets at prices and conditions similar to those for any other oil-consuming country.

Table 14-1. **Australia's Remaining Identified Economic Non-renewable Resources**

Resource	Date of measure	Units	Quantity Demonstrated	Demonstrated plus inferred
Crude oil and condensate		bbl x 10^6		
In situ	June 80		6,133	6,302
Recoverable[a]			2,428	2,522
Sale gas		ft^3 x 10^{12}		
In situ	June 80		36.0	40.6
Recoverable[a]			21.6	24.5
LPG		bbl x 10^6		
In situ	June 80		1,260	1,449
Recoverable[a]			776	857
Black coal		t x 10^6		
In situ	Dec 81		51,500	529,000
Recoverable			29,400	302,000
Brown coal		t x 10^6		
In situ	Dec 80		39,300	43,600
Recoverable			36,200	40,200
Uranium		t		
In situ	Dec 80		358,000	764,000
Recoverable[b]	June 81		294,000	558,000
Total		toe x 10^6		
In situ			48,340	361,380
Recoverable			32,075	210,748

Source: Bureau of Mineral Resources.
[a]Recovery factor of 60 percent has been assumed for condensate, sales gas, and LPG.
[b]Australian Atomic Energy Commission estimates.

In recognition of the importance of energy resources to Australia's national wealth, policies have been developed to respond to the changing pattern of world energy supplies, in order to try to minimize uncertainty for the future and to take full advantage of the opportunities arising from the oil situation by developing other energy sources that can substitute for oil in a wide range of uses in both domestic and export markets.

The nature and implementation of these policies are influenced significantly by the fact that government in Australia is a federation with two tiers—the commonwealth and the states—each having constitutionally defined powers. The state governments exercise substantial control over energy resources, including responsibility for exploration, production, distribution, and the provision of related infrastructures. The commonwealth government has responsibility for economic and energy policy on a national level, a responsibility which includes taxation powers, the power to control energy exports, and responsibilities for foreign investment but which entails only limited, indirect powers in regard to energy pricing. Crude oil pricing is subject to specific commonwealth government policy decisions. This paper focuses on the policies of the commonwealth government.

POLICY OBJECTIVES

The commonwealth government's energy policies have been formulated within the framework of the following broad objectives:

- achieving a balanced approach to energy supply and demand, including taking account of all indigenous energy resources, both current and prospective;
- promoting the timely development of indigenous energy resources and technologies, since a diversified energy supply base will permit smoother adjustment to changes in the world energy scene;
- maintaining a high level of self-sufficiency in liquid fuels, thus reducing dependence on uncertain oil imports and assuring supplies, particularly for transport fuels for which alternative energy sources are generally not suitable; and
- contributing, through exports, to the fulfillment of the energy needs of less energy-rich nations.

More specific objectives, with particular relevance to the area of liquid fuels, are as follows:

- to conserve energy, particularly liquid fuels, in all sectors;
- to encourage replacement of oil by more abundant energy sources;
- to encourage the exploration and efficient development of indigenous energy resources, including synthetic fuels; and
- to make adequate preparations to withstand sudden and severe short-term shortages of imported oil.

POLICY INITIATIVES

The commonwealth government believes that demand for energy should be influenced by the market mechanism and that the development of energy resources, particularly petroleum resources, should continue to be the responsibility of private enterprise. However, some utility functions—electricity generation and gas pipelining—are traditionally carried out by government agencies, particularly at the state level.

In the development of Australian energy resources, the government has sought to rely on general framework policies—a stable and favorable economic climate for investment, a clear recognition of the importance of market forces, and considerable efforts to ensure that Australians share in the benefits of resources development—supplemented where appropriate by a number of specific policies to achieve more particular objectives. The more specific policies are reviewed below.

Import Parity Pricing for Oil

One of the more important specific policies is to ensure that domestic consumers appreciate the real value of oil they are using. A policy of import parity pricing of indigenous crude oil was introduced in the 1978–79 budget. All domestically produced crude oil is now priced to refiners at a price equivalent to that for Saudi Arabian light crude oil, with appropriate allowances for freight and quality differences.

This pricing policy has had a wide range of effects on both supply and demand. It has encouraged exploration and development of indigenous energy resources while at the same time encouraging conservation and substitution. It is therefore of fundamental importance to Australian energy policy.

Supply Initiatives

On the supply side, additional government initiatives include the following:

Mining and exploration incentives. Generous capital allowances are available for exploration and development (including infrastructure) for all mining, including that for energy resources.

Incentives to oil exploration and development. Taxation incentives have been introduced since 1976 to encourage domestic oil exploration and development, specifically:

- receipt, by producers, of the world price for newly discovered oil, free of the government levy applying to oil discovered before 1976;

- the accelerated write-off of allowable capital expenditure on development and on transport facilities;
- allowance of petroleum exploration and development expenditures as deductions from income from any source;
- inclusion of the cost of a gas liquefaction plant as an allowable capital expenditure;
- an investment allowance of 18 percent of the cost of allowable capital expenditures; and
- a shareholder rebate scheme.

Encouragement of alternative liquid fuels, including synthetic fuels. The government has recognized the potential longer term contribution to Australian energy supplies of liquid fuels from the development of alternative energy sources, including oil shale, oil from coal, and renewables for which Australia has extensive resource feedstocks. The policy of allowing locally produced oil to be priced at world levels has provided a considerable stimulus to the development and use of alternative fuels.

Support for research, development, and demonstration (RD&D). The government recognizes the need for appropriate new technologies to meet medium- and long-term energy needs. In response to this, it established the National Energy Research, Development, and Demonstration Program. In the four fiscal years 1978–79 to 1981–82, the government committed $A80 million under the program. Apart from funding Australian energy RD&D, the program provides an avenue for supporting international cooperative projects involving Australia.

International cooperation. The government is an active participant in a number of regional and multilateral fora, including the International Energy Agency (IEA), the Commonwealth Heads of Government Regional Meeting (CHOGRM), and the Association of Southeast Asian Nations (ASEAN), all of which promote and work toward international cooperation in energy matters.

Demand Initiatives

On the demand side, initiatives include the following:

Conservation. Realistic energy prices are the central element of the government's conservation policies, but it is necessary to supplement market signals. Measures include the following:

- *The National Energy Conservation Program.* This program

was launched on October 15, 1979, with the objective of increasing the level of public understanding in energy matters.

• *The National Industrial Energy Management Scheme.* This scheme is designed to provide information to industrial managers. It was initiated because there had been reluctance to invest in energy-efficient plants rather than expanded production.

• *Fuel consumption goals.* Voluntary fuel economy goals for new cars have been agreed upon by manufacturers and the government. The aim is to reduce gasoline consumption by new cars from 10.0 liters per 100 kilometers (equivalent to 23.5 miles per US gallon) in 1981 to 9 liters per 100 kilometers (equivalent to 26.1 miles per US gallon) by 1983, with a further reduction to 8 liters per 100 kilometers (equivalent to 29.4 miles per US gallon) by 1987 agreed upon in principle.

• *Taxation concessions.* Incentives to residential energy conservation have been provided in making fully tax deductible the insulation costs assumed by people buying or building their first home after October 1, 1981.

Fuel substitution. Replacement of oil by other energy sources offers considerable scope for Australia to extend the life of its liquid fuel resources. The greatest scope for such change is in the industrial and commercial sectors, where the major alternatives include coal, natural gas, and coal-derived electricity. Considerable gains have been made in encouraging the wider use of natural gas, particularly in industrial applications in place of heavy grades of oil.

Although it is technically more difficult to find replacements for transport fuels, LPG offers scope as an alternative automotive fuel and as petrochemical feedstock.

FOREIGN INVESTMENT

A fair return to Australia of the benefits of resource development is a major policy objective with bipartisan support. This has led to the implementation of a comprehensive policy approach toward foreign investment in Australia.

The government's well-established and accepted foreign investment policy welcomes foreign investment in Australian energy and raw material resources where this investment supplements Australia's industrial and technological resources. The government considers that wherever practicable, Australians should participate with overseas partners in major projects. Proposals for the development of new natural resources projects are examined by the Foreign Investment Review Board against the government's broad objective of having 50 percent of the equity and at least 50 percent of the voting strength held by Australian interests.

EXPORT POLICY

The commonwealth government considers it the role of private enterprise to seek out markets and to negotiate contractual terms and conditions. This is no less true for energy exports—coal, uranium, LPG, and LNG. However, in certain circumstances, the government exercises control over the exports to protect the national interest.

All crude oil produced in Australia is required by the government to be processed in Australian refineries. For petroleum products, the government policy is to approve exports when these are in excess of Australia's requirements or in a limited range of other circumstances. For natural gas and LPG, the government will continue to give priority to domestic requirements, but reasonable exports of gas are expected in the future. Export controls are also administered on coal and on uranium and other materials of nuclear significance.

The government has indicated that consideration will be given on a case-by-case basis to specific product-sharing proposals for synthetic fuels, following a full assessment of all the factors relevant to a particular project.

ENVIRONMENTAL POLICY

The commonwealth government shares responsibility with the states for environmental protection. Although the states have the primary responsibility in this regard, if a project that is likely to have significant environmental effects requires approval by the commonwealth government for, say, foreign investment or export, the commonwealth minister giving the approval is required to take the environmental effects of the proposed project into account. In most cases, a state environmental impact statement may be sufficient to satisfy both the commonwealth and the state requirements.

ENERGY SECTOR REVIEWS

Energy use and supply patterns in Australia during the 1980s are expected to exhibit considerable change. The main features are expected to include the following:

- a substantial decline in the growth of demand for total primary energy to an average of 3.6 percent per year (compared with an average of 4.7 percent per year over the twenty years prior to 1979–80);
- a significant switching from oil to gas and coal-based electricity;
- an increase in liquid fuel self-sufficiency, with a reasonable prospect of achieving 80-percent self-sufficiency by 1989–90; and
- a considerable increase in net energy exports due to significant increases in coal, gas, and uranium exports and to a lower dependence on oil imports.

Past and projected changes in the demand pattern for primary fuels are illustrated in Table 14–2. Table 14–3 shows Australia's 1979–80 energy balance, including end uses by market sector. Brief reviews of the major components of Australia's energy sector are given below.

Table 14-2. **Australia's Demand for Primary Fuels by Market Share**

	1969-70	1979-80	1989-90
Crude Oil[a]	50	44	32
Coal[b]	43	39	48
Gas[c]	1	12	16
Other[d]	6	5	4
Total	100	100	100

Source: Department of National Development and Energy.
[a]Includes petroleum fuels used as petrochemical feedstock.
[b]Black and brown coal.
[c]Natural sales gas and ethane used as fuel and petrochemical feedstock.
[d]Includes hydro, wood, and bagasse.

Oil

In 1976, Australia was about 70-percent self-sufficient in liquid fuels, and consumption of petroleum was growing at a rate of 2.6 percent per year. At that rate, existing reserves were being rapidly depleted, and exploration for and development of additional reserves was virtually at a standstill. The level of self-sufficiency was expected to fall to 50 percent by the early 1980s and to under 20 percent by the end of the century. It was against this backdrop that the government took its major oil pricing steps in 1978 and introduced measures to encourage petroleum exploration and development.

Production levels are now expected to be maintained and even increased during the 1980s, but unless significant discoveries are made in the near future or existing discoveries are substantially upgraded, the level of self-sufficiency in liquid fuels could fall to around 50 percent during the 1990s. However, there have been promising "shows" recently in the Perth and Canning Basins, and development programs in Bass Strait and the Cooper Basin hold out hope for an improved outlook. In addition, exploration activity is currently at a high level for Australia.

On the demand side, sales of petroleum products peaked in 1979–80, and demand fell by an annual average of 2.2 percent between 1978–79 and 1980–81, with the largest reductions occurring in heating and fuel oils and a considerable reduction occurring in the rate of growth in transport fuel demand. In its June 1981 Forecast of Energy Supply and Demand, the Department of National Development and Energy estimated that petroleum demand would increase by an average of only 0.5 percent per year throughout the 1980s.

Emergency arrangements. Along with other industrial nations, the Australian government has decided, as part of its energy policy, to make contingency plans for possible liquid fuel (oil) supply disruptions. These arrangements include preparation of a contingency allocation system for petroleum products; participation in the IEA's Emergency Oil Sharing Scheme (EOSS); and ensuring that appropriate oil stocking levels and storage facilities are maintained by oil companies and major consumers.

Coal

Australia's most abundant energy source is coal, representing over 80 percent of its identified economically recoverable energy reserves. However, Australian coal reserves represent only 4 percent of total world reserves. Black coal is mainly found in Queensland and New South Wales.

Production in 1980–81 of raw black coal was about 106 million tons, having increased by some 18 percent over the previous

Table 14-3. **Australian Energy Balance, 1979-80** (toe x 10^6)

	Black coal	Brown coal	Oil and NGL[a]	Natural gas	Uranium[b]	Bagasse	Wood	Electricity Hydro	Electricity Total	Briquettes	Total
Supply											
Indigenous production	47.6	7.4	22.9	8.8[c]	9.4	1.4	.7	1.2	1.2		99.4
Imports			14.2[d]								14.2
Exports	30.3		3.2		13.3						46.8
Stock changes[e]	+3.4		−1.8[d]		+3.9						5.5
Total primary energy supplied	20.7	7.4	32.1	8.8		1.4	.7	1.2	1.2		72.3
Conversion[f]											
Briquetting		.7[g]								(.7)[h]	
Electricity generation[i]	13.2	6.6	1.2	2.2			.1	1.2	(8.2)[i]	.3	16.6[k]
Electricity transmission losses[l]									1.2		1.2
Petroleum refining			2.4	.2					.1		2.7
Gas manufacturing			.1[m]	.5[m]							.6
Total final energy demand	7.5	.1	28.4	5.9		1.4	.6		6.9	.4	51.2
End Use[f]											
Agriculture			2.1						.1		2.2
Mining			.6	.5[n]					.4		1.5
Manufacturing[o]	7.4	.1	4.9	3.9		1.4	.1		2.6	.3	20.7
Transport											
Road			14.1								14.1
Rail			.6						.1		.7
Air			1.9								1.9
Sea			2.4								2.4
Domestic/commercial	.1		1.8	1.5			.5		3.7	.1	7.7
Total final energy use	7.5	.1	28.4	5.9		1.4	.6		6.9	.4	51.2

Source: Australian Department of National Development and Energy.

[a]Natural gas liquids (NGL) include condensates and liquefied petroleum gas.

[b]Uranium content in "yellowcake."

[c]Includes natural gas of noncommercial quality for field and plant use.

[d]Includes an estimated 1.0 Mtoe of imports which are used for nonenergy products.

[e]Includes stock changes and statistical discrepancies. Negative stock drawdown.

[f]*Source: Demand for Primary and Secondary Fuels in Australia: 1960-61 to 1979-80* (Department of National Development and Energy: 1981).

[g]Excludes use of process heat obtained during production of electricity—about 0.3 Mtoe.

[h]Energy content of briquettes produced from brown coal.

[i]Includes fuels used for public and private generation.

[j]Net output generated.

[k]Losses in generation of thermal electricity.

[l]Includes own use, electricity used for pumped storage, and transmission and distribution losses.

[m]No end-use analysis is available.

[n]Includes gas transportation by pipeline to city gate; gas distribution is included with gas manufacturing.

[o]Includes water and sewerage industry.

fiscal year, with salable black coal totaling 87.4 million tons. At current rates of production, Australia's economic black coal reserves would last for over two hundred years.

Australia also has substantial brown coal resources, principally in Victoria. At a current consumption rate of about 33 million tons per year, the resource life of brown coal could extend for over three thousand years.

Domestic consumption of black coal was about 38 million tons in 1980–81 of which 25 million tons was used for electricity generation. Brown coal consumption in the same period—nearly all for electricity generation—was about 33 million tons.

In June of 1981, the Department of National Development and Energy estimated that domestic demand for coal would increase by 5.9 percent per year throughout the 1980s, largely as a result of forecasted increases in electricity demand.

The June 1981 estimates also show that Australia could be exporting 130 million tons of black coal in 1989–90. This would represent a major expansion from 47 million tons in 1979–80, especially in steaming coal (10.6 million tons in 1979–80, projected to rise to around 70 million tons in 1989–90). However, these forecasts should be viewed with caution. They were made when prospects for world coal trade were brighter than they are now. Changes in world economic growth prospects have affected demand for other fuels, particularly oil, and coal demand in Japan, which is expected to remain Australia's major coal market, is likely to be less than previously anticipated.

The government believes that on a resource basis a substantial expansion of coal exports is achievable, and, together with the relevant state governments, it has taken measures to ensure the timely availability of suitable infrastructures.

Australian resources of brown and black coal also provide considerable scope for coal-based synthetic fuel production.

Natural gas

Australia is relatively well-endowed with natural gas. Most of this is located on the Northwest Shelf off the coast of northwestern Australia and in Bass Strait and the Cooper Basin in southern Australia. Total resources are not large by world standards (24.5 trillion cubic feet of recoverable reserves, or just over 1 percent of world reserves), but when compared with Australia's current annual consumption of around 320 billion cubic feet they represent over seventy years of supply if the consumption level remains static.

However, Australia's demonstrated natural gas resources are generally not well placed in relation to local markets, which are primarily in major cities. Approximately half of Australia's current gas production is from the offshore Gippsland Basin and is supplied to the Victorian market. The remainder of current gas production is from onshore fields and is piped long distances to markets. A major new project costing a total of $8 billion is under way on the Northwest Shelf. The project will be in two stages, the first for the domestic market and the second for the export market to Japan. The export stage of the project provides for 6 million tons of LNG per year to be exported for up to twenty years. In addition, when the project is fully operational a further 1.4 million tons of condensate and 0.6 million tons of LPG could be available for export.

Uranium

Australia's demonstrated economic uranium resources represent some 17 percent of the western world's demonstrated recoverable reserves of low-cost uranium, and the prospects for the discovery of additional uranium in Australia are excellent. Limited exploration has already resulted in major finds.

There are no current plans for Australia to have a nuclear power industry. Thus, uranium is available for export. Since the government's decision in 1977 to allow further development of uranium, major markets for Australian U_3O_8 (uranium oxide) have been established with the United States, Western Europe, and Japan. Exports are expected to increase during the 1980s but will be restricted to countries with whom satisfactory safeguards agreements have been entered.

The rate of increase in exports will depend on the pace of development of nuclear industries overseas, which in turn will depend on public acceptance in the countries concerned. The government's policy toward nonproliferation and safeguards should be helpful in this respect.

Although no nuclear electricity generation is planned for Australia in the near future, a private consortium is currently examining the prospects for a uranium enrichment capability. Development of enrichment, if economically feasible, would be consistent with government objectives to encourage greater processing in Australia of indigenous raw materials.

Synfuels and Renewables

New discoveries of conventional crude oil have the potential to add significantly to Australia's liquid fuel supply, but these are not expected to completely satisfy domestic needs, particularly for transport fuels. It will probably be necessary to develop fuels for the longer term that are not dependent on crude oil, in order to enable Australia to maintain a reasonable level of independence from increasingly scarce imported oil. Of all the known technologies, oil shale and oil from coal hold the greatest prospects for Australia. The government takes the view that market forces should be allowed to determine the timing of the private sector's development of synthetic fuel projects.

Oil from coal. Australia has considerable scope for coal-based synthetic fuel production. The feasibility of using selected coals and conversion processes to produce ranges of liquid products such as gasoline and diesel fuel has been the subject of a number of studies. Two important developments are as follows:

- Nippon Brown Coal Liquefaction Company (NBCL) has signed an agreement with the Victorian government for construction of a 50-ton-per-day dry coal pilot plant using Victorian brown coal and costing $A237 million.
- A joint Australia/Federal Republic of Germany study (known as the Imhausen Study) of the feasibility of using selected coals from New South Wales, Victoria, and Queensland was completed in late 1981. Participating state governments and the commonwealth government shared half the $A4 million cost of the study.

Oil shale. Australia also has very large resources of oil shale (equivalent to 17 billion barrels of oil), mainly in Queensland. Major high-grade deposits have been identified at Rundle and Condor in Queensland. Production of oil from these and other deposits is currently being examined, although current indications are that it would not be commercially feasible at this time. Major feasibility studies are proceeding.

Renewables. Australia has the technical potential to obtain a proportion of its energy needs from renewable sources such as ethanol, solar power, and wind power. Although large-scale development of many of the technologies may not be commercially or economically viable at present, there may be some scope for their adoption (e.g., in remoter areas) and for small-scale domestic solar heating to supplement conventional energy supplies.

Research and development into alternative energy technologies within Australia will continue (with considerable assistance from the government's National Energy Research, Development, and Demonstration Program). Opportunities for export to countries where the technologies may be commercially viable could result in the shorter term.

Electricity

Australia's future energy demand and supply is likely to place increasing emphasis on electricity (of which 80 percent is already derived from coal) and on natural gas. Demand for electricity grew at a rate of over 5 percent per year in the three fiscal years to 1980–81, while consumption of oil has fallen. Over the ten years from 1979–80 to 1989–90, the supply of electricity was expected to increase from 19.1 million tons of oil equivalent to some 30.4 million tons of oil equivalent. Some 80 percent of the forecasted extra domestic demand for coal between 1979–80 and 1989–90 was expected to be used for electricity. Some reduction of these forecasts may now be required.

Demand for electricity is very much influenced by the development of electricity-consuming energy-intensive industries, such as aluminum smelting. Proposed large-scale projects were placing considerable pressure on state electricity utilities to meet increasing demand for reliable and competitively priced electricity; however, recent deferrals of some projects will affect previous demand forecasts, and development of new power stations may not proceed as rapidly as previously envisioned. The resource base and the opportunity for development remain unchanged, and projects could be reinstated when the level of international economic activity improves.

ENERGY-RELATED RESOURCE DEVELOPMENT

Following the rapid oil price rises of 1973–74 and 1979–80, a major change began to occur in investment economics, particularly in energy-intensive raw materials processing. With rising transport fuel costs it became more attractive to process raw materials where abundant, assured energy resources were available rather than near the point of consumption. As well as being richly endowed with energy, Australia has an abundance of most key minerals. It possesses major deposits of bauxite, copper, gold, iron ore, lead, manganese, mineral sands, nickel, phosphate, silver, tin, tungsten, and zinc.

Alumina and aluminum are prime examples of raw material processing in Australia occurring in response to changing circumstances. As a result, four large-scale alumina refineries were established at Gladstone, Gove, Kwinana, and Pinjarra, and others are planned. The existing aluminum smelting industry in Australia is small by world standards, but new world-scale aluminum smelters are now under construction. Other planned aluminum developments may well proceed when world aluminum markets recover from their current depressed levels.

SUMMARY OF ACHIEVEMENTS

The government's energy policies have achieved considerable success for Australia:

- Investment in energy development has increased markedly, and domestic production capacity has increased accordingly. Production of salable black coal expanded from around 64 million tons in 1974–75 to 87.4 million tons in 1980–81; natural gas production increased from 136 billion cubic feet to 255 billion cubic feet over the same period; uranium production increased from 120 tons in 1975–76 to 2,250 tons in 1980–81. Prospects for sustaining a high level of liquid fuel self-sufficiency to the end of the 1980s and beyond have improved. In 1976–77 Australia faced a bleak prospect for self-sufficiency in liquid fuels. Today, we are still 68 percent self-sufficient, and we expect that level to be maintained until at least 1985, even without additional discoveries of crude oil—and prospects for such discoveries are good. In June of 1981, the Department of National Development and Energy was able to point to a reasonable prospect of a liquid fuels self-sufficiency level of about 80 percent by 1990.
- The latest Department of Industry and Commerce survey of investment in mining and manufacturing in Australia shows that of the planned $A32 billion investment in mining and manufacturing projects in Australia in the coming decade, three-quarters can be identified as energy-related development. While timetables for some of these projects are being adjusted in the light of world economic circumstances, the proposed projects are a useful indication of longer term investment projects in Australia.
- Australia has achieved a fortunate position among industrialized nations in attracting investment in energy-based resource development and processing and in becoming a net energy exporter, with accruing benefits for national wealth.

CONCLUSION

While rapidly rising oil prices and supply shortages in recent years have focused governmental attention on that energy source, the Australian government has recognized the need to implement policies to stimulate development of a diversified energy base and to avoid overreliance on any one energy source, be it oil, coal, or electricity. This experience, and the prospect of further changes in world energy markets, highlights the need for flexibility and diversification in the development of energy resources and technologies.

There is a need to be cautious about overreaction to short-term fluctuations in the world energy market. To be effective, energy policy must be based on sound long-term perceptions of the world energy outlook. This is not to say that long term perceptions will not change from time to time, but such changes should be the result of careful study and assessment over a reasonable period of time. In its efforts to implement energy policy, Australia is seeking to follow a consistent long-term approach to achieve a smooth adjustment to a more diverse and reliable energy balance.

The realization by other countries of the need to diversify energy supplies, prompted by events in the world oil market, has been of benefit to Australia. Based on the development of its abundant energy resources (with the exception of oil), Australia's energy industries are being expanded to meet increased local and overseas demand. Industrial development in Australia, based on the processing of Australia's abundant raw materials, has been stimulated by changes in the world energy scene, and this has been of major significance to the Australian economy in recent years.

SELECTED BIBLIOGRAPHY

"Forecasts of Energy Demand and Supply—Primary and Secondary Fuels. Australia, 1980–81 to 1989–90" (Department of National Development and Energy: June 1981).

"Australian Energy Statistics, 1981" (Department of National Development and Energy).

"Australia's Energy Resources, 1980," National Energy Advisory Committee Report No. 14 (1981).

"Energy Policy and Related Resource Development" (Statement by the Prime Minister, the Rt. Hon. Malcolm Fraser, to the House of Representatives on August 26, 1980).

"Petroleum Exploration and Development in Australia, March 1982" (Department of National Development and Energy).

"Major Manufacturing and Mining Investment Projects, December 1981" (Department of Industry and Commerce).

"Your Investment in Australia—A Guide for Investors, 1981" (Department of the Treasury).

CHAPTER FIFTEEN

The Republic of Korea's Present Energy Picture and Major Policy Implementation Plan

Hyo Joon Hahm
Vice President
Korean Institute of Energy and Resources

It is indeed a pleasure to have this opportunity to share the energy experience in the Republic of Korea* with an audience of eminent scholars and distinguished businesspeople who are here with the betterment of the world energy situation in mind. I would like to present briefly Korea's present energy picture and its future direction on energy, the problems with which it is faced, and its countermeasures and policies to effectively cope with these problems.

ENERGY PROBLEMS IN KOREA

Korea has few indigenous energy resources. Thus far, no oil has been discovered there, despite continued exploration efforts. Coal deposits are small and of poor quality. Due to increasing mine depths, coal production costs have accelerated. Korea's potential for hydropower generation is limited to 1.8 million kw, and its other renewable sources are also limited. Its energy resource imports have grown rapidly during the past ten years of high economic growth and were especially great in the latter part of the 1970s. In 1976, the level of dependence on imported energy resources was 62.3 percent of total energy consumption. By 1980, this level had increased to 73.7 percent.

This limited resource base, combined with rapid economic

---

*Or South Korea; hereafter referred to in this chapter as Korea for brevity's sake. [eds.]

growth starting just before the extraordinary petroleum price increases of the 1970s, has given rise to four major energy problems:

- *A rapidly growing dependence on imported energy resources.* In 1965, 21 percent of the energy consumed in Korea was imported. In 1980, 80 percent was imported—all of its oil, gas, and nuclear fuels, and one-third of its coal. Continued economic growth and a limited resource base means that this dependency will continue to increase.

- *An increasing financial burden.* During the same fifteen-year period, the percentage of export earnings needed to pay for these imports grew from 16 to 36 percent. This increase occurred despite an extraordinarily rapid rate of increase in export earnings. It will take continued rapid growth of exports plus a measure of luck with respect to world energy prices to keep this burden from increasing further in the future.

- *A heavy dependence on petroleum, which until recently was the cheapest and most convenient fuel to import.* In 1965, petroleum products accounted for 12 percent of total energy consumption; in 1980, they accounted for 58 percent. While this percentage is expected to decline in the future, the absolute level of imports is projected to continue to increase.

- *A heavy concentration of suppliers.* Ninety percent of Korea's petroleum purchases come from Saudi Arabia, Iran, and Kuwait. Uranium and coal purchases are equally concentrated.

Of less importance but growing in severity are environmental problems associated with energy use. In 1977, only Seoul had sulfur oxide levels above the World Health Organization's standard. By 1981, this standard was also surpassed in Pusan and Ulsan. Other energy-related pollutants and environmental problems are mounting as well but cannot easily be documented because of a lack of data. The burning of coal within cities is probably the principal cause of energy-related pollutants, but exhaust from internal combustion engines is rapidly becoming an important contributing factor.

Sometimes mentioned as an additional dimension of Korea's energy problem is a high overall intensity of energy use. In 1978, Korea's energy/GDP ratio was 64 percent above the average of all middle-income countries. Such a comparison, however, can be misleading since it does not take into account differences in purchasing power parities, climate, status as an oil importer or exporter, per capita income, economic structure, or geographic dispersion of population and economic activities.

KOREA'S ENERGY POLICY

Korea's energy policy is designed to lessen its future energy burden. This policy is predicated on four basic goals:

- Ensuring the supply of energy necessary for continued economic growth.
- Diversifying energy resources.
- Developing petroleum resources, domestic and overseas.
- Increasing conservation and fuel substitution.

Enhancement of Oil Supply Security

Currently the bulk of Korea's oil imports, about 89 percent, are from the politically and militarily sensitive Middle East. This high geographic concentration of import sources exacerbated energy problems during the last two oil crises. Korea's energy plans call for a wider geographic diversification of import sources, although this may result in oil cost increases. The additional cost would reflect the price of improved diversification. The target for diversification is to reduce the Middle East sources to about 75 percent.

The current low level of oil stockpiles severely limits the country's ability to weather short-term disruptions in the international oil markets. The current stockpile level—equivalent to 45 days of consumption, including the refineries' normal operating inventories—is simply inadequate. It is planned that the stockpile level will be increased to a 90-day equivalent by 1986. The government and the refining industry will share the stockpile cost.

This level of stockpiling, while smaller than the 120-day stockpile recommended by the International Energy Agency for its members, is ambitious for a developing country. Once in place, the 90-day stockpile should provide a reasonable degree of security against a sudden disruption in supply. The stockpile program ought to be supplemented, however, by the development of an emergency rationing and allocation scheme prepared for implementation in advance to cover the possibilities of either a disruption occurring before the stockpile is in place or a disruption requiring more than a 90-day supply. Indeed, whether the 90-day stockpile is appropriate at all depends on how much of a reduction in consumption could be achieved by such emergency rationing and allocation measures: if such measures could stretch out supplies for a substantial period, it might be appropriate to cut back on the ultimate size of this very expensive stockpile program.

Reduction of Petroleum Dependence

Fuel substitution will be most important in the electricity generation sector, which has become heavily dependent on oil. Oil currently accounts for 79 percent of power generation (with a total of 9.4 million kw of installed capacity), the remainder being shared by nuclear (9 percent), coal (7 percent), and hydro (5 percent). It is planned that this fuel mix will undergo a substantial change during the next ten years. As planned, petroleum will by 1986 account for 35 percent of the total generating capacity, whereas the nuclear portion will increase to 27 percent. The remainder will be shared by LNG and increased coal. By 1991, petroleum use will decline further to a mere 19 percent, with nuclear expanding to 42 percent.

In addition to the rising importance of nuclear power, coal use in power generation will also increase. By the mid 1980s there will be four new units operating on bituminous coal with a combined capacity of 2.12 million kw, and in the latter part of the 1980s there will be four additional units operating on bituminous. There will be two new units using domestic anthracite added to the existing total of twelve units with a combined capacity of 750 thousand kw.

Several oil-fired power plants currently in operation will switch to either LNG or bituminous coal. Those located near the Seoul metropolitan area will use LNG instead of relatively high-sulfur heavy fuel oil. The LNG will penetrate the premium urban residential/commercial markets in the latter part of the 1980s, thereby reducing these sectors' high dependence on petroleum and on anthracite briquettes. It is expected that the use of gas (including LPG in the residential and commercial sectors) will increase from the current 10 percent (used mostly for cooking) to about 30 percent (for cooking and heating) by 1986.

The decision to retire oil plants as quickly as possible is based on an analysis by the Korea Electric Company showing that the total generating costs of coal and nuclear are now substantially below just the fuel cost of oil. The decision to move ahead as fast as possible with nuclear in preference to coal is based on the following considerations:

• Nuclear is substantially cheaper than coal, even when one assumes no increases in fuel costs in the future. (If such increases are assumed, nuclear becomes even more favorable because of its smaller proportion of fuel costs to total costs.)
• Coal requires large quantities of social overhead capital (harbors, transportation, and stockpiling facilities), which nuclear does not.

• Capital from abroad is available on very favorable terms (currently, at negative real interest rates). This factor is probably the most important financial reason involved.

Expansion of Investments in Energy Development

A great deal of effort will be directed toward exploring for oil in offshore Korea. According to a recently prepared report of the US Geological Survey, onshore deposits of oil or gas are highly unlikely, but the report estimated that there is a 5 percent probability that offshore resources-in-place could be as high as 1.4 billion barrels of oil with an additional 0.44 trillion cubic feet of gas.

Korean energy plans call for more active drilling in two promising offshore blocks—blocks 7 and 4. Block 7 is under a joint exploration and development agreement with Japan. Drilling there has already started, and it is expected that by 1987 at least eleven exploratory wells will have been drilled. Block 4 will be explored and developed jointly with an American oil company, and drilling there is to begin early next year.

Korean firms will also be active in exploration overseas. An agreement with Pertamina of Indonesia for joint exploration in offshore Madura was the first of its kind. Several Korean firms are evaluating the prospect of joint exploration and development in Peru and other South American countries.

Emphasis will be given as well to increasing mechanization in coal mining. The ratio of mechanization is currently a mere 18 percent, but this ratio is expected to increase to 35 percent by 1986. To expedite the mechanization of mines, the mining industry plans to utilize foreign expertise as much as possible and will push for more unification of small mines. As a result of the latter, it is expected that by the mid 1980s the mining industry will consist of five large consolidated mining companies.

The investment in coal will also cover an increased coal stockpile. The current level of coal stockpiling is about 6 million tons. By 1986 the stockpile level should rise to 8 million tons. Plans call for an increased investment to upgrade the coal transport system. Investments will increase for coal loading facilities, and there will be more investments directed toward improving the living and social environments of mining villages.

The energy plans also call for expansion of equity investment in overseas mines and mineral deposits, as part of an overall effort to enhance supply security. As stated earlier, the level of dependence on imported energy resources is about 74 percent. Dependence on imports of some key minerals is even higher: iron ore, 94 percent, copper, 99 percent. By 1986, the level of dependence on imported energy resources will rise to 82 percent; iron ore, 96 percent; and copper, close to 100 percent. Several Korean firms have already entered into joint venture agreements or are negotiating with foreign mining and minerals interests. The government plans to provide broad financial support and incentives for overseas investment. It also plans to upgrade its capability of gathering and analyzing energy and other resource information worldwide.

Conservation and Efficiency in Energy Use

The importance of conservation and efficient energy use is well recognized in Korea, where the economy is especially energy intensive. According to a survey conducted in 1979, energy waste in Korean manufacturing industries amounted to a surprising 22 percent of total industrial energy consumption. Korean residential structures are also found to be extremely energy wasteful: for example, only 5 percent of all recently built houses are equipped with insulation materials, and old houses are devoid of any insulation. A survey of building energy use revealed that energy waste amounted to 33 percent in 1979. The potential for energy conservation is very high in Korea.

Conservation efforts in the industrial sector consist mainly of replacing energy-inefficient boilers, kilns, furnaces, pipes, and so on. Financial subsidies to this purpose are provided. Also, energy plans call for expansion of cogeneration capabilities. Currently, there are twenty-three manufacturing plants equipped with cogeneration facilities capable of generating 328 kw. It is planned that by 1986 a total of fifty-three additional manufacturing plants will be equipped with cogeneration facilities with a combined capacity of 265 thousand kw. In addition, energy use will be closely monitored at the plant level in order to reduce the energy requirement per unit of output. The Korean government plans to impose mandatory energy audits for heavy energy users and will if necessary regulate energy use to improve efficiency. There are about 2,500 manufacturing establishments which are defined as heavy energy users. The conservation program will also emphasize the importance of training and the transfer of technical information and know-how. Heat managers and auditors will be required to attend short courses in energy management each year.

Future energy demand is expected to increase most rapidly in the transportation sector, due to increases in the number of personal autos and the amount of freight transportation. Transport demand for gasoline and diesel is currently only 14 percent of total refinery output, but within the next five years, it is expected to rise to more than 40 percent. Improving energy efficiency in the transportation sector will thus become increasingly important. The auto manufacturing industry plans to improve fuel efficiency of popular compact models from the current 12 km/l to 16 km/l by 1986. In addition, the government plans to design and enforce fuel efficiency standards for different classes of autos. The energy efficiency of the Seoul metropolitan subway system will increase from its current 62 percent to 90 percent within the next five years. To improve the efficiency of inland transportation, a number of large-scale freight terminals will be constructed.

The demand for electricity will continue to increase, albeit at a somewhat slower rate than in the past, as economic growth continues in the future. In the last five years, a 1-percent growth of real GNP was accompanied by a 2.4-percent growth of electricity consumption. However, it is expected that in the next five years the elasticity of electricity consumption will be reduced to 1.5, resulting in an 11.1-percent annual growth rate for electricity. It is imperative that the electricity sector cut its energy loss as much as possible. The state-owned power company plans, by retiring small-scale inefficient plants, to increase total generation efficiency by about 2 percent, attaining a 37-percent efficiency level by 1986. The company also plans to reduce transmission losses to about 7 percent by 1986.

Conservation in the residential and commercial sectors has long been neglected. The energy plans call for mandatory insulation of new buildings and provide general financial support for retrofitting. Multiple housing structures that have heating systems will be equipped with individually controlled thermostats in each unit. The makers of home appliances will be required to display energy efficiency ratings in order to facilitate consumer selection of high-efficiency home appliances. And the public campaign for conservation will continue.

CONCLUSION

This, then, is Korea's present energy situation and its future energy goals and plans. Although it has not been possible to cover in detail all of the aspects of Korea's energy problems and policies, I hope this has contributed to an understanding of the Korean energy situation, which, as in all countries, is unique in its predicaments and solutions.

Let me conclude by saying that the importance of such a gathering as this International Energy Symposium cannot be overstated. It is through this kind of encounter, where ideas and prospects on universal energy problems are exchanged among different nations, that the valuable purpose of mutual understanding and cooperation, which will ultimately lead to the solution of energy problems, can be realized. I therefore personally hope to see increased opportunities in this area in order to promote international cooperation on energy in the future.

CHAPTER SIXTEEN

The Republic of the Philippines' Renewable Energy Strategy

Pedro Dumol
Executive Director
National Rural Electrification Program
Republic of the Philippines

I represent a developing country which has received both financial and technical assistance from many countries and institutions represented around this table, and for that, I would like to express our gratefulness for your generosity.

Now, to give you some background about the Philippines. The Philippines has 50 million people living in about 8 million houses. We have 30 million hectares of land, of which 10 million are cultivated, another 10 million are still virgin forest, and the remainder are grasslands and denuded forests. The Philippines is blessed with an annual average of about 2,000 hours of sunshine and about 2½ meters—that is, about 100 inches—of rainfall (although many areas have over 5 meters of rainfall per year). We have a considerable geothermal resource supply—one of the highest in the world; we have moderate deposits of low-grade coal; and we have a very limited supply of oil and gas. In 1980, our total commercial energy consumption was 90 million barrels of oil equivalent, of which 80 million was oil—95 percent of it imported. Our oil imports cost approximately 2.5 billion dollars, which is about half the return on our total exports. That, in summary, is our situation and our problem.

Our policy as an immediate or intermediate goal is to shift away from oil. And to do that, we are pushing our geothermal development to the limit; we are pushing our coal plants; we are pushing our hydros—big hydros; and we will commission our first nuclear plant by 1984 or early 1985. We hope to reduce our oil dependence from 83 percent to 50 percent in 1985 and to less than

30 percent by 1990. In our long-range plans, we intend to get away from oil completely through the development of our renewable resources—primarily geothermal, hydro, and dendrothermal. It is on this theme of renewable energy that I would like to speak to you.

First, if we are to get off oil, then we have to consider where the oil is being used. In the Philippines, 25 percent of our oil is used for electricity, about 40 percent is used for transportation, and about 35 percent is used by industry.

In terms of electricity, our total requirement is currently about 3,500 mw, and by the turn of the century, it should be in the vicinity of about 10,000–15,000 mw. But our geothermal resources equal over 10,000 mw; our big hydro resources equal about 10,000 mw; our mini hydro resources equal about 5,000 mw; and our dendrothermal resources are estimated to equal close to 100,000 mw. So, we will have sufficient energy for our electricity needs in the long run.

Now, in transportation, our problem is to replace oil, but we have developed gasifier units that can power our vehicles with wood—I think we are the only country in the world that has a factory for manufacturing gasifiers—and we intend to develop 400,000 of these units within five years. To support this with wood, we have to plant fast-growing trees on about 700,000 hectares within about five years, and that again is a problem which I will touch on further below.

In industry, wood can be used instead of charcoal; charcoal can, of course, be used instead of coal; coal can be used instead of oil—thus, wood can be used instead of charcoal and coal. And so, we think that we can also solve the problem of our industrial requirements by using wood.

Now, let me explain how our wood can be used to generate electricity. We currently have a program for seventy power plants of the 3-mw class. Of these power plants, seventeen are in installation or manufacturing stages. We are going to inaugurate the first plants later this year and proceed at the rate of one power plant per month. The standard 3-mw power plant is supported by 1,000 hectares of tree plantation. These 1,000 hectares are divided into ten modules of 100 hectares each, and each module is owned and operated by a farmers' association of ten families. The power plant is owned by the cooperative and buys its wood from the tree plantation. The power plant also operates a cable way system to bring the wood to the power plant, since in general the power plants are located near rivers while trees are planted in the hills.

This transport system is similar to a ski lift, except that whereas in a ski lift you move people up the hill, in this case you are going to move wood down the hill, and in the process you will generate electricity. We are also going to provide housing for the people who will operate these tree plantations and power plants. Thus, this program of planting trees to generate electricity will reforest our country, save us from buying oil, provide livelihoods, and stabilize our rural areas.

Wood for transportation fuels presents a bigger problem: that of planting about 700,000 hectares to support the gasifier industry. We are approaching this problem in two ways. One is to plant 100 hectares in each municipality so that it can support its local wood requirements. However, the big communities, the big urban centers, will require bigger modules: 500-hectare modules. The wood here will be converted into charcoal for ease of transport.

As I mentioned, the intent of this program is to develop 400,000 gasifier units which will be used for transportation, for irrigation pumps, for fishing boats—at two o'clock, we are launching a fishing boat down on the river here that we brought from the Philippines and that is powered with wood chips. The fuel economy of these wood-fired vehicles is on the order of 1:5 in terms of gasoline—in other words, if you paid $5 for gasoline to go a certain distance, you will pay $1 for the wood, or charcoal, to go the same distance.

That, then, is a brief summary of some key aspects of our renewable energy program. The program is fairly well explained in the books that were distributed to you, and I will be available after this session if you have any questions.

ADDENDUM: THE ASEAN REGION*

I have studied the Association of Southeast Asian Nations (ASEAN) region for decades. I have studied the energy problems of the ASEAN region for the last ten years. For the benefit of those of you less interested in Asian affairs than I am, ASEAN is an organization established in 1967 which includes Indonesia, Malaysia, the Philippines, Singapore, and Thailand. It is a microcosm of the developing world. Two of the countries—Indonesia and Malaysia—export oil and natural gas (Indonesia is the only East Asian member of OPEC). On the other hand, the Philippines and Thailand are both oil-importing

---

*The statement below was volunteered by Dr. Guy J. Pauker following General Pedro Dumol's presentation.

industrializing countries; each currently spends about 2.5 to 3 billion dollars per year on oil imports. Singapore could be described as a mini Japan, with absolutely no natural resources but with a very vigorous economy and a reliance on market forces to cope with the repeated oil price shocks occurring.

What General Pedro Dumol told us a few minutes ago is of great significance, because the Philippines is, in my opinion, a pioneer in trying to break the bondage of oil imports. If that country succeeds in attaining independence from oil used for electricity generation by shifting to coal, geothermal, dendrothermal, and nuclear power plants, and if it also succeeds in reducing its dependence on liquid fuels used for transportation by shifting to car- and boat-mounted gasifiers, and perhaps gasohol at a later point, then it will have shown that at least tropical developing countries can overcome their dependence on imported oil.

The implication of this for the whole world becomes very vivid with just these few figures: at present, Indonesia consumes 450,000 barrels per day of oil; Malaysia, 100,000; the Philippines, 234,000; Thailand, 225,000; and Singapore, about 60,000. To sum up, their total oil consumption is about 1 million barrels per day. Yet these five Asian countries have altogether only about 260 million people, a small fraction of the whole developing world.

Indonesia is an oil exporter that has a production-to-reserve ratio now of about seventeen years—at its present rate of production, for domestic consumption as well as export, it will run out of oil in about seventeen years. Malaysia has a production-to-reserve ratio of twenty-seven years. By the end of the century, then, the two ASEAN oil-producing countries will have run out of oil (although such figures are, of course, rather speculative and controversial, as more oil is likely to be found).

If the current growth figures for energy demand in general and petroleum products in particular continue—and they will for Indonesia at least, as the figures firmly document a demand growth there of about 14 percent per year, or a doubling time of five years, which is a mind-boggling figure—if this continues and there is no transition from oil to other energy sources, by the year 2001 these five countries could require as much as 16 million barrels per day of oil, with no domestic oil production still available to them. Now, let's adjust these figures and assume that the ASEAN countries will be as successful by the year 2000 in reducing their oil dependence as Dr. Ikuta told us Japan hopes to be by the year 1990. If they reduce their oil dependence by 50 percent, they would require 8 million barrels of imported oil per day. If we then keep in mind, as Dr. Fesharaki just mentioned, that by the year 2000, OPEC production is not likely to exceed 30 million barrels per day, then we can see how the ASEAN region, this one small segment of the developing world, could become a very important source of demand pressure on the available oil resources of the world. Therefore, the kind of pioneering efforts that General Dumol told us about have enormous significance, not only for the ASEAN region, where cooperation between these five countries is increasing very markedly in the energy field, but also for the rest of the world.

There are alternative sources of energy that can be developed. Indonesia has perhaps 31,000 MW of ultimate hydro power capacity, of which only 480 MW have been developed; Malaysia, 3,700 MW, of which 265 MW have been developed; the Philippines, perhaps 10,000 MW, of which 933 MW have been developed; Thailand, 17,000 MW, of which only 900 MW have been developed. Altogether, 4 percent of the hydroelectric potential of the ASEAN region is developed.

The coal resources there are also substantial. Indonesia may have as much as 18 billion tons of coal, of which quite a lot is poor-quality lignite but 150 million tons are proven reserves of good quality. Malaysia has almost half a billion tons in reserves; the Philippines, almost a billion tons; Thailand, over half a billion tons. Coal use could be developed, perhaps by first building up the infrastructure through the imaginative Philippine proposal for a concessional export program from the United States, Australia, and other major coal-producing countries to the oil-importing developing countries for the purpose of replacing oil with coal for power generation.

IESS Communiqué: Process and Result

Editors' Note

As explained in the Preface, a central outcome of the Symposia Series was to be a communiqué suggesting ways to help manage the world's energy problem. Although presented at the close of Symposium III, the communiqué was to represent the approach of not only that conference but also its two predecessors. It was thus to be an amalgam that, at Symposium III, would be accepted by informal consensus.

Partly by design and partly de facto, the final communiqué (see chap. 19) evolved through an iterative process. As a springboard for discussion, a draft communiqué was prepared by a small committee of participants who, by virtue of their early and continuing association with the Series, could bring an integrative perspective to the statement. The draft was then presented at a plenary session of Symposium III on the afternoon of Wednesday, May 26, after which the draft was the subject of full debate by the Symposium III participants. This debate resulted in a sense that substantial changes in the draft were needed. Responding to the comments that had been made, a revised approach was proposed at the end of the discussion period; refined by the drafting committee; further discussed at a late-afternoon ad hoc session of Symposium III participants; and turned into document form for S. H. Roberts, Jr., who, as President of The 1982 World's Fair, was to deliver the final communiqué. He reviewed the document, primarily for its clarity and concision, and then presented it at the Symposium's closing session on the morning of May 27, 1982, at which time copies were released to the press and the public.

Two factors complicated the above process, at times threatening to irrevocably disrupt it but in the end adding to its dynamism. First, there was an implacable paradox due to timing: the final communiqué was intended to integrate the sense of all three Symposia, yet the third Symposium had just gotten under way as the draft was being prepared. And second, as noted in the Preface, some of Symposium III's participants had attended the prior Symposia, but many were new to the Series and held quite different views from former participants. Thus, there was to some extent a gap between the ideology developed during the first two Symposia—an ideology which necessarily formed the context for the draft communiqué—and the ideology developed at Symposium III.

This ideological gap can be seen in Chapter Eighteen, where comments from the Wednesday afternoon discussion session have been selected to show the diverse reactions to the draft. But those reactions, while not always favorable, proved to be extremely valuable, as did the whole evolutionary process of the communiqué: the comments are evidence that *conflict resolution by discussion can work.* They thereby exhibit one of the most striking and admirable aspects of Symposium III—the way in which the conference participants, individually and collectively, were able to move through conflict to coalescence, and do so in a remarkably short time.

To all those who contributed to the final communiqué's development, both directly at Symposium III and by providing a context at Symposia I and II, thanks are extended. And to William E. Fulkerson, who presented the draft communiqué, and Ishrat H. Usmani, who moderated the subsequent plenary session discussion, a special note of appreciation is due for all their contributions to the communiqué and the Series as a whole. Finally, the support and understanding of S. H. Roberts, Jr., in terms of both the communiqué and the Series, should not pass without recognition: his efforts on the Symposia's behalf made possible the results they have achieved.

CHAPTER SEVENTEEN

Draft Communiqué*

PREAMBLE

"Energy is the Spirit, and the Spirit is with us." We all have an inner energy which, when called upon, is manifested by imagination, creativity, and courage. In this age of technical miracles and enormous disparity among nations, one of the compelling challenges and opportunities is to focus that inner energy on international problems and the attainment of cooperation. And one of the most persistent of problems is and will remain energy.

Understanding of energy—not only energy technology but energy's social, economic, and environmental ramifications and the pervasive influence of time—has improved enormously over the past decade. This World's Fair is testimony to that new understanding.

However, the full extent of our options and of the constraints under which they operate, including the fact that there are no technological panaceas, is still being revealed—a continuing process. This Symposia Series therefore holds no sudden revelations, but it does offer the opportunity in a unique context to rethink, relearn, reaffirm . . . and also to move toward consensus and recommendations.

In doing this, we must remember that energy is only a part of a larger problem—lagging economic progress, degrading environments, political instability, and the consequent risk of war—but, partial though the world's energy problem is, it must be addressed in the context of these larger issues. We must also remember that there is no universal, final answer to either the larger problem or the energy problem—instead, we are and will be continually faced with choices resulting in wise or unwise decisions. Finally, we

*As noted in this section's introduction, the draft communiqué was prepared by a small group of participants at Symposium III and was presented by Dr. William E. Fulkerson to a plenary session of the Symposium on the afternoon of May 26, 1982.

must remember that energy choices must consider both the resources available and the demands on them, now and in the future—and, hardest of all, must consider these things in terms of both immediate and long-term, local and global concerns.

FINDINGS

The world's population of nearly 4½ billion can be expected to nearly double in the next half century. Demand for the services which energy provides can also be expected to rise on a global scale, especially because of the need for dramatic improvement in living conditions in the less developed countries. Thus, it is likely that more energy will be needed in the future, a situation which requires both more energy production and higher energy productivity.

We are not running out of energy but, despite temporary oil gluts, fossil fuels cannot last indefinitely, will be precarious because of political uncertainty, and, during the transition to sustainable energy systems, will become more expensive and may provoke more environmental problems. Furthermore, this transition will not come easily; inertia must be overcome to realize sustainable energy systems. And throughout, now and in the future, it must be kept in mind that all of our actions have side effects, sooner or later, across space and across time: this is the tragedy of the commons.

No two nations are alike. The world offers rich variety, but it also holds tremendous inequity and strife—inequity in the distribution of natural resources and technological advances, strife from the attempt to get what one doesn't have in order to develop economically, or simply keep from slipping backwards. And today's less industrialized energy-deficit countries have a particular handicap in this development: they do not have the cheap, high-grade fuels that were abundantly available to countries which achieved industrialization in the past.

This situation illustrates an important point: although it is each nation's responsibility to address its energy problem, the management of that problem inevitably and appropriately involves ties with other nations. These ties, or interdependencies, must be assumed with caution, but they should not be rejected out of hand. Energy interdependence only means national vulnerability when it entails too great a risk to supply security or national sovereignty; it otherwise can contribute to energy self-reliance, by attaining a more diverse network of resources than might otherwise be possible.

Furthermore, there is cause for optimism: confronted with the energy problem, human ingenuity is achieving technical, social, economic, and environmental adaptions and innovations. In particular, energy productivity has increased much more rapidly than expected and holds the possibility of greater end-use efficiencies in the future.

There has also been a revolution in other aspects of the energy equation's demand side: a remarkably rapid and effective response to rising prices. This response shows the possibility of both self-imposed restraint in energy use and the partial replaceability of energy with other production factors.

Taken together, these trends hold particular promise for the less developed countries. Such countries now have the possibility of avoiding their energy handicaps: they may be able to bypass the traditional phase of energy intensiveness in development, using less energy as their economies develop than was feasible in the formative stages of the now-industrialized countries. However, realizing this possibility will require special assistance, which will take special multilateral relationships.

Some steps have already been taken to facilitate international cooperation and attain a sense of global interdependence, but in many instances these relationships need further development. Nevertheless, there is reason to think that this can be achieved. As this Symposia Series has shown, there is a deepening understanding of the global energy problem's complex nature and of the need for integrated approaches to its management at international as well as national levels. This understanding has shaped our process and its outcome.

CONCLUSIONS AND RECOMMENDATIONS

The first two Symposia attempted to identify and then to analyze the issues surrounding the world's energy problem. From this process, the third Symposium has tried to draw conclusions—conclusions which are embodied in this communiqué and which represent not formal positions of the participants' native countries, but a consensus of the IESS participants themselves. And this consensus should be taken in the spirit that, although not all agree with all that is said, there is sufficient support for the points covered here to adopt the text as a whole. It should be remembered that the conclusions set out below are not exhaustive; many other meritorious points were brought out and are recorded in the *Proceedings* of the Symposia. But the following conclusions, in particular, convey our sense, derived from the Symposia Series as a whole, of some directions in which we should be moving to deal with the world's energy problem.

It is, of course, each nation's right and responsibility to deal with its own unique energy situation in the way it deems best. There is no perfect, universally applicable energy technology (or approach). Each country must seek the system of energy supply and use which is deemed best for it, and the situation will change over time. An appropriate mix will provide resilience to accommodate change and uncertainty and to protect against contingencies. Furthermore, actions by one nation may affect others both because of the way energy is used and because of the influence of these actions on world energy markets.

Therefore, each nation should carefully assess and audit its energy situation on a continual basis and develop its strategy with due consideration not only to its own opportunities, constraints (e.g., technological, resource, social, environmental), and desires for its future, but also with due concern for the impact of that strategy on other nations. And in this assessment, planning and policymaking cooperation between nations can help through technical assistance, exchange of information and methods of analysis, training, and directed cooperative research.

As a moral and humanitarian principle, and from pure practicality—when one is better off, all are better off—countries should adopt attitudes that go beyond purely national concerns. In particular, industrialized countries should assist less industrialized countries, especially the extremely poor ones, to improve their lots, particularly regarding energy. And furthermore, all countries, especially those that are better off, should pay particular attention to ameliorating or avoiding the long-term environmental or other disruptive effects of high energy use. We do not own the earth absolutely, but only as stewards.

Normal market mechanisms do not directly deal with these necessary matters, leaving governmental, intergovernmental, and nongovernmental organizations as possible effective institutions. We recommend the strengthening of the international institutions via formation of regional organizations, global ones such as UN specialized agencies, and international nongovernmental organizations with substantial dedication to dealing with these long-term and equity issues.

Other recommendations that came out in the past Symposia related particularly to the problems of the less developed countries. These are encapsulated in the following points.

- The high cost of oil has had a profound impact on the economies of all countries, but it is having a devastating effect on the very poor, energy-deficit countries. An extraordinary international effort should be mounted, ensuring massive financial and technical assistance flowing from the groups of countries which are energy rich and/or technology rich to the very poor, energy-deficit nations. This would be a sort of Marshall Plan type effort. For this purpose an experimental program spread over five years in several poor, energy deficit countries of Asia, Africa, and Latin America should be launched so that the impact and cost effectiveness of such an international effort can be monitored and evaluated.
- While there has been progressive liberalization of trade, there still exist barriers to imports by the industrialized nations that impede exports from developing countries. This is especially troublesome in a period of economic tightness when protectionism is apt to make headway. Removal of remaining trade barriers is an urgent necessity.
- The present geographic distribution of oil production would suggest that most of the developing energy-deficit countries have no oil occurrence. This is not likely to be true, but it will take both financial and technical assistance from OPEC and industrialized nations to explore and test the assumption.
- Provision of capital for the developed countries has become increasingly complicated because the terms for investment in the countries are unattractive and the security of capital and return not assured. Yet foreign investment in the developing countries, in energy as well as generally, can bring substantial benefits. At the same time, OPEC countries complain that developed countries do not provide incentives for investment of OPEC surplus balances, especially in a period of high inflation. In both instances it is highly important that governments endeavor to improve the investment climate.
- The potential for nuclear proliferation constitutes a potent impediment to expanded use of that energy source. While at least one control mechanism now exists, it is limited in scope, and its effectiveness has been challenged. Apart from revitalizing it, other paths should be pursued such as different nuclear reactor systems that greatly reduce the attendant proliferation potential.

Solar resources have been utilized for centuries (some for millenia) and provide primary energy for perhaps half of the present world population. Today they continue to provide the best energy hope for the future for billions of people. It is very fortunate, if not providential, that ecological sciences and the development of biotechnology are moving so rapidly, because they provide real cause for optimism for substantial advances in how we use the sun. Different nations have different things to contribute to a cooperative effort, including plant materials (e.g., seeds) as well as technical expertise. We identified several actions that merit pursuit in this regard.

- International cooperative actions to identify, collect, and preserve plant species as a "bank" of biochemical producers—relevant not only to energy but also to food, chemicals, and fiber.
- Establish a new institute (or a new mission in existing institutions) to apply new biotechnology methods to improve biomass and to increase international cooperation in developing ecological systems analysis methods to enable multiple plant, multiproduct biomass production. This cooperation can be critically important in anticipating and avoiding potential energy/food/fiber/chemicals conflicts.
- Establish and support pilot "village-level" energy systems in poor rural areas with the aim of providing basic amenities such as illumination, food refrigeration, communications, and water. Priorities should be given to using local fuel resources with high efficiency and to developing methods that are widely transferable.

There was almost universal agreement that, for developed countries and less developed countries alike, energy productivity (the efficiency of energy use) can and should be significantly increased in most human activities, and it can be increased in ways which are economically justified. This is an area ripe for productive international cooperation and the development of new markets and opportunities for private investments. Nations should accelerate this trend toward increased energy productivity by appropriate pricing or equivalent policies, by encouraging technology and information transfer, and by supporting research.

Finally, there were a series of conclusions and recommendations related to expanding or at least continuing the efforts of communication and interaction begun at these Symposia.

- The spirit of these International Energy Symposia should be continued through meetings convening biennially in Knoxville to evaluate successes and failures in managing the world energy problem. Such a series would encourage further dispassionate, careful thinking and would be a permanent memorial to the efforts of The 1982 World's Fair to promote international understanding and cooperation. The first meeting of this continued series, held in 1984, should be devoted to the topic, "Managing the Energy Transition." It is proposed that a secretariat be established and housed in the current US Pavilion and that it be supported by a perpetual endowment, perhaps including contributions from the anticipated profits of The 1982 World's Fair plus other public and private sources.

- The need exists for an international energy organization to collect, analyze, and distribute information and to institute programs of research and education, particularly between the developed and developing nations. Some of the areas of study and investigation that have been proposed for such an institute are (1) biomass technology, (2) energy planning and forecasting, (3) energy requirements of urban and rural social systems in both industrialized and industrializing countries, (4) fuel mix transitions, and (5) tragedy of the commons issues. But perhaps the organization should begin with the problem of efficiency improvement, since there is universal agreement about the need. The organization might be housed in the current US Pavilion at The 1982 World's Fair, a logical extension of its current use as a demonstration of the Fair's theme, "Energy Turns the World."

- The findings and recommendations of these Symposia should be forwarded to appropriate governments, international organizations, and private entities.

Participants from many nations, reflecting an extraordinary diversity of economic status, resource availability, technological sophistication, and political systems, have contributed to these Symposia. The commonality of views on energy issues has been remarkable. Although national problems differ, the fundamental challenge is strongly shared—so strongly that more extensive international cooperation and the continuation of dialogues such as these are imperative if the nations of the world are to achieve the goal of a just and sustainable energy future.

CHAPTER EIGHTEEN

Selected Comments

ALVIN M. WEINBERG

As I read this elegantly phrased and perceptive document, I am concerned whether, in fact, it represents a full consensus or even an adequate consensus of what was presented during the three Symposia. It is my impression that the document is very strongly influenced by those members of the Symposium who basically believe that the world's energy salvation is to be found in the sun. I don't think that this represents the views of many of the representatives around this table, and I very much hope that the final document will somehow place in better perspective and put in better balance the role of the sun, even for the underdeveloped countries.

As it stands, I think that if I were a representative of an underdeveloped country I would take profound issue with this document, because in saying that the underdeveloped countries must depend upon the sun, we are almost surely committing those underdeveloped countries to a future of unmitigated poverty. For example, at the beginning it is stated that "such countries now have the possibility of avoiding their energy handicap: they may be able to bypass the traditional phase of energy intensiveness and development, using less energy as their economies develop than was feasible in the formative stages of now-industrialized countries." I don't think very many representatives of underdeveloped countries would concede that their countries' paths of development are going to be so totally different from those of the developed countries, and indeed, if you look at the four countries that have moved most strongly from a state of great underdevelopment toward development—Korea, Taiwan, Hong Kong, Singapore—this is not the path that they have followed.

Then, when one looks at the energy production modalities that are proposed, I find one short and very pessimistic paragraph about the possibilities of rectifying nuclear energy problems—pessimistic even for those countries that are capable of using nuclear energy on a very wide scale and thereby reducing the pressure on the other energy modalities—and for countries not prepared for nuclear energy I find the statement, "They [solar resources] continue to provide the best energy hope for the future for billions of people." I would say that if this is the best energy hope for billions of people, then there is little hope for billions of people. And I don't think that we ought to concede that point; I don't think that that is really the sense of this Symposium.

Again, it states, "It is very fortunate, if not providential, that ecological sciences and the development of biotechnology are moving so rapidly, because they provide real cause for optimism for substantial advances on how we use the sun." Was that really brought out in this Symposium? Do most of the representatives around this table concede that this in fact represents the situation in ecology and biotechnology? I would like to have that explained before I, for example, would be able to sign that statement.

ULF LANTZKE

I want to speak on language. I want to make a few remarks about the balance of this document. I have a very strong feeling that if the balance of this document isn't better struck, it will be very difficult to achieve even a consensus view. In the conclusions—and I am not talking about the preamble or findings; I am talking about the conclusions and recommendations—if the major conclusions of this Symposia Series were restricted to what we have before us now, I am afraid the Symposium would have missed the whole point that the energy problem poses.

First, the document in its concrete conclusions deals nearly exclusively with the situation in developing countries. That is an important issue, but it is not the most important one, because I don't think we can manage the energy problem if industrialized countries don't take on themselves the burden of restructuring their energy economies—and that is even, in my view, the most important issue for developing countries. I think that we would miss the whole point if we didn't say that.

Second, in the document's choice of examples, we are given biomass and solar. I would fully agree with Dr. Weinberg that this distorts the overall picture. I think the consensus view in this room would be that at least until the end of the century there will be only four important energy sources—five, if you like. The first is oil; second, coal; third, nuclear; fourth, gas; and fifth, if you like, hydro. Those are the ones which are really important, and I think that is a second point which should be made if you want to reach consensus over this document.

Third, the choice of concrete proposals. In relation to developing countries, the first priority, in my view, would still be the deforestation or firewood problem. The second would be, probably, that of energy supplies in rural areas. And the third would certainly be what is the action catalogue from the Nairobi conference—the analysis of developing countries' problems and the development of solutions to those problems.

Only if you follow that course do I feel that you would strike an overall balance which would do justice to what this Symposium has been all about and to what has been said here. With that, I have been too long, but this is a very difficult problem that I bring to the floor, and I thought I should do it at an early stage.

GUY J. PAUKER

First, I would like to ask whether this document is supposed to carry the signatures and therefore the formal endorsement of all of us. If it is to be signed only by its authors, then in some ways I don't feel very strongly about it. However I, like so many others in this room, have given quite a lot of time to this Symposia Series over the past two and one-half years, and I therefore have some feelings about it.

I am not prepared to endorse this document in the form in which it is written. I am not discussing its literary quality or the spiritual values it embodies. I think that, as Dr. Weinberg also said, it is substantively very misleading. I question in particular the statement already cited by Dr. Weinberg: "Today they [solar resources] continue to provide the best energy hope for the future for billions of people." I think this is grossly misleading, and I do not want to be associated with it.

Furthermore, I think I owe it to all of us to ask those who drafted this document what its purpose is. If it is meant to be included in the final volume of this Series' *Proceedings*, then it has one purpose, and the more philosophical it is—the more spiritually uplifting—the better, because it will be in a book and will have lasting value, and God knows that we all need a bit more uplift. The Platonist spirit or the spirit of St. John pervading the preamble's first paragraph is certainly very welcome in that light. But it is not welcome if the document is intended to give these Symposia wider publicity, by being picked up by the wire agencies, because the wire agencies will not pick up Platonist statements since the agencies do not regard them as newsworthy.

Therefore, if you just want a very fitting conclusion to a volume which, judging from the previous two, will be of very high quality—and I want to compliment the editors for what they have been able to do after the October, 1980, and November, 1981, Symposia—this document could if anything be expanded in terms of its spirit, its concept. But if you also wish to catch the attention of the media, the newspapers, and so on, then may I suggest, with all due respect for those who drafted this document, that it does not have a single catch phrase which would make a newspaper editor want to even recognize that these Symposia have occurred. Now, there are others that are, I am sure, much more talented than I am in public relations, but I wanted to raise this issue, because I think it is an important one.

As far as the content is concerned, I think that Dr. Lantzke expressed so well most of what I would have said that I can save you any further comments on the substance of the document per se as it addresses the energy problem.

ISHRAT H. USMANI

First of all, I would like to say that consensus does not mean unanimity. In a diverse group such as this, there will never be unanimity. You can always reserve your position if you disagree with a particular conclusion. In any case, there is no compulsion for anyone to sign on the "dotted line." What I wish to see is whether there is a general consensus on the spirit behind the document. Although not all of us may agree with everything that is said in the final document, there should be sufficient support for the points covered here to adopt the text as it emerges. That is all. I don't think the organizers of the Symposia Series expected anything more from us.

At this point, it might be a good idea to call upon Jack Gibbons, the chairman of the IESS Program Committee, to say a few words on the whole issue of this document before us.

JOHN H. GIBBONS

I want to respond to some of the important points made so far this afternoon.

One is that as I look at this text in the light of these discussions, there are several things which we who drafted it took implicitly but which clearly need to be made more explicit. For example, consider Dr. Lantzke's point about where the major energy sources are to be derived over the next twenty years or more: it strikes me that there's such a universal agreement about that matter that it scarcely needs to be said. But these discussions make it clear that we need to make that agreement more explicit.

I think there are some other words that we should readdress carefully. For example, consider Alvin Weinberg's concern about the paragraph regarding the developing countries' ability to bypass the traditional phase of energy intensity in their economic development. This was the notion that one can introduce, with the assistance of nations that have already been through it, means for improving energy productivity (that is, lower energy intensiveness in the development of an economy). I have spent a number of weeks, Alvin, in developing countries, witnessing them bypass the peak of energy intensiveness that America went through in its course of industrialization. They are doing this by using the technology available from around the world. We must be more careful with our words. I believe you were trying to make the same point that we were attempting to make. The point is valid; I've been there; I know it happens. And I think it has come out in many instances at these Symposia that the new paths of development don't have to follow the old paths of high energy intensiveness. The old paths are more expensive paths. Goods and services can be provided with half or less of the energy intensiveness that was required in the United States. That is the message that was intended.

The complaint about the short paragraph on nuclear energy is appropriate, I think. It seems to me that what's needed is an expansion of thought—a more careful introduction to the nuclear options than is in the draft's conclusions and recommendations.

Dr. Pauker asked about the intent of this communication. I think the intent should be defined by ourselves. The draft is an attempt to wrestle with all of the things that have come before the many participants of these Symposia representing many nations and points of view—an attempt to distill from these many papers and discussions some meaningful statement, if for no one else than ourselves, about what we find at the close of these three Symposia.

I will only repeat that there are some things that are quite well understood, accepted, and therefore implicit in energy discussions that were not intended to be brought out explicitly in the draft document—rather, it looks to the next step. Judging from the discussions today, that may be a basic fault which will need some more work this afternoon and tonight.

PETER S. VAN NORT

I'd like to make three points.

The first is that I believe this document should be responsive to what one perceives the press is going to do with it. These *Proceedings* will never make the light of day as far as public discussion is concerned, and so whatever we want the world to know about this Symposium is going to have to be carried in this communiqué. And in that context, Jack, I think it's very important that we include the things that we believe are well understood and implicit, because some people do not know those things. As you and I are aware, the media in the United States will distort to the maximum extent possible what we say in here. If we leave out something implicit, like the comment about the four major sources of power, that won't ever appear. I think it's important to recognize that.

I think we also need to define in this document what we're about. The problem that we're addressing doesn't jump out at you in it. I was not at Symposia I and II, but my review of their *Proceedings* indicates that we ought to be able to define the problem. I think one of the issues is clearly the long-term availability of oil, which is the basic foundation of everybody's energy economy. We've got to deal with that problem, and you can't find that in here in a blaring headline, but it seems to me that one is needed. So, a definition of the problem is important.

The draft also immediately jumps to the term "transition," and again, I am not sure that anybody is going to know what we mean by "transition" without some statement about what that is. General Dumol from the Philippines described his country's transition [chap. 16]; other people have described their countries' transitions—this document just talks about it.

The last point I would like to make is to pick up on a comment that Mrs. Marcos made at the end of her keynote address [chap. 1].

She said, "I hope God does bless America, because as He does He blesses us all." Everybody who has spoken here today has talked about the plans their countries have for energy. The United States has no such plan. I believe that if we agree with what Mrs. Marcos said, one of the things this Symposium should say up front is that the United States in its leadership position had better get its act together or the rest of the world's countries are going to be in trouble. Now, I'm an American saying that, and I won't fight for that if other countries don't feel that way. But if you do, I think it is important that that come out of this Symposium—that somebody say to the United States, "For God's sake, get with it, or you're going to take us all down with you."

MARCELO ALONSO

Of course, I recognize that the effort which has gone into preparing this document is tremendous, and the authors deserve our recognition. But there are some things which I believe require further consideration.

First, I believe that the document does not reflect clearly the energy problems we face ahead in the short term. For example, as Dr. Lantzke very correctly pointed out, at this moment we cannot hope to use any other energy sources for the next twenty years— substantially, I mean—except the five he mentioned. This understanding is very important, because it will help to enlighten people. Then, we can supplement that understanding by saying, "Nevertheless, we have to make even more serious efforts to develop alternative energy sources." And the alternatives are not just biomass, which is the only one mentioned here; the alternatives include improving the use of those energy sources we now use.

How can we use existing energy sources in a better way? One tactic, of course, is "move away from oil." Well, that is easier said than done. I heard M. Rimareix with interest today—I asked him a question, and I must say that I am not fully satisfied with his answer, because I don't think you can do in ten years what he said France is going to do to improve its energy elasticity and energy efficiency.

So, I think we should put into proper perspective the problems we are facing as a world—not just as developed or less developed countries or as industrialized or less industrialized countries. And I want to make the suggestion that we do so.

I also think that in Symposium II, through the efforts of the work sessions, a great number of ideas about more specific problems we are facing—let's say in biomass; let's say in nuclear power; and so on—emerged. I think that we should inform people of how we have looked at those problems.

I agree that we have to define better what we mean by "energy transition." We should not leave those terms dangling. By "energy transition," do we mean we are not going to use oil or do we mean we are just going to depend on the sun? I think that we need to be more specific.

Another point of a general nature that is missing here is the role of government. This document should consider that somewhere. It is in the technical paper [chap. 3], and I think it should be emphasized here.

The problem of adjusting demand is another problem that is not fully mentioned here. We have a social responsibility to help people use energy in an improved way—I don't know which improved way, but reorienting demand is a problem that is not even touched on in the document.

In addition to that, I have some suggestions about some of the document's terminology and paragraphs—suggestions which I have already passed to those who undertook this excellent effort for their consideration—so I won't take your time with that now.

DENIS J. IVES

Some of the points that I'm interested in have already been touched on, but they are points of substance and I do want to emphasize them for the record.

The first point I want to raise is that there doesn't seem to be enough recognition in this document that progress with adjustment to a better energy mix is being made, and quite considerable progress has been made. That needs to be recognized, and I'll separately provide some specific words to suggest on that.

A further point, also of substance, under the conclusions and recommendations: first of all, conventional energy resources available at reasonable costs have been expanded considerably in recent years, a fact which is not sufficiently recognized in the document and which indicates that conventional energy sources in general have been neglected there.

Similarly, I think that, like it or not, the evidence at this Symposium is that many countries are devoting increasing attention and emphasis to the use of the market mechanism, and that's not mentioned anywhere in the document. Now, I am sure we are not going to reach a total consensus on that point, but there is a factual position that many countries are devoting increasing attention to the use of that mechanism.

The next point I wish to raise concerns the first bullet point under the list of other recommendations for less developed countries. I am surprised that some other speakers haven't already commented on this. There is a real headline-grabbing proposal set out there—a proposal which has been given very little attention or very little discussion—but if you want to know what will appear in the international wire services, it's probably that point. Is this Symposium really proposing an extraordinary international effort with massive financial and technical assistance of a Marshall Plan type? I haven't heard that in the last couple of days, and I don't want to be negative about the concept of cooperation; I think that there is a need to work with our colleagues in developing countries. But I am not at all convinced that the proposal spelled out here for consensus support is at all what we have discussed in recent days.

And finally, I lend my support to the comments that have been made about solar and the reference to its being the best energy hope for billions of people. I don't think that is a satisfactory or reasonable statement.

In conclusion, I'd be inclined to say that there does seem to be a consensus about a communiqué, but it doesn't seem to be this one. Instead, we need one that picks up most of the points which have already been mentioned in the last half hour. It seems to me that many of the comments that have been made today reinforce one another and do suggest a consensus.

KEICHI OSHIMA

Most of the things I was going to say have been said already, but I would like to repeat them for emphasis.

As Dr. Gibbons said, some things that are well understood have not been made explicit in the draft communiqué. Nevertheless, some important issues should be stressed there. For example, the effort to solve energy problems, especially in the industrialized countries, is not as vigorous as before—it's slowing down in some countries. One thing which should be repeatedly emphasized is that the industrialized countries' efforts to use energy rationally and to exploit new energy sources are important not only to them but also to the whole world, because those countries are the largest energy resource consumers.

My second point refers to the conventional energy resources already mentioned by several people. First, I fully endorse what Dr. Lantzke said about the major alternatives to oil being nuclear and coal, not solar and biomass, and I think this has to be put in the document somewhere. But I especially want to say one thing about nuclear. This document seems to say that because of the risk of nuclear weapons proliferation, the countries which have nuclear power should consider nonproliferation as a first priority. If that is the case, it can lead to the conclusion that the only countries to use nuclear power will be advanced industrialized countries. As you saw in this morning's presentations, most of the advanced countries are pursuing nuclear power very aggressively, but I think it would be inappropriate for nuclear power's benefits to be restricted to them. Instead, there should be more emphasis on how all available energy resources (in this case, nuclear) can be used by developing countries in appropriate ways—although not necessarily in the same ways that they are used in the highly industrialized countries, with their higher energy consumption levels. One specific point—and this was discussed very little at this Symposium—is that some kind of regional collaboration can help solve this problem. For example, the possibility of some form of regional collaboration on nuclear power is already being explored in the Pacific region.

In conclusion, I just want to emphasize that traditional energy resources, if they are appropriately adjusted to a country's needs and used with technical and financial collaboration or assistance, will be much more advantageous for the development of the less industrialized countries than some renewables such as solar, biomass, and wind.

ULRICH ENGELMANN

The problem of this document is that it is a mixture of findings, facts, and considerations and political recommendations, and the last are one-sided. This is the problem of this communiqué, and I have great difficulties with this approach to the international energy problem.

Take the preamble, for example. If the message to the public is that energy is a global problem; that it is linked with other problems, at least with sound economic development; that no group of countries can be excluded; and that the developed countries, the oil-producing countries, and the developing countries have a common responsibility—then this is not the message spelled out. Read naively, the preamble gives the impression that there is a problem which has no structure and is not manageable and that we are in danger of making unwise decisions.

The reality is otherwise. It is the common opinion, in the meantime, that we are on the right track: there is increasing understanding between the oil-producing countries and the developed countries; the developed countries have adopted similar policy lines—namely, to adapt their structures, save energy, find substitutes for oil, and develop other energy resources supplies; and there is agreement that oil-importing developing countries have a special problem. The first message should be that the global energy problem is being managed, that progress is being made in different policy categories.

And there again, I have difficulties understanding the balance of the document. For example, I have difficulty understanding the statement that in principle the market-oriented approach is not suited to the energy problem. Who can change the picture and therefore solve the energy problem? In this document it is not mentioned that those who can change the picture are investors, consumers, and then governments. What we should recommend is that the consumers go ahead with their policy of saving energy and using substitutes for oil. In addition, we must ask the investors to invest in alternative energy supplies, especially in nuclear and coal and perhaps in new technologies. From this paper, people may get the impression that it's only up to international institutions and governments to change the picture. The reality is that the economic forces are in the process of changing the energy structure. The role of governments is to support that and to give the investors and consumers room to maneuver.

I also have difficulty in seeing that an energy symposium should take up the subject of trade barriers. I know from international discussions what a problem that is and that it is not only a problem of energy. Thus, I don't think it fits into the scope of this document.

I have similar problems accepting the proliferation issue as the impediment for adopting nuclear power. In West Germany the impediment is the public resistance in terms of safety and in terms of what happens with radioactive waste disposal; the problem is not proliferation, since West Germany does not have atomic weapons. So I think that the proliferation subject is much too complicated to be incorporated here in such a short document.

I also find it unrealistic for the Symposium to make proposals concerning new institutions, Marshall Plans, and other such things. This opens the door to unrealistic expectations. What we are doing in international energy cooperation is increasing multilateral aid and bilateral aid. However, no one is in favor of new institutions, and I would like to warn the Symposium against taking up this subject.

So, coming to the end, my feeling is more that the final communiqué could be a collection of headlines, but as far as political recommendations are concerned, I think it is impossible to get a balanced consensus in this circle here.

DAVID LE B. JONES

Could I say first that, having attended two of these Symposia, I think those who prepared this draft have done a very good job on a very difficult and intractable problem. Despite the criticisms which have been made, we should recognize this. The main problem with this sort of communiqué is to strike the appropriate balance between meaningless generalizations and highly specific and political recommendations with which it would be difficult for some of us to concur—particularly those of us who come from governments. I think it is, in fact, possible to strike that balance, but in a slightly different way from what this draft does. In the hope that it will move things forward, I would like to put some suggestions as to the sort of points which I think the communiqué should make, which I think it would be useful to make, and on which I think we could agree.

First, the communiqué should state very firmly that energy is still a problem and that it still matters. The problem hasn't gone away because the oil market is temporarily easy. Now, that is recognized in the preamble, but it is recognized in a very long-term sense about fossil fuels eventually running out and so on. We should also bring out the short-term risks of the situation and the need to see that energy does not again become a constraint on economic growth throughout the world in the way that it did in 1979 and 1980. That's the first point.

The second point I would like to see made is Hans Landsberg's from yesterday: that we are dealing with a problem and not a crisis, that we are managing a process and not a situation. That is an important message to get across.

Third, we should recognize that energy is a world issue which the oil producers, the industrialized countries, and the oil-importing developing countries all have a common interest in solving—for different reasons, but all basically pointing to the same solution.

Fourth, in looking at solutions, we should recognize as the draft does that each country will have to deal with its own situation in its own way. I also think we should recognize the need for the five elements which Dr. Lantzke brought out and not have quite the degree of emphasis on the sun which is in this draft.

Fifth, I think we should say that governments alone cannot deal with this problem and solve it. I don't think we should necessarily talk about the market, because some of those present do not come from wholly market economies. But one of our nonmarket-economy friends yesterday talked about the right division of responsibility between governments and companies. It's a question of governments, companies, and individuals working within a policy framework which will produce the right answer.

Finally, I personally would prefer to see omitted the specific recommendations about institutions, a massive new aid program, and so on. But if that causes difficulty with some members of the Symposium, then perhaps it could be somehow expressed in terms such as "among the suggestions which were made but which did not necessarily command the support of the Symposium as a whole were *a, b,* and *c.*"

That's the sort of approach which I would like to see to the communiqué. I think it would get across some valuable points on which we would be able to agree.

Finally, two specific comments. I agree with Denis Ives about the danger of headlines on this new Marshall Plan, although I was happy to hear from the version that was read that the sentence about the Marshall Plan seems to have disappeared. But I think the risk is still there, and we need to be careful about it. And I agree very much with Ulrich Engelmann that the paragraph about trade barriers, which has not got a great deal to do with energy, or at least directly with energy, should come out.

HANS H. LANDSBERG

I have been listening very carefully, because against my better judgment I have been involved in this effort, and I would like to make a few comments which I hope will be helpful. It's all right to dream the impossible dream, but it is very difficult to draft the impossible draft, and that's what we have been trying to do.

I am very much taken by what David Jones has been saying. It does mean one turns out something that is two or three pages and not twelve and that stays fairly general but makes a few points. There's a problem which we have never resolved—whether, in fact, such a communiqué is a good idea. There has been discussion about it, and it's certainly an open question. There are many reasons for this. The first is that we are trying to reach out to two past Symposia. The people who have been working the hardest on the draft have combed through the *Proceedings* of Symposia I and II and have pulled out ideas that were in there. We are not simply summarizing what has happened during the last two days—nothing of the sort. We are trying to summarize what has happened over a period of two years—a period in which, I must remind you, the parameters of the situation have drastically changed. So it is a very, very difficult thing to convey the sense of some degree of consensus here.

Now, we have tried in the document as it stands to qualify that consensus precisely because we have no formal voting structure; we have no structure at all. And what we have been saying in the document is that nobody necessarily agrees with every point but enough agree with the general orientation to give their approval. That is about the best one can do, and sometimes it works and sometimes it doesn't. I do think the situation is particularly difficult for people who have official positions in their governments, and if I did I would have a lot of trouble committing myself to even one sentence that I knew was anathema to my government, my party, or whatever. That is a real problem. Therefore, if we go the Jones way we might be able to avoid that, and I, for one—and again, I am only one of several—I don't know what we will do come five o'clock, when the redrafting begins, but I think that's a possible way to avoid a great many difficulties.

There's also a question of "credibility" here, if you want to use that awful word (I have used it now). Namely, there will be no chance after we leave this room to discuss this draft all over again. So it is important that the people who have been working on it take note of the points being made, as they have been doing since we started here this afternoon—and I fortunately have found very few points with which I would have any trouble, beginning with the remarks that Alvin Weinberg made or that Ulf Lantzke made. And I think Jack Gibbons was quite right; one falls into a trap here. Some things seem so obvious that one doesn't want to put them in—whether or not the press picks up the communiqué, I don't really care—but these points are so obvious that one forgets about them, and this does badly distort the balance. Now, as one looks at the communiqué—as I look at it—it is quite obvious that what has been omitted ought to be said, because people from the outside will read it, and say, "What is the matter with these people? Don't they understand?" In fact, I think that in the paper we presented, the so-called technical paper, there were some paragraphs about what we have to live with—coal, oil, gas, nuclear, and so forth—for the balance of the century, because the other energy sources are fairly far off in time. And so, there are a number of things that have been said this afternoon that strike me as very good points.

But we have a very practical difficulty now: as I see it, we have no procedures, no structure, no further occasion for debate, and there fore the best we can offer—when I say "we," I mean the drafters, who again were not elected officials; the organizers grabbed people who were foolish enough to say they would be willing to devote themselves to this, so the drafting group has no official standing—the best I think we can offer is to listen very attentively, and after five o'clock see which way we want to go, trying to reflect most of the things that have been said. Some points we will reflect by omission, because they seem to create problems in people's minds. We did not set out, in either the first or the second or the third Symposium, to write a comprehensive review of the energy problem. I would not have written any of this myself; I would have written it quite differently and so would everybody else around this table. But we did not set out to write another energy book; there are already many on the shelves, and this was not to be one. The special merit and at the same time the special problem of this group was its very mixed composition—more mixed than I have ever experienced in terms of backgrounds, nationalities, professions, disciplines, and so on—and the idea was to see what would emerge as some kind of consensus on a number of aspects of the energy problem. The communiqué is not comprehensive, and I am not particularly disturbed that some things are left out, as I am not terribly disturbed that some things were pulled in, so to speak. An example of the latter is the trade problem, though it has a relationship: if the less developed countries can't export, they have fewer funds and their energy problems become worse. But I see no problem with leaving out the trade problem. It doesn't have to be there.

So my message at this point really is this: let us try to get as many people as possible to the microphones to give us ideas, either about what to leave out or what to include, and have them wish us good luck and provide us with a minimum degree of enthusiasm for doing this, so that we can spend as much time as is available to try to do another draft. It is quite possible that that draft will also be unsatisfactory, and that would not be the end of the world. If these Symposia had never happened I doubt that the world would be very different in the future, and if there is no communiqué I think the same thing goes. It would be good to have it, because it is worthwhile not to just find new truths but to reaffirm and rethink and review what has been said before by different groups of people. There is a famous story about a former us Secretary of the Treasury who came to the traditional Monday morning briefing, and somebody pointed out to him that agenda point 14 was the same as agenda point 1, whereupon he said, "If it is good enough for point 1, it surely is good enough for point 14." So there is no great harm done by reviewing some old wisdom.

One more comment and then I'll disappear. A question has been raised about what the media will pick up. I just don't think we can outguess the media. If they never print a word of the communiqué, so be it; if they pick something up, so be it. What is important is not to write things they can easily take out of context and headline. We have to be aware of that possibility. Years ago I participated in a conference in Aspen which was on human values, technology, and so on and which I remember with mixed emotions. But in any event, there was finally to be an Aspen declaration—the same kind of thing, a communiqué to the world. It took days; competitive drafts were circulated; and so forth. Finally one was adopted, and it said at the top, "Embargoed until 11:00 A.M. Tuesday." One participant observed, "I don't see why you bother to embargo it; no self-respecting newspaper would ever print it." So let's not worry excessively about our image.

NAIM AFGAN

I would like to join those who have expressed their appreciation to the drafters of this communiqué. We all know that the participants in this Symposia Series are not a very unified group in many respects—we recognized that from the very beginning, at Symposium I. But that's an advantage of this kind of meeting, and I think its polyvalency, if we may call it, gives a different approach from that seen at many specialized meetings.

Nevertheless, it is very important that the communiqué be

balanced. If we took a very simple criterion to decide what the balance should be—the time spent here on certain subjects—really, the draft does not respond to this criterion. First of all, the nuclear issue is, as you probably know, a very important issue, and we have to stress this importance since the world's future will greatly depend on the development of nuclear energy. But in this draft, breeder reactors or fusion reactors or other such things are not even mentioned at all. So I would say that in this respect the draft requires some adjustment in order to attain the necessary balance. Second, there is no word about coal; the draft ignores the fact that we have spent a lot of time listening to what efforts are being made in different countries concerning the development of coal as an energy resource. Third—returning to nuclear—it is my impression through these discussions that many countries, especially developed countries, are aiming their energy programs at the nuclear option, and I hesitate to number all those who have explained here that after the year 2000 the main source of energy will be nuclear. And I don't see an alternative for those countries that are now recognized as developing because they, or at least many of them, aim to be developed by the end of this century. They could not become developed countries on the basis of solar energy—I really cannot imagine how that would be possible.

So, if we are going to suggest anything, I would say that a balance should be somehow attained. Instead of devoting four points to solar energy and its use, we should adjust the draft a bit and make it sound reasonable, so that it becomes evident that this serious Symposia Series, which has gathered three times, has really weighed all the subjects from different angles. And I would be glad if this was reflected in the final document, because most of us, when we return to our countries, should be trying to publicize it and give it life in our surroundings. But I am afraid I would find it difficult to do so with the document that is being proposed to us.

ISHRAT H. USMANI

First of all, I would like to say that as participants in the Symposia Series, we have all contributed to, discussed, and debated the various issues entirely in our personal capacities, without the commitment of the organizations from which we come. For example, my views are personal and are not necessarily those of the United Nations department that I serve. The same is true of those of us here who may be serving their national governments. So let this point be very, very clear: the consensus that is sought, as expressed in the form of an agreed communiqué, would be entirely that of the participants serving purely in their personal capacities as invited by the organizers of this Symposia Series.

My second comment is meant to help you concentrate on two points. One is that from our discussions, it is clear that of five conventional energy sources (coal, oil, gas, hydro, and nuclear), the world will largely rely on oil and nuclear for its energy until the end of the century. The second is that both of these sources are too expensive for the poor of the Third World to use for their development, and therefore the alternative of the renewables cannot be ignored in the transition from the oil/nuclear economy to the nonoil/nonnuclear age. In fact, as far as the Third World is concerned, the renewables offer the only hope in the short, mid, and long term. What is needed is intensive R&D and extensive demonstration of various applications of these sources' technologies in varying climates and terrains.

A word about nuclear—and I think I have some credentials to talk about nuclear power, since I was the one who first introduced it in Pakistan, a truly poor and bullock-cart country. Some people think that a nuclear power reactor is a foolproof "black box" which can generate power at any level we want. This is not so. First, the technology of nuclear power generation is extremely complex and sophisticated, and second, the minimum size of a commercially available power reactor is about 600 MW. To integrate it into a national grid, the total generating capacity of that grid should be at least 3,000 MW. Now, out of about one hundred ten developing countries, hardly ten or twelve have grids of that size. So nuclear power cannot be regarded as a power source for the large majority of the developing countries. Even countries that could install nuclear power reactors would then become dependent on millions of dollars worth of fuel, spare parts, and expertise, all imported from advanced countries—a fact which is generally ignored by nuclear enthusiasts. Food and energy are two areas where every country must become self-sufficient and self-reliant. Nuclear power does not satisfy these criteria. There are also the political overtones connected with the issue of nuclear weapons proliferation, safeguards, and so forth.

So I think we should be very realistic and realize that there is no single energy source that can be a panacea for all countries for the foreseeable future. Each country will have to evolve its own mix of sources, but all of them will have to prepare for the transition from overwhelming dependence on oil—a depletable source—

to a variety of sources. This is precisely the balanced view which is proposed to be reflected in the final communiqué of this Symposia Series. There is no need to become emotional or be counted as for one source or against another source. We who have assembled here in our personal capacities as energy enthusiasts, energy planners, energy economists, and energy technologists must give our collective wisdom to solve the complex energy issues being faced by all countries of the world.

DAVID J. ROSE

I suspected that something like this would happen, because what we ask for and what everybody calls for is very difficult to produce. One asks for the eloquence of John Donne, the cunning of Machiavelli, the wisdom of Lao-tse, and furthermore, all in something that sounds politically acceptable—and furthermore, in no time. John Galbraith pointed out that the kind of casual eloquence that one finds in good documents comes in the sixth draft. Now, here you see the first draft, for which I and others bear some responsibility. Having been through all three of these Symposia, I'd like to respond to several questions that have been raised here.

First, Symposia I and II said many things, many of which have not been said here, and whose spirit needs to be caught. The draft that you heard does try to do some of those things. Second, several topics were mentioned this afternoon that need emphasis and should be included. For example, Ulf Lantzke's five transition fuels—things of that kind; the comment that nuclear power is not handled adequately in a number of ways; other topics, too. I tend to agree with most of these comments, although not all.

Guy Pauker raises a very important point, to wit: "Who will sign the communiqué, and who is responsible for it?" At the end of this Symposium somebody is going to ask, "What did you do?" And so a communiqué was planned which somebody will read tomorrow and say, "Here's what I think we did." It's pretty clear that not everybody is going to be asked to endorse this document with statements like "I hereby subscribe to this document"—that isn't going to happen. It's nice to say that this Symposium's participants are here in personal capacities, and sure enough, I guess they are. But that doesn't save them, of course, when they go back, because if somebody—say, a deputy minister—signs such a document and his minister then says, "Why did you sign that?" He replies, "I signed it in my personal capacity," and the minister will say, "My God, I didn't realize I had such persons with such capacities," and other uncomplimentary things. Regarding personal capacity: I remember Keichi Oshima's marvelous comment last year, when somebody said, "Were you wearing your official hats?" and he said, "No, we may have no hats and even no hair, but still we wear our hats." (I think that's what you said.)

There is a way out. Those working on the communiqué can try to catch the spirit of all these comments and put out something. Now, nobody need subscribe to it precisely. Some say, "Well, I went there and we had a good argument; I didn't agree with some things, but I did agree with others"—each of you can agree with things as you wish. So I think the worst objection raised by Guy Pauker could be handled, because the communiqué is not an official statement of all the people here but could be interpreted as a statement of the people who are organizing this thing.

Now, regarding some of the details. There is little time. To produce something of this complexity requires a long time, and so anything produced by tomorrow morning is bound to be incomplete—and what we have seen here is an effort to catch the spirit of things that people have been wrestling with for years. Some of the difficulties are quite easily resolvable. For example, the solar/nuclear debate which Alvin Weinberg pointed to is resolvable—first of all, by a difference in the tone of the statements; second, in that it can be incorporated with Ulf Lantzke's transition fuels and so on, by recognizing that there are a number of time scales involved here, and that on different time scales, different things will come in. That will need continuing discussion. I am much in favor of emphasis on the problems of biomass and traditional fuels, because, as Dr. Usmani said, half of the world lives on those things, and they live in conditions that many people in the middle of the United States and Europe have not seen.

Regarding what we shall do, I am taking notes as fast as I can, and I don't intend to go to the dinner this evening.

JOHN W. SHUPE

I declined the initial opportunity to comment for two reasons. First, I'm from Hawaii, so I probably represent the smallest constituency here. Second, I was satisfied with the communiqué as it was presented. I agree in general both with its philosophy and with the emphasis on the renewable energy sources.

As I listened to the discussion during the first hour, however, I felt more and more compelled to comment. I have attended each of the three Symposia, listened to all of the discussions, and feel that the ideas conveyed in the communiqué are not as far from the essence of these three meetings as one would judge from the discussion this afternoon. Fortunately, Dr. Usmani has given a very positive response to the communiqué, which I endorse strongly.

Hawaii has more in common with the developing nations than with the industrialized countries, as far as its resources are concerned. Regarding one of the comments that Dr. Engelmann made regarding the normal market mechanisms—whether they do govern or do not—I would like to present a brief case study. In 1976 we drilled the hottest geothermal well in the world—it had a 358°C (676°F) downhole temperature, and the quality of the geothermal fuel was excellent. However, there is a very limited market for geothermal power on the island of Hawaii, as well as a high risk factor in drilling for geothermal energy in an active volcano rift zone. Therefore, it took public funds to get that test well drilled and the initial power plant constructed. We had endeavored to get Union, Chevron, Shell, and others to develop geothermal in Hawaii, but there was little interest due to the market and risk situation. Now that we have proved the resources, there are three consortia developing geothermal power with private capital.

It seems to me that for the developing countries, the normal market mechanism will not always apply. Particularly in resource assessments or in establishing inventories of the potential of the developing countries' various renewable resources, public support may be necessary to get these programs under way.

Regarding the early discussions on the communiqué, I do not disagree markedly with your comments, Dr. Weinberg, or with the majority of the remarks made. These have been made by people who are articulate, authoritative, and forceful, and who represent the accepted conventional wisdom which usually dominates this type of discussion. I'm sure these comments are pertinent to the countries which these people represent. The point I wish to make is that the committee working on the communiqué should not overreact to these comments but should retain much of its initial philosophy and emphasize the importance of renewable energy resources, particularly for the developing nations.

JOHN H. GIBBONS

It may be my eternal optimism, but the rich discussion this afternoon actually persuades me that we don't have a great deal of basic disagreement. We have strong feelings about words, and if we are careful with our words, I believe we have a remarkably strong sense about what things are most important in our energy futures. What has been illuminated this afternoon is the fact that there are some very important implicit assumptions that need to be made explicit. I, for one, am prepared to try to incorporate those modifications.

I think the opportunity we have tomorrow and in the future to share some of what has gone on in these three Symposia is an important and worthy task. Whether it's a statement prepared for Bo Roberts that has anonymous authorship or whether only four of us sign it is not a matter of great concern to me as long as the statement is faithful to the events that have transpired. We have an opportunity to do something that is meaningful, especially given the input this afternoon. If it's the sense of the group that you are ready now for us to prepare something shorter that incorporates the illuminations and alterations provided by you, I am prepared to go and do it if as many of you as possible will meet with us in an hour and go over the outline of what we intend to say. I would even be prepared, if you wish, to give you right now my own preliminary outline.

What I have in mind is a briefer statement than the draft we have been discussing, although drawing quite largely from that statement. The first half would be an affirmation of energy's importance in our lives, the reality and nature of the energy problem, the reality and value of interdependence. The second statement has to do with the need for sustained attention and action. We may even want to note the recent paucity of us government attention. The third is to point out that progress is already quite evident, although quite mixed. Fourth, we would make it clear that there are important options for both supply and efficient utilization. There are also time constraints in the system. Now, these are a series of observations, but they provide an improved context for the remainder of the statement.

Then to recommendations, and I only draw here selectively from what we have already written. The first recommendation that emerged in the draft has to do with what we call national "assessments," or "audits." I refer to assessments about energy—resources, options, goals at the national level. It is hoped that there will be an opportunity later to share and combine these national goals into an international perspective. But to begin with, each nation must develop its own statement of where it is and where it wants to go with respect to energy. The second recommendation would speak to the legitimacy and self-interest of wealthier nations providing technical advice and material assistance to certain especially impacted nations. The third recommendation is that, while we use our existing options, there is an imperative for improving and developing *new* options. This would include everything from solar to nuclear to increased efficiency and productivity. And finally, we would place an emphasis on increased instrumentalities—that is, nations sharing through existing international institutions—we don't have to talk about creating new institutions. I'll give you two possible examples of subjects for international cooperation. Number one, how can we make nuclear power more acceptable and utilitarian in a variety of world contexts? Number two, how can we combine symbiotically the richness of plant material that is mostly found in the Third World with the richness of biotechnology that's in the industrial world?

Now, I think most of this is already in the draft before you—it's a matter of reshaping and reemphasizing. If you like the approach I've outlined, I volunteer our original group—and I'd love to have David Jones join us—to spend the next hour putting together a more detailed outline—perhaps some text—and then have you critique it at 5:30. If it looks promising to you, we will turn it into prose tonight and deliver it to Bo Roberts by tomorrow morning.

J. ERICH EVERED

I feel compelled to set the record straight. The allegation that the US government does not have an energy policy is not a consensus. I most strenuously disagree with that statement. I could go into significant detail about the policy which we do have, one which is largely based on less government intervention, but I will leave that honor to Secretary Edwards, who will share his thoughts with us tomorrow.

CHAPTER NINETEEN

Final Communiqué:
The Outlook for a
Sustainable Energy Future*

The following statement attempts to express the central message from this series of International Energy Symposia, a series of three related meetings that has sought to develop some convergence of understanding of the world energy problem. It has been prepared by a small group of participants who, by virtue of their early and continuing association with the Series, can bring an integrative perspective to this statement. Because the Series has been an evolving process, and because only a portion of the participants here today attended the past two Symposia, the statement may not necessarily represent the views of all who have attended this or previous Symposia sessions. Nevertheless, it is an effort to convey the sense of the Series as a whole.

---

*As explained in the introduction to this section, the final communiqué of the International Energy Symposia Series was prepared by Symposium III participants following a plenary discussion of the draft communiqué on May 26, 1982. The final communiqué was then reviewed and presented by S. H. Roberts, Jr., President of The 1982 World's Fair, at Symposium III's closing session on the morning of May 27.

FINDINGS AND OBSERVATIONS

Energy: The Nature of the Problem

The theme of The 1982 World's Fair in Knoxville, Tennessee, is "Energy Turns the World." And indeed it does.

Energy is important . . . to industrial production . . . for raising crops . . . for the individual, in making life more livable. These verities need no proof.

We discover how much we need energy when we do not have as much as we believe we need. Such a moment came nearly ten years ago. Most economies of the world have not yet fully recovered from the 1973–74 upheaval in world oil prices and its aftershocks. The crucial role of energy in the modern world could not have been demonstrated more sharply. Ever since, we have had "the energy crisis." Those who believe that it has been "solved" are wrong and are in for many unhappy surprises.

In the short run, abundant supplies of energy at the right time and place can no longer be taken for granted. In the long run, depletion of resources and the adverse effect on the environment raise serious questions of where to turn. These are real, not imagined, problems. For the next two decades we must depend for most of our energy supplies on what have come to be known as the conventional sources. Most of these sources have serious difficulties in production and use. Yet, the promise of low-risk, abundant, nondepleting sources at affordable prices is on a distant horizon. That is the core of the problem: to manage wisely what we have while searching with sustained urgency for what we want.

Nor is this problem just one country's concern. Most energy sources are concentrated in widely distant parts of the world, and the action of any one country touches the fortune and fate of all others. Interdependence, through trade and through deliberate cooperation, is a necessity in the energy field. It carries a risk of vulnerability, but it can also benefit all who participate.

Sustained Attention

It is both correct and useful to speak of the energy *problem*, not the energy *crisis*. While a crisis can often occur—a temporary shutdown, a disruption, an accident—this is not the essence of our energy concerns. Instead, we are dealing with a set of issues that can no more be solved than other complex issues of society such as world hunger. What we have is not an event but a process that continues over time. That makes it hard; a process needs sustained attention. It lacks the kind of excitement and gratification brought by "victory" over adversity, as can occur in a crisis. Effective energy actions tend not to be dramatic, and their effect is often not easily determined or even visible. Moreover, when the pressure eases, there is a tendency to turn to other things. Thus, insistence on sustained attention is critical.

Because energy is so pervasive and so strongly linked to economic performance, there are of necessity many actors. Some believe that it is government's role to manage energy matters; others assign that role largely to markets or, more broadly, to the actions of individuals. In reality, there is a role for both. In market economies, individuals, or the private sector, exercise choices—in the amount and kind of energy used. Government sets the framework in which these choices take place. Of equal importance, it performs those functions that are dictated by the broad national interest but that individuals are incapable of undertaking. Thus, in response to national realities, strong government leadership—though not necessarily of an interventionist kind—is important if not essential. Leadership is expected especially from those countries that play a large role as either consumers or producers of energy. Their actions as nations impinge most heavily on the destinies of others.

Options and Futures

The energy options differ for different countries at different times. One thing they all have in common is an inevitable transition to sustainable energy technologies.

For the currently most industrialized countries, the principal options *for the next twenty to thirty years* are as follows:

- Continued use of oil, but at a decreasing rate.
- Continued use of gas, determined by cost and availability.
- Selectively increased use of coal, with increasing attention to its environmental and other problems.
- Development of nuclear power, as safely as possible, with technologies that are proliferation-resistant.
- Selective development of hydro power and other renewable resources, particularly solar energy.
- Attention to increased efficiency of use, for which many opportunities exist.

This last item is especially important, because (1) industrialized countries use the bulk of the world's energy, and therefore increasing energy productivity has global benefits; (2) it eases the transition to sustainable sources by buying time; and (3) it displaces the costliest and least attractive sources, both now and later.

For later, the principal options of the currently most industrialized countries are as follows:

- Completion of a transition already started, to substantially decreased use of fossil fuels, and to increased use of renewable or virtually inexhaustible energy sources. There are only two major ones: solar power in various forms, and nuclear power in various forms. If the timetable shortens, so much the better.
- Continued improvement of energy productivity.

For the currently less industrialized countries, the principal options *for the next twenty to thirty years* are as follows:

- Continued use of oil, gas, and other fossil fuels as governed by economic circumstances.
- Increased development of domestic fossil fuels via independent or cooperative international programs.
- Adoption of nuclear power at an appropriate scale, in countries in which the requisite infrastructures clearly exist.
- Improvement of the use and supply of biomass in environmentally sound ways, with special attention to the deforestation problem.
- Development of hydro power, large and small, and other renewable resources, particularly solar energy.
- Improved efficiency of energy use.

For later, the principal option of the currently less industrialized countries is as follows:

- The energy programs of the industrialized and currently less industrialized countries will, if all goes well, approach each other much more closely than they do at present; therefore, as seen imperfectly at the current time, the same options should apply.

Every present and future option has defects or difficulties (otherwise it would have been adopted and we would have no energy problem); the transition period of 20–30 years, while seemingly long, is deceptively short for developing these major options on a global scale.

Progress

Over the past decade we have dramatically improved our

understanding of global energy resources and uses. That understanding now provides the basis for meeting current needs, identifying potential long-term solutions, and moving from one to the other. The transition, requiring decades, is primarily driven by the changing economics of energy and is strongly influenced by changing technology. It was initially triggered by the sudden change in oil prices that occurred in 1974, but the conditions had been laid long before. It consists of moving from an oil-dominated supply system to a successor system of a variety of energy sources that, taken as a whole, are more resilient and will last longer. It also consists of a shift to substantially higher energy productivity— that is, wringing more out of each unit of energy.

As each nation progresses in this transition, its success or lack of success reflects upon other nations. This fact of interdependence carries special weight in the case of the largest energy consumers. For example, small gains in productivity for them can mean large differences in energy available to others.

Much progress is already evident, even though the transition is less than a decade old. Supplies are being developed, and many former users of oil are shifting to other fuels. Very impressive gains in energy productivity have been achieved in many countries, and much more is possible. Unfortunately, the progress is mixed. Some countries are doing much better than others. Those that have been forced to be especially energy-conserving and have developed actions and policies to that purpose have made the most progress. Whether the rate of progress can be maintained and accelerated (or finally begun, in some cases) will determine the shape and magnitude of the problem we will face in the future.

CONCLUSIONS AND RECOMMENDATIONS

Assessments

Each nation rightly deals with its unique energy situation in the way it deems best. There is no perfect, universally applicable energy technology strategy. Each country must seek its own mix of energy supplies and uses, and this mix will change over time. An appropriate mix will provide resilience to accommodate change and uncertainty, and to protect against contingencies. Therefore, each nation should carefully assess its energy options on a continual basis and develop its strategy with due consideration for its unique opportunities and constraints (e.g., environmental, technological, economic, resource, social). In this assessment, cooperation among nations can help through technical assistance, exchange of information and methods of analysis, education and training, and cooperative research. Efforts should be made to remove barriers to the free flow of information and technology.

As stated before, actions by one nation may affect other nations, because of the way energy is used and because of the influence of these actions on world energy markets. Thus, each nation should be sensitive to the consequences of its actions on others, and there should be a broadening of international opportunities to measure and compare the progress of national energy strategies, to assess how equitably the world's total energy burden is being borne.

Advice and Assistance

The world's less developed countries face numerous difficulties as they seek to raise the quality of life for their people. Many of their problems, including population growth, lack of investment capital and export markets, and deforestation, are linked with and exacerbate their energy problems. While each country should look primarily to its own resources, the least fortunate countries merit special help from others who are well endowed in technology or other resources. This help could take the form of technical assistance as well as financial and material aid. Such assistance could give critically needed near-term relief. It could enable developing countries to use less energy as their economies develop than was feasible in the formative stages of the now-industrialized nations. One example of such assistance could be to establish and support pilot village-level energy systems in poor rural areas, using local energy resources with high efficiency, with the aim of providing production inputs such as irrigation water and basic amenities such as illumination, refrigeration, communications, and water supply.

New and Improved Options

All available energy production and productivity options may be needed and used, but in different measures by nations according to their circumstances. For the next several decades the major supply burden will be borne by the sources mentioned earlier. But given the inertia of energy systems, it is imperative to develop and evaluate new options to assist the transition in the energy resource mix and in end-use technologies. The menu of potential future options is extensive, but three technology areas, at least, can benefit from cooperative efforts—efficiency improvement, nuclear, and solar. In each there are significant opportunities, and also significant difficulties to be overcome. Efforts should be made to use existing international organizations as well as bilateral and multilateral arrangements to pursue development and evaluation of new and existing options. Two examples illustrate this:

- Rapid developments in ecological sciences and biotechnology (including, for example, genetic engineering) provide cause for optimism about advances in how we use the sun. Different nations have different things to contribute to a cooperative effort, including plant materials (e.g., seeds) as well as technical expertise.
- Concern about nuclear weapons proliferation stands in the way of the universal availability of nuclear power. If the two could be unambiguously separated, many of nuclear power's other problems (such as safety and waste management) could be more easily addressed in a cooperative spirit.

Continuation

The spirit of these International Energy Symposia should be continued through meetings convening biennially in Knoxville to evaluate successes and failures in managing the world energy problem. Such a series would encourage further dispassionate, careful thinking and would be a permanent memorial to the efforts of The 1982 World's Fair to promote international understanding and cooperation. The first meeting of this continued series, held in 1984, should be devoted to the topic, "Managing the Energy Transition."

Participants from many nations, reflecting an extraordinary diversity of economic status, resource availability, technological sophistication, and political systems, have contributed to these Symposia. The commonality of views on energy issues has been remarkable. Although national problems differ, the fundamental challenge is strongly shared—so strongly that more intensive international cooperation and the continuation of interactions such as these Symposia are imperative if the nations of the world are to achieve the goal of a just and sustainable energy future.

Closing Session

Editors' Note

Symposium III's closing session was held in the World's Fair amphitheater and was open to the public. This session featured the final communiqué's presentation by S. H. Roberts, Jr., President of The World's Fair (see chap. 19). In addition, a special paper was presented by Michel Carpentier, Director General of the Commission of the European Communities (see chap. 7); a closing address was given by James B. Edwards, Secretary of the US Department of Energy; and brief speeches—excluded here because of space limitations—were made by diverse people associated with the Fair or the Symposium. The session concluded with remarks by Walter N. Lambert, an Executive Vice President of the Fair who, together with Nelda Kersey, an Assistant Vice President, had primary responsibility for the Symposia Series. The editors extend appreciation to them and their staff for their impressive work in coordinating this and the prior Symposia.

CHAPTER TWENTY

Closing Address

James B. Edwards
Secretary
United States Department of Energy

For more than a decade now, we have been gripped by a crisis
spawned by higher oil prices and the need to develop alternative
sources of energy. This crisis has been exaggerated by the attempts
of government, the media, and the universities to turn energy from
a commodity to a cause, from a technical matter to a highly
charged political issue.

I want to take the opportunity during these closing remarks at
this International Energy Symposium to summarize what I think
are the major challenges facing us. I am an optimist. I am convinced that we will continue to persevere. I am convinced that we
are learning how to cope with our energy problems. I am convinced
that we will one day be able to put the energy crisis behind us. I am
convinced that most of you in this audience agree that, with
appropriate dedication, our future progress internationally will not
be limited by shortages of energy.

We are in the midst of a long, sometimes very painful transition to new forms of energy. There are no instant, magical answers.
There are no universal energy truths awaiting discovery. There are
no secret formulas for turning base minerals into oil. And there are
no governmental miracles. Our only tools are hard work, devotion,
prudence, and creativity.

The Knoxville World's Fair symbolizes our confidence in the
future. A city of this size was not supposed to be able to sponsor a
fair of this scale. That didn't stop the organizers. A city of this size
was not supposed to be able to turn as conflict-ridden a subject as

energy into a symbol of human hope. It did. A city of this size was not supposed to be able to draw as distinguished an audience as this, or those that participated in the earlier Symposia. But it did.

One thing on which we can all agree: we are leaving that dark era where fears about energy shortages threatened our way of life, resulting in a loss of confidence in the future, a loss of confidence in technology, a loss of confidence in mankind's ability to wisely harness nature, and a loss of confidence in our fellow human beings.

The problems are not solved, but the solutions are coming into focus. The energy crisis is not over, but we can put the siege mentality that it spawned behind us.

What have we learned during the last decade? There are six essential lessons on which nearly all of us agree.

First, we realize that it was counterproductive to advocate reliance on a single energy source as our salvation, or to rule out particular energy sources. We need a mix of energy sources. There is a bumper sticker that reads, "Split wood, not atoms." Anybody with that slogan on his car has not split much wood. I have, and it is not easy work. And for the less developed countries that rely on wood as the main source of fuel, there is an urgent need to find alternatives to the rapidly depleting stands of wood that remain. We cannot afford the cultural myopia that dominates the thinking of some of the most affluent people in our midst. In short, we need to split wood and atoms and everything in between.

Second, we realize that the centralization of decisionmaking about energy—turning over to government the whole job of managing and regulating energy—didn't work. It only made matters worse. There is a role for government in the sponsorship of long-term, high-risk research. The Reagan administration has increased spending on basic energy sciences. But we have learned that the private sector works best. Government officials are no better at allocating resources, regulating prices, and predicting the future than the man on the street. Energy is a commodity, albeit an especially valuable one.

President Reagan ordered the immediate decontrol of oil on January 28, 1981. Contrary to some prophecies, the price of oil has gone down, as have oil company profits. Deregulation has been good for the American consumer. The Reagan administration also intends to accelerate the decontrol of natural gas. Keeping the price of any fuel artificially low encourages the inefficient use of that energy. Until the price of natural gas rises to the level of oil and other fuels, few Americans will invest in solar hot water heaters and other renewable technologies that are currently not cost effective.

Third, the world is not running out of energy. We are running out of cheap energy. The rising cost of energy has had a very detrimental impact on the world economy. The rapid increases in the price of oil during the last decade were politically motivated. In the long run, however, the price of oil was destined to rise. As the price rises, there is more incentive to look for more oil and gas. I am confident that, contrary to some dire predictions, we will maintain worldwide reserve levels longer than was anticipated just a few years ago.

Yet there is no doubt that oil is a finite resource. It has to be used wisely. And we have to develop alternatives, including coal; unconventional oil resources like shale, tar sands, and heavy oil; nuclear; and solar and other renewables. Technically, we know that we have the raw materials and the technologies we need. Economically, we're still not sure how and when to use them.

Fourth, we realize that there is a tremendous elasticity between Gross National Product and the consumption of energy. We should be proud of the progress we have made in conserving energy and, as the theme of this Symposia Series highlights, improving our productivity. The Reagan administration's energy policy is built on two pillars: on increasing production and on conservation. The two are complementary and are equally vital to the future well-being of the world.

As the economics of the United States and other countries recover from recession, the demand for energy will rise only modestly. The conservation ethic has become a habit; there is a thriving conservation industry, and most importantly, the price of energy will continue to spur conservation. In short, we are not about to go off on a wild energy-wasting binge.

Fifth, we realize that it is the "resource-poor" developing nations that have suffered the most from the rapid rise in oil prices. And it is generally this group of countries that are seeing their demand for oil grow the fastest. It is in the interest of oil-consuming and -producing nations to moderate prices and to encourage this group to develop their own resources. These countries have to remove the barriers that hinder their ability to utilize their own resources and adopt new technologies.

Finally, we all agree that while all nations have a natural desire for self-sufficiency—a goal few nations ever have hope of achieving—all nations also have responsibility to share the global burden. The United States realizes that. Even if we were to reduce our oil imports drastically, we would not be secure so long as our friends and allies, who aren't so well endowed with natural resources, remain dependent on imports. The United States intends to stand by its commitments. The United States intends to maintain its commitment to the International Energy Agency. The United States also intends to continue strengthening its exports of coal and advanced energy technology, including nuclear power plants.

Where do our nations go from here? We have learned that there are many roads to follow and many forks along those roads that are worth exploring. We have learned that there is no single path to follow.

Let me speak with you for a few minutes about the various roads along which America is trodding. For the Reagan administration, energy has been one of the brightest spots. The year 1981 was the year of oil. Largely as a result of the President's decision to immediately decontrol oil, we saw drilling and seismic activity reach all-time peaks. At one-point, there were 4,520 drilling rigs and 744 seismic crews at work. Nearly 80,000 wells were drilled.

Oil imports have declined significantly. They are half the level of only five years ago. Most of that savings is due to conservation.

We have accelerated the filling of the strategic petroleum reserve. We have more than a quarter billion barrels in reserve, more than any other nation in the western alliance. We're currently adding 200,000 barrels per day.

Last year, we laid the groundwork for the renewal of nuclear power. We expect to pass legislation on high-level nuclear waste, to adopt dramatically streamlined licensing rules, and to remove some of the barriers that have created unfair financial hardship on utilities.

Unlike previous administrations, we shy away from policy-making based on detailed quotas. We are convinced, however, that, as is the case with most countries, the electricity sector will gradually provide a growing share of our primary energy. We need to be assured of a reliable electricity supply. That means starting construction of power plants, the capacity of which will not be needed for another decade. We can't afford to be shortsighted about future needs.

Until 1977, when the us Department of Energy was created, federal energy functions were spread throughout the government. There was a need to consolidate most of those functions, but there was no need to create a separate department. In fact, creating a separate department was a mistake. It led to the growth of a large bureaucratic entity that has had as its main function the regulation of energy. The Reagan administration has moved a long way toward deregulating and plans to continue that process. We intend to strengthen our ability to manage our energy problems and to encourage the development of long-term technologies for which the government bears most of the responsibility.

The administration's reorganization proposal is not meant to signal the demise of energy as an issue. It is meant to put energy in perspective under an efficient, sensibly sized umbrella. The United States will honor all of its international commitments. The new organization, which we are asking Congress to enact, will enable the United States to be a more reliable supplier of coal and advanced technologies.

Energy should be a source of strength for all of our countries. It symbolizes mankind's ability to safely harness the forces of nature. In recent years, energy has been portrayed as our Achilles' heel. Energy should be seen as a source of cooperation rather than conflict. Energy should be seen as a source of hope rather than despair. The United States is doing its part to put the crisis mentality behind us. Many other nations are also doing their parts. Our nation must strengthen those efforts and intensify our bilateral and multilateral relations for the good of all humankind.

CHAPTER TWENTY-ONE

Closing Remarks

Walter N. Lambert
Executive Vice President
The 1982 World's Fair

In July of 1980, when I was approached about assuming responsibility for the direction of the three-part International Energy Symposia Series of The 1982 World's Fair, significant work had been done. An international program committee and a local organizing committee had been established, and a basic scheme for the Series had been developed. It was an ambitious, perhaps even audacious, idea. It said that it was possible to bring together in Knoxville, Tennessee, in conjunction with a world's fair, a group of energy technicians, energy policy experts, and government officials from nations around the world to examine over time the critical issues in relation to energy production and productivity in the world. I must admit that at first glance it seemed an unlikely idea. Further examination showed that it was supported by a group of people who were capable and willing to make it work.

Now, on May 27, 1982, we have seen the culmination of more than three years of work on this International Symposia Series. We have seen the experts that were anticipated from around the world come together and join with the government policymakers and opinion leaders to examine energy production and productivity in terms not of technology but of the impact of energy shortage or availability on humankind.

In fact, the overall shape of this conference evolved directly out of the work and knowledge of these people. The establishment of energy in its total context—which is political, which is social, which is human—became an essential part of the Series' success. Keeping the questions raised in their appropriate global context

also became crucial to any long-term importance of this conference.

As had been planned, the first Symposium established a range
of questions that must be dealt with if we are to consider energy as
it affects our lives. Such questions then became the basis for
careful, in-depth analysis in seven major working sessions at the
second Symposium and, finally, led to a set of national statements
and a group of papers in this, the third and concluding Symposium.
From these three Symposia has grown a communiqué which will
set the tone of examination of the energy question for years to
come.

All of this did not happen by accident. It happened, first,
because the organizers of The 1982 World's Fair decided not to
have only the required "Education Program" necessary to comply
with the regulations of the Bureau of International Expositions;
instead, they decided to undertake an International Energy Symposia Series which had the potential of making a truly significant
contribution. This required courage on the part of the organizers at
the time this decision was made in 1977. Special thanks are due to
the Board of Directors, paticularly to the Management Committee, and most particularly to S. H. Roberts, Jr., President of The
1982 World's Fair, for having the courage and the willingness to
devote a considerable amount of the Fair's corporate funds, at a
time when funds were extremely scarce, to this examination of the
Fair's theme.

Support from the us Department of Energy, coming as it did at
a crucial period in 1980, made the Symposia Series a reality. More
important than the cash support which we have received from the
Department of Energy has been the strong support of that staff
throughout the course of the Symposia Series.

The great faith and confidence and hard work displayed by the
Commissioners General of the participating nations in The 1982
World's Fair has also been an essential part of the success of this
Series. Their willingness to work with their energy departments in
their home countries and to encourage participation by those government officials at the policymaking level has been a critical part
of what we have done.

The local organizing committee of the Symposia Series has
given untold hours in advising, assisting, hand-holding, encouraging, chastising, and ever shaping the nature of this Series and
moving it forward. The international program committee has been
essential to the Series' success. In the early days we quite simply
borrowed the prestige of this distinguished group to make people
believe that Knoxville was a worthwhile place to be at the time the

three Symposia were to be held. The program committee members have been free with their advice, with their knowledge, and with their skill. More importantly, they have been people with whom it has been superb to work. I know it is unwise to single out individuals in such a listing of support, but there are three individuals who have been members of the international program committee without whose dedication this Series could not have happened, and I personally want to express my sincere gratitude to Dr. John H. Gibbons, Mr. Hans H. Landsberg, and Professor David J. Rose for being not only great minds but great people. I have never known three men for whom I have had greater professional regard, and, more importantly, for whom I have had more personal respect. If there is any flaw in the world today, it is that there are too few people like these three in it.

Finally, a special thank you to the staff of the International Energy Symposia Series of The 1982 World's Fair; to the staff from the Energy, Environment, and Resources Center at the University of Tennessee—particularly Bob Bohm, Lil Clinard, and Mary English—for their continued hard work and support; and to the staff of The 1982 World's Fair, headed by Nelda Kersey, whose dedication and organizational ability always managed to make the highly disorganized director of this Symposia Series appear to know what he was doing. A finer staff was never assembled nor worked harder to make the success of a program.

During the first Symposium, a participant said to me that there were three potential outcomes from the Series. The first two would be easy; the third not as easy. The participant said that the Symposia Series would certainly attract attention to the energy problems of the world by being associated with an event like a world's fair, and that would be a good thing. Second, it would attract attention to The World's Fair itself and make clear that The World's Fair organizing staff members were serious about their commitment to meeting energy needs in the world, now and in the future. The participant felt that both of these outcomes would certainly occur. The participant then observed that finally, if we were very lucky, we might make a significant impact on the way people thought about energy availability, now and in the years to come. I am convinced, as I stand here today, that we have met all three of those goals, that all three of those good outcomes have happened, and that they are as good as we had hoped they might be. That is true because of the quality of people who have associated themselves with this endeavor, and I will be forever grateful to each of them.

Appendices

Symposium III Program

The 1982 World's Fair
INTERNATIONAL ENERGY SYMPOSIUM III
Toward an Efficient Energy Future

May 24–27, 1982

Symposium Chairman: Armand Hammer
Chairman of the Board and
Chief Executive Officer
Occidental Petroleum Corporation

Monday, May 24, 1982

8:00 p.m. - 9:30 p.m. **Opening Session**

Keynote Address
Imelda Romualdez Marcos
Minister of Human Settlements
Republic of the Philippines

Tuesday, May 25, 1982

8:30 a.m. - 9:15 a.m. **Presentation of Technical Paper**
Parts A & B

David J. Rose
Professor of Nuclear Engineering
Massachusetts Institute of
Technology
United States

John H. Gibbons
Director
Office of Technology Assessment
United States Congress

9:15 a.m. - 11:30 a.m.   **Comments by Symposium II
Chairmen/Integrators**

11:30 a.m. - 12:00 noon   **Address by Symposium III
Chairman**
Armand Hammer
Chairman of the Board and
Chief Executive Officer
Occidental Petroleum Corporation

1:30 p.m. - 2:15 p.m.   **Presentation of Technical Paper
Part C**
Hans H. Landsberg
Senior Fellow
Resources for the Future
United States

2:15 p.m. - 3:00 p.m.   **Comments by Symposium II
Chairmen/Integrators**

3:00 p.m. - 5:00 p.m.   **General Discussion Among
Symposium Participants**

Wednesday, May 26, 1982

8:30 a.m. - 12:00 noon   **Presentations of National Energy
Policies and Positions by
Ministerial/Cabinet-Level
Participants**

1:30 p.m. - 2:00 p.m.   **Case Study: Italy's Public/Private
Cooperation in Energy Technology
Transfer**
Giacomo Elias
Director
National Research Council
Italy

2:00 p.m. - 3:00 p.m.   **Presentation of Draft Communiqué**
William E. Fulkerson
Director, Energy Division
Oak Ridge National Laboratory
United States

3:00 p.m. - 4:30 p.m.   **Working Session:**
Discussion of Draft Communiqué

Thursday, May 27, 1982

9:00 a.m. - 11:30 a.m.   **Closing Session**

Special Paper: International Energy
Cooperation from a European
Community Perspective
Michel Carpentier
Director General
Commission of the European
Communities

Presentation of Final Communiqué
S. H. Roberts, Jr.
President
The 1982 World's Fair

Closing Address
James B. Edwards
Secretary
Department of Energy
United States

Closing Remarks
Walter N. Lambert
Executive Vice President
The 1982 World's Fair

Symposium III
Participants

Philip II. Abelson
Editor
Science
United States

Naim Afgan
Professor
Boris Kidrič Institute of Sciences
Yugoslavia

Yumi Akimoto
General Manager
Nuclear Energy Department
Mitsubishi Metal Corporation
Japan

James E. Akins
Former Ambassador to Saudi Arabia
United States

Marcelo Alonso
Executive Director
Florida Institute of Technology Research and Engineering, Inc.
United States

Ishag A. Bashir
Senior Energy Planner
Ministry of Energy and Mining
National Energy Administration
Sudan

Giovanni Briganti
Administrative Counselor
National Council for Research and Development on
Nuclear and Alternative Energy
Italy

Anthony R. Buhl
Vice President of Operations
Technology for Energy Corporation
United States

Michel Carpentier
Director General
Commission of the European Communities

José Andres de Oteyza
Secretary of Patrimony and Industrial Development
Mexico

Pedro Dumol
Executive Director
National Rural Electrification Program
Republic of the Philippines

James B. Edwards
Secretary
Department of Energy
United States

Giacomo Elias
Director of the Energy Project
National Research Council
Italy

Ulrich Engelmann
Director General
Department of Energy
Ministry of Economics
Federal Republic of Germany

J. Erich Evered
Administrator
Energy Information Administration
Department of Energy
United States

Fereidun Fesharaki
Research Associate
East-West Resource Systems Institute
United States

William E. Fulkerson
Director, Energy Division
Oak Ridge National Laboratory
United States

John H. Gibbons
Director
Office of Technology Assessment
United States Congress

Richard L. Grant
President
Boeing Engineering and Construction Southeast, Inc.
United States

Armand Hammer
Chairman of the Board and Chief Executive Officer
Occidental Petroleum Corporation
United States

Hyo Joon Hahm
Vice President
Institute of Energy and Resources
Republic of Korea

Toyoaki Ikuta
President
Institute of Energy Economics
Japan

Denis J. Ives
Deputy Secretary
Department of National Development and Energy
Australia

David le B. Jones
Deputy Secretary
Department of Energy
United Kingdom

Robert W. Kiernan
Director of Energy
National Association of Manufacturers
United States

Donald L. Klass
Vice President
Institute of Gas Technology
United States

Zsolt Kohalmi
Science Attaché and First Secretary
Embassy to the United States
Hungarian People's Republic

Hans H. Landsberg
Senior Fellow
Resources for the Future
United States

Ulf Lantzke
Executive Director
International Energy Agency
Organisation for Economic Co-operation and Development

Amory B. Lovins
Friends of the Earth
United States

L. Hunter Lovins
Friends of the Earth
United States

Edward Lumsdaine
Director
Energy, Environment, and Resources Center
The University of Tennessee
United States

Winjones Lyombe
Joint Project Manager
Petroleum Conservation Association
Tansania

H. G. MacPherson
Consultant
Institute for Energy Analysis
Oak Ridge Associated Universities
United States

Imelda Romualdez Marcos
Minister of Human Settlements
Republic of the Philippines

Alejandro D. Melchor
Board of Directors
Asian Development Bank
Republic of the Philippines

G. Wayne Meyers
Vice President and General Manager
Atomics International Division
Rockwell International Corporation
Untied States

Keichi Oshima
Professor Emeritus
University of Tokyo
Japan

Guy J. Pauker
Senior Staff Member
Rand Corporation
United States

R. Raghavendran
India

Gaston Rimareix
Principal Private Secretary of the Minister for Energy
France

David J. Rose
Professor of Nuclear Engineering
Massachusetts Institute of Technology
United States

Robert Sadove
Senior Advisor for Energy
World Bank

M. Y. Shana'a
Gulf Organization for Industrial Consulting
Qatar

John W. Shupe
Director
Hawaii Natural Energy Institute
Univesity of Hawaii at Manoa
United States

Ishrat H. Usmani
Inter-Regional Energy Adviser
Department of Technical Cooperation for Development
United Nations

Dan V. Vamanu
National Council for Science and Technology
Romania

Peter S. Van Nort
Vice President of Quality and Technical Services
Daniel International Corporation
United States

Alvin M. Weinberg
Director
Institute for Energy Analysis
Oak Ridge Associated Universities
United States

Symposium III Organizers, Contributors, and Staff

ORGANIZING COMMITTEE

The Organizing Committee is composed of representatives from major energy related organizations in the Knoxville area. Primary responsibilities of the Organizing Committee are to advise Symposia personnel regarding overall operation in areas of finance, program management, facilities, services and hospitality, and communications.

Nobert J. Ackermann
Technology for Energy Corporation

Ben Adams
Adams Craft Herz Walker

William Bibb
United States Department of Energy

Tony Buhl
Technology for Energy Corporation

Harvey I. Cobert
Union Carbide Corporation—Nuclear Division

Pete Craven
Science Applications, Inc.

Kenneth E. DeBusk
The University of Tennessee

William E. Fulkerson
Oak Ridge National Laboratory

Ron Green
System Development Corporation

Robert F. Hemphill
Tennessee Valley Authority

Eugene Joyce
Attorney-at-Law

Walter N. Lambert
The 1982 World's Fair

Robert Landry
First Christian Church

Robert L. Little
The University of Tennessee

Lillian Mashburn
Goodstein, Hahn, Shorr & Associates

Wayne Range
United States Department of Energy

Don Riley
Clinch River Breeder Reactor

S. H. Roberts, Jr.
The 1982 World's Fair

Selma Shapiro
Oak Ridge Children's Museum

Ernest G. Silver
Oak Ridge National Laboratory

H. Brown Wright
Tennessee Valley Authority

PROGRAM COMMITTEE

The Program Committee is composed of internationally known experts in energy-related areas. The primary responsibility of the Committee is to screen participants and identify speakers for the Symposia.

James E. Akins
Former US Ambassador to Saudi Arabia

Kenneth E. Boulding
Chairman of the Board
American Association for the Advancement of Science
Professor Emeritus
University of Colorado

John S. Foster, Jr.
Vice President
Science & Technology
TRW, Inc.

John H. Gibbons
Director
Office of Technology Assessment
United States Congress

Denis Hayes
Executive Director
Solar Energy Research Institute

Hans H. Landsberg
Senior Fellow
Resources for the Future

Henry R. Linden
President
Gas Research Institute

Amory B. and L. Hunter Lovins
Friends of the Earth, Inc.

Guy J. Pauker
Senior Staff Member
Rand Corporation

David J. Rose
Professor
Massachusetts Institute of Technology

Mohammad Sadli
Professor
The University of Indonesia

John C. Sawhill
Director
McKinsey & Company, Inc.

Ishrat H. Usmani
Inter-Regional Energy Advisor
United Nations

Alvin M. Weinberg
Director
Institute for Energy Analysis

LOCAL CONTRIBUTORS

Boeing Engineering and Construction Southeast, Inc.
Delta Airlines, Inc.
Hyatt Regency Knoxville Hotel
South Central Bell
Pilot Oil Company

SYMPOSIUM III STAFF

Management Staff

Robert A. Bohm
Traci R. Brakebill
Kim Bridges
Lisa Bridges
Lillian A. Clinard
Mary R. English
Leigh R. Hendry

Richard D. Jacobs
Nelda T. Kersey
Walter N. Lambert
M. Nan Lintz
Edward Lumsdaine
Sheila McCullough
Katherine Murphy

Supporting Staff

The 1982 World's Fair Executive Staff
Jake F. Butcher, Chairman of the Board
S.H. Roberts, Jr., President
James E. Drinnon, Sr., Executive Vice President
  and General Manager

The 1982 World's Fair Executive Vice Presidents
William R. Francisco
Edward S. Keen
Walter N. Lambert

George M. Siler
Charles K. Swan, III

The 1982 World's Fair Vice Presidents

Jim Benedick
Peter H. Claussen
William C. Carroll

A. G. Forrester
Theotis Robinson, Jr.
Charles D. Smith

The 1982 World's Fair Assistant Vice Presidents

Joe Brunet
Marc Grossman

Nelda Kersey

The 1982 World's Fair Staff

Jeannie Boyle
Jon Brock
Jimmy Cannington
Ed Cureton
Emmett Edwards
Jame Eppes
Donna Hankins
Cathy Higdon

Pat Hutsell
Marian Kozar
Dora McCoury
Sam Roberts
Martha Theobald
John Underwood
Jerry Wiggs

The University of Tennessee
Energy, Environment, and Resources Center

Mitzi Broyles
William Clemons
Nancy Gibson
Helen Hafford
Daniel Hoglund
Alan Johns
Betty Moss
Carole Purkey

Joe Stines
Carolyn Srite
Rica Swisher
Peggy Taylor
Joyce Troxler
Tse Wei Wang
Beverly Worman

Hyatt Regency Knoxville

Paul Sherbakoff
   General Manager
Pam Caldwell
Scott Caldwell
Willie Cannon
Mike Cowell
Arthur Davis
Barnes Goutermout
Sherri Harrell
Ruth Hauk
George Hoch
Karl Holme
Bob Iantosca
Patti Lewis

Dan May
Richard May
Jo Marsh
Vaughn McCoy
C. J. McDaniel
Margaret Ogle
Sally Peach
Henrietta Pendergrass
Joyce Roth
Karen Stranathan
Sanford Swann
Mary Lou Wardell
Susan White

U.S. Department of Energy
John C. Bradburne, Jr.

Oak Ridge National Laboratory
William Fulkerson
Andrew Locbl
Jeff Rexhousen

Ernest Silver
Tom Wilbanks

The University of Tennessee
Bob Allen
Bill Baird
Dan Evans

Sheldon Reaven
David Van Horn

Knoxville/ Knox County Metropolitan Planning Commission
Wayne Blasius

Tate Godfrey

City of Knoxville
Randy Tyree, Mayor
Patricia Ball

Jim Humphrey

Miscellaneous Support

Diane Abernathy
Patti Anderson
Tom Barnard
Maxine Byrne
David Cash
Lynn Clapp
David Conkling
Candace Dreyer
Charlie Faires
Jack Fagan
Love Gossett
Eleanor Grace
Joe Hach
Donna Hankins
Rebecca Henderson
Sylvia Lacey
Ann Lambert
Ann Lockridge
Lillian Mashburn
Sam Maynard
Jean McClain
Roma Misra

Lisa Murphy
Donna Pack
Daniel Parrish
Robert Roach
Marcia Roberts
Conie Robledo
William Roland
Helen Roth
Joy Shanks
Rich Sibley
Julian Sptizer
Ray Suarez
Lance Tacke
Martha Theobald
Jim Thorpe
Ann Walker
Julia Walker
Lee Ann Wells
Sharon Wells
Virginia Wheeler
Elaine Williams